Essentials of materials management

Essentials of
materials management

Ted Barker

Training Consultant with Purchasing and Materials Management Services

McGRAW-HILL BOOK COMPANY

London · New York · St Louis · San Francisco · Auckland
Bogotá · Guatemala · Hamburg · Lisbon · Madrid · Mexico
Montreal · New Delhi · Panama · Paris · San Juan · São Paulo
Singapore · Sydney · Tokyo · Toronto

Published by
McGRAW-HILL Book Company (UK) Limited
MAIDENHEAD · BERKSHIRE · ENGLAND

British Library Cataloguing in Publication Data
Barker, Ted
Essentials of materials management.
1. Materials management
I. Title
658.7

ISBN 0-07-084197-7

Library of Congress Cataloging-in-Publication Data
Barker, Ted.
    Essentials of materials management/Ted Barker.
    p.   cm.
    Bibliography: p.
    Includes index.
    ISBN 0-07-084197-7
    1. Materials management.   I. Title.
TS161.B38   1989   88-32410
658.7——dc 19.

Cover photograph: Forklift trucks. *Foreground*: Lansing Foer
15.1 (Electric); *Background*: Lansing Seven 2.5 (Diesel).
Supplied by Lansing Bagnall.

1234 B&S 8909

Typeset by
STYLESET LIMITED · Warminster · Wiltshire

and printed and bound by Billings & Sons Limited

To Kathleen
*For her encouragement and forebearance
during the writing of this book*

Contents

Preface

Materials management requires the right blend of technical and commercial expertise operating within the framework of an appropriate and good organizational structure if it is to provide the efficient and effective service demanded of it. Increasingly, sophisticated techniques are being applied to all functions within materials management. It is not, however, the aim of this book to examine in detail all such sophisticated techniques. These are dealt with adequately in some of the specialized text-books listed in 'Recommended reading'. The aim of this book is to consider the basic essentials of the inter-functional activities, general techniques and practices embraced by materials management and, hence, to have a wide appeal. The book is aimed at students taking IPS and BPICS examination and non-examination courses, and practitioners working (or seeking to work) within materials management, supplies management or operations management. They should find the book helpful and also gain a better appreciation of the activities, and commitments of colleagues in interrelated functions.

The management of materials is thus considered in its widest sense. There can be no one ideal solution to its operation. The book considers, therefore, the different approaches which may be pursued by any organization to manage materials. There is no restriction. An organization may be large or small, manufacturing or non-manufacturing, or in the public or private sector.

Chapter 1 considers the various approaches which are adopted to manage materials. The subsequent chapters follow in logical sequence (related to first-time buy material) commencing with demand/supply/resource analysis. Function/activity sequencing is, therefore, not related to degree of importance. Indeed, all have particular importance. Thus, for example, production control is separated from material/production planning by a number of chapters.

Acknowledgements

I wish to thank many former colleagues in the steel, shipbuilding and general engineering industries and the North West Regional Management Centre, present colleagues with Purchasing and Materials Management Services (PMMS) training consultants, and many students I have had the pleasure to work with over the years. Ideas have been stimulated working with them from which it has been possible to develop much of the material used in this book.

I also wish to thank companies who have supplied photographs of their equipment included in Chapters 10 and 13. These are Dexion (Impex Shelving System), Lansing Bagnall (Fork-lift trucks) and Mannesmann Demag (Automated Warehouse System). Lansing Bagnall are also thanked for supplying the cover photograph.

Finally, I wish to give special thanks to Paul Steele, Managing Director of PMMS, for the help and advice he has given me during the writing of this book.

The management of materials

Introduction

Much progress has been made in recent years to develop professionalism in all functions concerned with the management of
materials, aided, of course, by computer application. A major
factor that has demanded the need for such progress has been
the greatly increased cost of capital, which has risen from 3–4 per
cent in the 1950s to 10–15 per cent in the 1980s. However, while
successes have been achieved, progress towards the development
of a soundly based management-of-materials philosophy has
been generally disappointing. The importance of logistics
management has long been understood. It has been applied particularly successfully in the Armed Services, where men, equipment and materials have to be directed to the right place at the
right time. Within industry, commerce and the public sector,
organizational structures such as supplies management, operations
management and materials management have been introduced
and developed. Indeed, all these structures are established
throughout the United Kingdom. The concept of 'input' and
'output' management of materials has been propounded by a
number of writers. However, the fundamental problem has been
that increasing professionalism within purchasing, stores,
production planning and control, inventory control, materials
handling, warehouse and distribution has tended to be developed
mainly in independent compartments. This has produced an
insular, restricting and uneconomic approach. What is needed is
a philosophy of integrated professionalism. Staff cannot operate
well unless they appreciate the needs and problems of colleagues
in interrelated functions. Such awareness cannot by itself
produce desired results. These are achieved by each function
translating awareness into action and all staff working as a team
to achieve corporate objectives. Managing materials must be
viewed as a total concept, which is in balance with other major

functions such as marketing, sales, production, engineering, finance and personnel.

Major manufacturing industries in the United States have long recognized that materials management should be viewed as a total concept. The majority of directors, executives and managers in the UK now appreciate the need for materials to be better managed. The one point that appears to be at issue is how such an objective can best be achieved and over what time-scale. Organizations differ greatly in the nature and size of their operations and in their individual strengths and weaknesses. The market opportunities open to them and the threats they face may be dependent on widely differing influencing circumstances. Hence, there cannot be one common, standard approach to the management of materials.

Factors affecting choice

The particular approach adopted or pursued by an organization may depend on many factors, which are:

- Type and size of the organization, i.e. manufacturing, process, supply, service or transport industry, and public or commercial enterprise
- Organization independence or membership of a group of companies and operating at one or more locations
- Nature of its product(s) and or service(s)
- Profit centre accountability for a product or product range
- Relative importance of functions and their actual or potential contributions to total profitability
- Centralization or decentralization of the supplies, purchasing and stores operations
- Traditional custom and practice and extent of probable resistance to change
- Calibre of management and staff
- Computer system selection, application and development
- Extent of successful application of materials management within associated companies

In considering the various options for managing materials, the approach should be selected that seems most appropriate to needs, capabilities and practical application. This requires careful consideration being given to available options. The importance of seeking 'best value at the point of use' needs to be understood.

Materials management objectives

While organizations differ greatly in type and size, they all share a common essential need: that is, to be financially viable. This requires the achieving of two primary objectives, which are:

1. The improvement (or maintenance of an existing standard) of the quality of goods and services provided to customers
2. The reduction (or containment at satisfactory levels) of total annual expenditure to meet budget targets internally or externally set

These objectives cannot be achieved unless secondary or subordinate objectives are also met. These will obviously relate to the nature of the enterprise (e.g. manufacturing or non-manufacturing) and include the reduction in:

- Cost of bought-out goods and services
- Capital invested in stocks
- Transport, packaging and handling costs
- Value of work in progress
- Product throughput time
- Materials for disposal
- Research and development costs
- Total organization administrative costs

Other important objectives are the improvement in:

- Utilization of machines and other facilities
- Utilization of manpower
- Quality and specification of the product(s) and service(s)

A manufacturing company's resources should be considered in terms of the 'seven Ms' (i.e. management, money, machines, men, materials, methods and marketing). Most of these apply equally to the transport, supply and service industries in both the public and private sectors. Each of these areas may be considered separately, but they are interdependent, with some degree of overlap. Taking materials as an example, management, money and methods could influence greatly specification, choice of suppliers and prices paid. Also, management of materials must be intimately concerned with the management of men. The two cannot be disassociated.

Functional activities

Functional activities embraced will depend on the nature and size of the enterprise. Let us, therefore, next consider material flow in its simplest terms, which is shown in Fig.1.1.

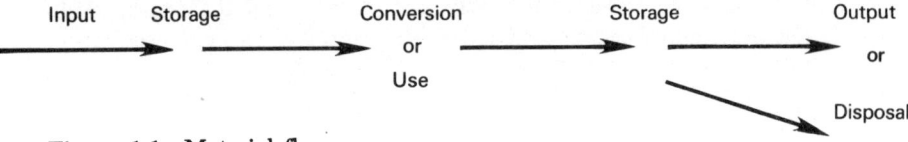

Figure 1.1   Material flow

In a manufacturing company, production materials are processed, converted or assembled and ultimately will form part of the saleable product. In a non-manufacturing organization, materials are withdrawn from stores for internal use, e.g. bedlinen, drugs and foodstuffs in the National Health Service.

Whatever the nature of an organization and its material flow, many activities are common, such as:

- Forecasting anticipated demand
- Authorizing material expenditure
- Sourcing to locate capable suppliers
- Issuing enquiries, evaluating quotations, negotiating and placing orders with suppliers
- Administrating orders placed
- Receiving goods
- Handling goods and putting into storage
- Controlling stock levels
- Issuing goods to users

In a manufacturing environment, additional major activities are:

- Material planning
- Work in progress
- Production control

So, too, might be finished-goods storage and distribution of goods to customers. In all cases, there is need for strict management and financial control of all functional activities.

Alternative methods of managing materials

Before we consider the different approaches used to manage materials, it is useful to define 'materials management'. The Institute of Purchasing and Supply (IPS) and the British Production and Inventory Control Society are working closely together to develop materials management in the UK. An IPS subcommittee has already defined materials management as follows:

> Materials Management is the concept requiring an organised structure which unifies into one functional responsibility the systematic planning and control of all materials from identification of the need to delivery to the customer.
>
> Materials Management embraces planning, purchasing, production and inventory control, storage, material handling and physical distribution. The objects of Materials Management are to optimise performance in meeting customer service requirements at the same time adding to profitability by minimising costs and making the best use of available resources.

Materials management is thus seen in a strictly manufacturing context. Most organizations in the UK do not and would not develop an organization to manage materials to this degree of sophistication. Let us consider, therefore, the various forms of organization structures used in the UK.

Traditional structure

This is the long-established traditional approach, where individual functions are independent one from another, a typical structure being as shown in Fig.1.2.

Each of these commercial activities, such as stores, purchasing and inventory control, operates within its own defined parameters to meet individual functional objectives against which achievement may be measured. Frequently, these objectives are in conflict. Purchasing may concentrate its efforts to obtain the keenest prices. Inventory control could seek to reduce stock levels. Stores might be preoccupied with storage and handling problems.

In manufacturing organizations, production planning and control are concerned with economic batch loading and utilization of machines and other facilities. The gulf between the commercial and production functions is often wide. However, in this

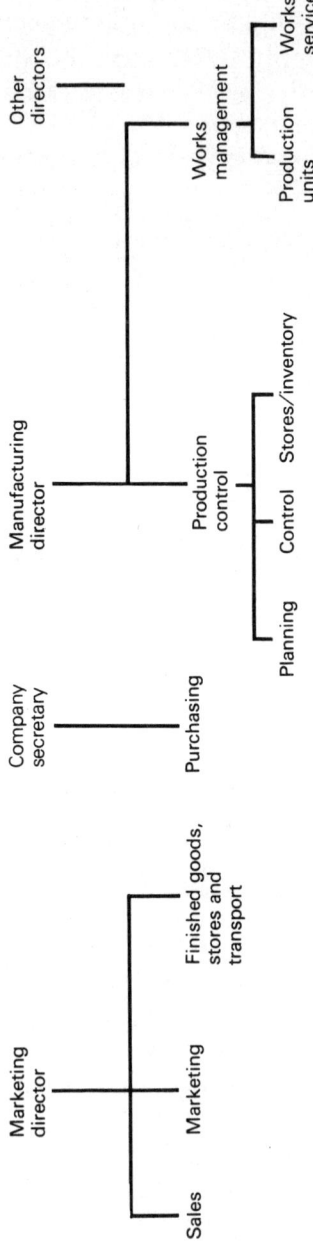

Figure 1.2 Traditional structure

approach to managing materials (and, indeed, in other approaches also), there is an awareness that commercially oriented staff must gain a better appreciation of the needs and problems of user staff. Increasing numbers of technical- and production-trained staff are being assigned to buying and inventory control work where such specialisms are considered essential.

There are some advantages to having independent commercial functions. This applies, for example, where the main contribution to a company's profitability is derived from the activities of one function. Consider the entrepreneurial skills and specialism of one person, the chief buyer. The nature of his job could require him to concentrate his attention almost exclusively on the supply market. The company's profits could flow very much from the skill of his decisions on how much to buy, when to buy and from what sources. Such a person needs to work closely with, and report directly to, a senior director or executive. It could be a gross misuse of his talents and flair to extend his reporting line or to burden him with unnecessary administrative responsibilities within, say, a supplies or materials management department.

Where the functions of purchasing, stores and inventory control are independent, the quality of coordination and cooperation between them will depend entirely on the attitudes and actions of individual managers, their directors and their staffs. It will be appreciated, however, that in a small company (and these form the greater majority of companies in the UK), the total workload of these three functions may be limited and so might be handled by very few people, in some cases by only one person.

Supplies management

This is a well established approach where all the supply market-oriented functions are brought together under one manager. This is the non-processing stage of input management. These functions normally include purchasing, physical storekeeping and inventory control. Transport may also be included. Many organizations in the public sector, including local, education and health authorities, have generally adopted this form of managing materials.

A typical supplies management organization structure is shown in Fig.1.3.

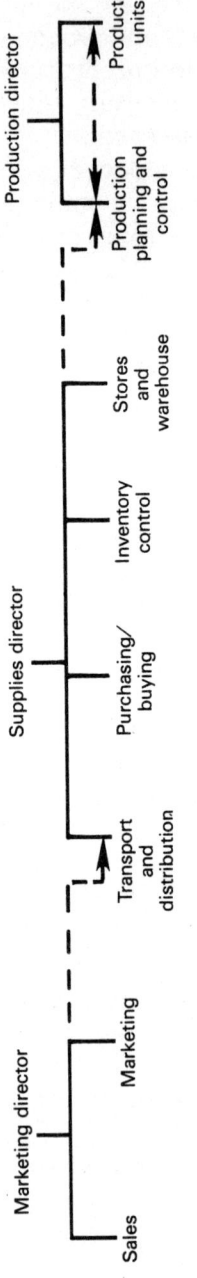

Figure 1.3 Supplies management structure

A supplies management structure provides good scope for coordinating these functions. The supplies manager can view the wider spectrum of the activities embraced and is able to arbitrate directly to deal with functional conflicts that arise between his subordinate section managers. His responsibilities include setting both departmental and functional objectives for his staff. His main objective is to ensure that they operate in the most effective and economical manner possible. This demands the right balance being sought and achieved in the following key cost/expenditure areas:

1. Expenditure on bought-out materials
2. Stockholding cost
3. Cost of non-availability of stock
4. Administration cost

The supplies manager has scope to optimize the whole of his resources of staff, equipment and facilities, deploying them to best advantage under changing situations. Because of his higher status, he has more influence at senior management or director/executive level. This is helpful, too, in his dealings with colleagues in finance, operations, production, engineering and sales. He will be mindful also that, in addition to the four areas of cost mentioned above, there must be full awareness of subsequent handling, processing or usage costs, which ultimately equate to the total cost.

Operations management
Operations management is applied to both manufacturing and non-manufacturing organizations. Let us consider first its application to a manufacturing company. In this approach, the functions included under supplies management (as discussed above) are combined with responsibility for manufacturing with its supporting production planning and control under one manager, the operations manager. The basic organization structure for operations management is shown in Fig.1.4.

This approach is adopted in some manufacturing companies where the manager responsible for the manufacturing or conversion process also has accountability for the cost-effectiveness of his profit centre operation. The person in charge of the operation may be a director or manager (for simplicity we refer to manager

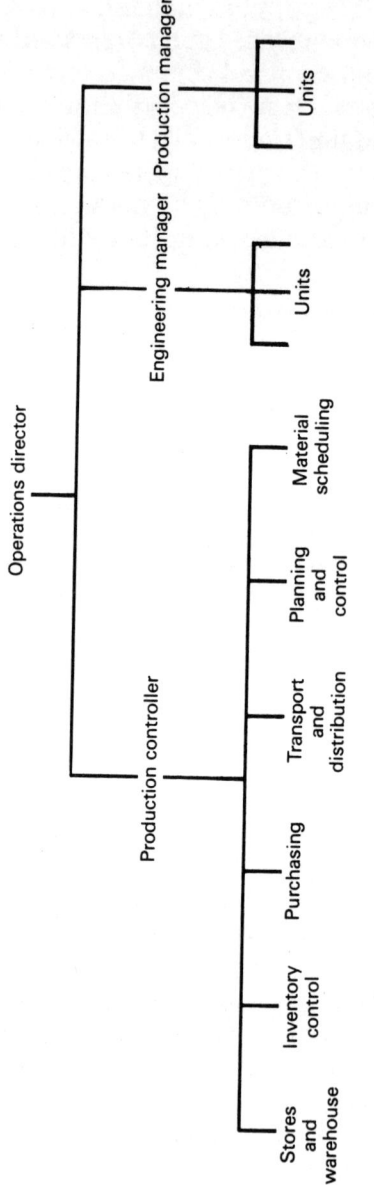

Figure 1.4   Operations management structure

only in this section). A very strong case can be made for one manager to control all the functions concerned that relate to the utilization of machines, materials, men and methods. The operations manager needs to have a more global view than the supplies manager. He, too, has to seek the right economic balance between aspects such as expenditure on bought-out materials, cost of stockholding, cost of non-availability of materials and administration cost. He will additionally, however, be particularly concerned with the cost of his production operation.

The operations management approach can have one major disadvantage. The manager is required to wear two quite different hats, a production one and a commercial one. Specialism is rapidly growing in these two widely differing fields and the operations manager must keep pace with developments in each of them. His skill is an ability to apply a broad expertise to manage effectively in both areas. One of an operation manager's main aims is to have competent functional specialists reporting to him.

In the non-manufacturing situation, the operations manager could be responsible for providing a service operation. For example, consider the operation of a city bus service. Here the operations manager's responsibilities include schedules, vehicles, facilities, manpower and materials. He could be responsible also for engineering maintenance and control of a central engineering workshop in which buses were serviced, repaired and overhauled to planned maintenance schedules.

Materials management
Materials management was developed initially in the United States within manufacturing industry. This concept was hailed by a number of major companies as a new, effective approach for dealing with material problems. There were high expectations that a new, coordinated approach to managing materials could be achieved under a senior manager. An organizational rather than a techniques solution should thus be sought. Materials management would be concerned with, but would not have actual control of, material processing or usage except for status reporting. It would be concerned with the long-term forecasting of demand, sourcing, acquiring, handling, storing and the planning and control of usage of materials.

When materials management was first introduced, it was considered that its application would yield significant contributions to profitability, far greater than could be gained in further reducing or containing labour costs. Later, a modified approach was developed that included similar functional groupings as before, but with one fundamental difference. Functional managers would not report to one senior manager. However, before we consider and compare these two quite different conceptual approaches, let us look at common benefits that are claimed from both these applications.

Common benefits
During recent years, surveys have been undertaken in a number of organizations that have adopted materials management of whatever form to determine what benefits have been gained. The main benefits claimed are:

1. Improvement in continuity of supplies, with reduced lead times
2. Reduction in inventories, with reduced obsolescence and surpluses
3. Improvement in cooperation and communications, with reduced duplication of effort
4. Reduction in material costs
5. Improvement in quality control
6. Improvement in status control, and hence quicker identification of problems

Materials management — 'organization'
The generally held view of authors on management is that better results are more likely to be achieved from good organization than from poor. Obviously, there are many cases where individual managers and staff achieve good results in spite of shortcomings in their organizations. However, there is little doubt that the consensus of informed opinion is that such performances would have been even better working from the sound foundations of good organization.

The basic materials management 'organization' structure is shown in Fig.1.5.

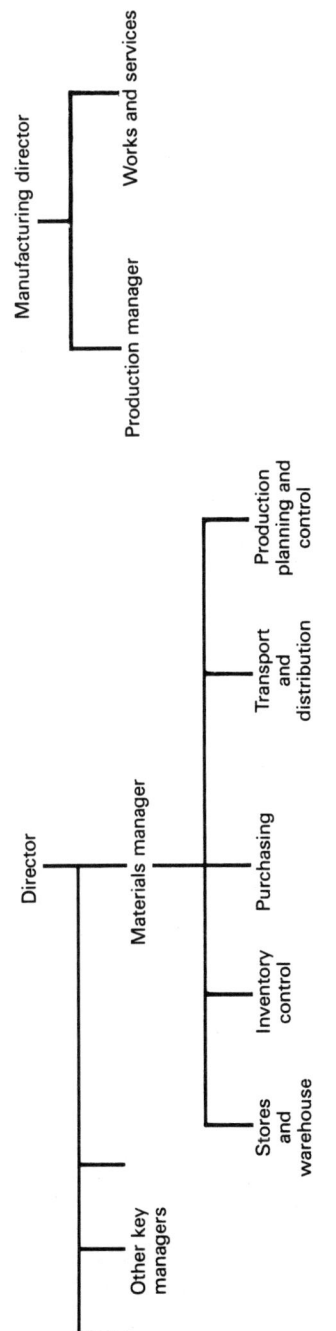

Figure 1.5 Materials management — 'organization' structure

Advantages

Insufficient research has been done to analyse adequately the results achieved by companies adopting the two approaches to materials management. However, many additional benefits are claimed by the proponents of the 'organization' approach, resulting mainly from the appointment of a senior manager. Let us consider the main points made relating to the scope of such a manager.

1. Sole ultimate responsibility and accountability.
2. Can view the total commitments on his department, produce a policy, set individual duties and responsibilities, and establish procedures and budgets.
3. Reports to a higher level in the organization. Thus greater scope to influence Board decisions affecting his area of operations and interfacing ones.
4. Is ideally placed to assess the capabilities and potential of professional specialists reporting to him. This enables him to select and train a possible successor.
5. Scope to evaluate the strengths and weaknesses throughout the whole of the materials management department. This facilitates optimum deployment of staff in changing circumstances.

Disadvantages

The opponents of the 'organization' approach claim that there are serious disadvantages to it, these being as follows:

1. Heads of the separate functions reporting to the manager lose status and could be demotivated.
2. Lines of communications lengthen to production and other user departments with some impeding of inter-functional communication.
3. An 'organization' approach is a major change of structure. Its introduction might create resistance to change with subsequent friction. It could adversely affect the relative balance of status and power with other functions such as marketing, finance and manufacturing/production.

Materials management — 'integrated system'

In the case of the 'integrated system' approach, an additional

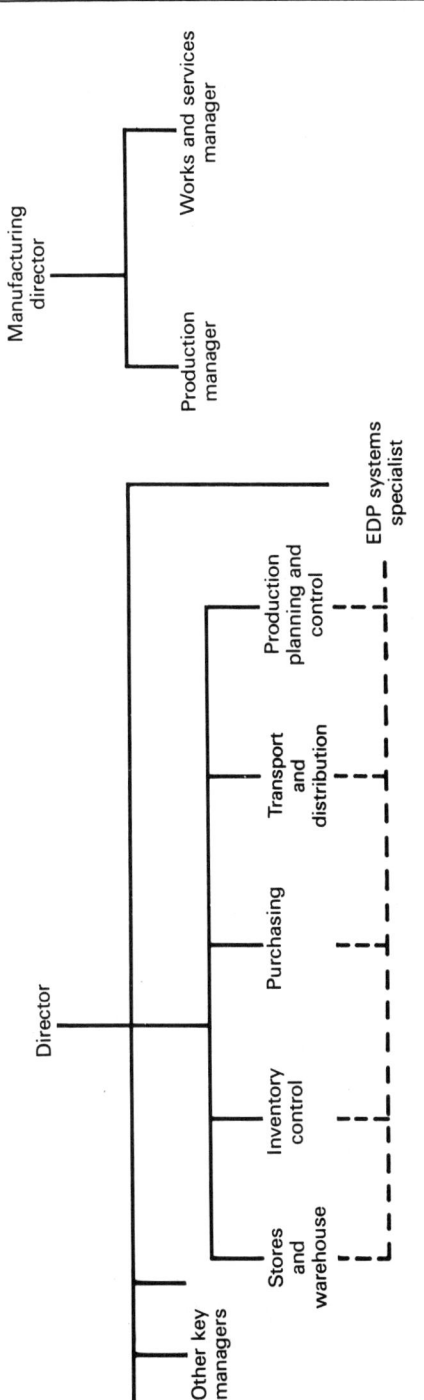

Figure 1.6 Materials management — 'integrated system' structure

level of management would not be appointed. Results would be achieved through coordination, cooperation and integration by consensus. All functional managers would be supported by a systems consultant working closely with them.

The basic 'integrated system' structure is shown in Fig.1.6.

Advantages

The particular additional advantages claimed from the adoption of the 'integrated system' approach are:

1. An additional level of management is not created.
2. Existing functional managers (e.g. purchasing manager, materials planning and control manager) do not lose status but continue to report to their directors or other executives as before.
3. As fundamental organizational change is not envisaged, there should be more support for such a system.
4. Lateral functional relationships continue as before, avoiding additional vertical links in communications.
5. There is more scope within the system for individual flair, initiative and the development of specialist skills, which are essential ingredients for the successful operation of materials management. The required pace of technological change cannot be achieved without specialism.

As a manager will not be appointed, the services of a consultant coordinator, specializing in materials management systems, is required. This assignment could be for an extended period depending on circumstances. The consultant must discuss functional objectives and roles with individual heads of sections. He would report direct to senior Board level.

Disadvantages

The proponents of the 'organization' approach claim disadvantages for this alternative approach, the main ones being the following:

1. No one person is in a position of knowledge and responsibility to deal promptly and effectively with major problems affecting any functional interface.

2. Resources cannot readily be redeployed to meet greatly fluctuating commitments on an individual function that result from overload, introduction of new procedures or absence of staff.
3. Expenditure on materials is a high percentage of a company's total annual expenditure. There would be no senior manager at an influential level to control it.
4. There would be no one person within the organization able to understand, without bias, the needs and problems of the integrated functions. There would be no one capable of promoting effective coordinated development to meet corporate plan commitments.
5. Finally, there would be no experienced senior manager responsible for the whole material management group who can concentrate his efforts to optimize the use of all resources, human, material, accommodation, equipment and facilities.

The materials manager

In selecting a materials manager, consideration would be given to an individual's capacity and ability to manage a materials management department, with all that this demands. Such a person must be equipped to handle a challenging job. This requires self-development as a professional manager. He must be alive to all significant developments taking place in materials management, with particular emphasis on the company's own field of specialism.

What sort of background experience and qualifications does the applicant need? This depends very much on the nature of the organization's operations. Consider, for example, two organizations. The first is heavily conversion process oriented. The second is very much supply market oriented. Thus the contributions required from the commercial and production functions could differ greatly. In the first case, an experienced production planner and controller might be the best choice as manager. In the other case, a supplies manager would seem to be better equipped to do the job, as a supplies management type of organization is required rather than a materials management one.

Where there is significant difference in the balance of contributions between production and supply market oriented functions, particular consideration must be given to the applicant's background. He must, however, be foremost a professional manager and not just a professional specialist. Results demanded from him will only be achieved through the coordinated efforts of his team of functional specialists and their staffs. He has to be a leader who can motivate people of greatly differing experience and backgrounds. They must be stimulated to work to the limits of their capabilities within a very demanding environment. Reduction in operating costs or improvement in services being provided should not be sought through badly conceived reorganization and grouping of functions under inadequately equipped managers. To seek to do so would be doomed to failure.

Measuring performance

Management embraces planning, organizing, coordinating and controlling. A key element of controlling is the measuring of actual departmental or functional performance to determine how they compare with planned. Measurement is concerned with identifying shortfalls in performance to facilitate necessary corrective action being taken.

To what extent do the different forms of organization structures that we have discussed facilitate realistic measurement of performance of all the functions concerned? To what extent may realistic evaluation be made of the cost-effectiveness of the various organizational options? These are two vitally important questions to which quantitative answers are required.

Ultimately, successful application of materials management of whatever form must be measured against the productive output or level of service provided and the costs incurred. Materials management must have its objectives, strategies and tactics. It must operate from a sound plan based on good reliable data.

Measuring the effectiveness of each of the functional activities requires a quantitative or qualitative approach depending on the aspects under consideration. Let us consider inventory control and purchasing as two examples.

Inventory control
In the case of inventory levels, for example, an inventory budget might be £1.5m but actual stock valuation is £1.62m (an over-investment of £120 000). Failure to meet target is thus clearly

demonstrated in financial terms. The resulting true total cost to the organization is not, however, so readily assessed. Careful analysis is necessary of all contributing factors. For example, a buyer advances delivery of a high-value order for materials to avoid paying a high price increase soon to be applied. He arranges early delivery of other material because of anticipated scarcity. Prior agreement is required in both cases where inventories will be inflated. However, imposing a severe reduction in inventory levels could seriously jeopardize the ability to meet specified service levels. Careful consideration is required of the possible consequences of such an action.

Purchasing
Purchasing's contribution to profitability is readily measurable on prices paid. Consider the following example, where the cost of bought-out materials is 50 per cent of a company's total return on sales.

Total sales turnover £100 000	Purchasing expenditure £50 000	Company profit £10 000 (10% of turnover)

If purchasing had been more efficient, it might have reduced the cost of bought-out materials by, say, 5 per cent. Had it done so, the above figures would have been modified as follows:

£100 000	£47 500	£12 500 (12½% of turnover)

Hence, a 5 per cent reduction in the cost of bought-out materials would have yielded a 25 per cent increase in profits. Alternatively, selling prices might have been reduced to increase sales volume to yield higher profits.

Purchasing's performance on price is thus measured against expenditure budgets, individual buyers being given annual targets.

Measurement of an individual function's performance must be considered in relation to the measurement of all the related functions, i.e. as one integrated entity. Savings made in one area can often be more than cancelled out by resulting losses made in another. In the example given on page 19 relating to purchasing, consideration is given to price but not to 'value at the point of use'. In applying measurement and seeking solutions to problems, there must be an awareness of possible implications across all interfaces.

Conclusions

Every organization needs to manage its materials in the most effective and economical manner possible, relating to its own circumstances. Consideration needs to be given to many points, which include:

1. Ensuring that there is no conflict with corporate plan objectives. The impact of proposed change on the attitudes of finance, sales, production and engineering departments must be anticipated and problems arising overcome.
2. Examining carefully organizational needs and selecting the method of operation that seems most appropriate to individual circumstances.
3. Being mindful of the capacities and capabilities of managers and staff to ensure compatibility with 2.
4. Ensuring that the benefits of proposed change are sold to all who are required to operate the new policies, systems and procedures. Their full and active cooperation is vital. Hence the need to avoid introducing counter-productive, demotivating measures wherever possible.
5. Giving necessary training, which is required early rather than later.
6. Setting realistic time-scales for implementing proposals.
7. Providing good management.

The provision of a framework within which materials are well managed is demonstrated in Fig.1.7.

Whatever form of approach is adopted to manage materials, the use of resources must be optimized. This requires answers being sought to the following questions:

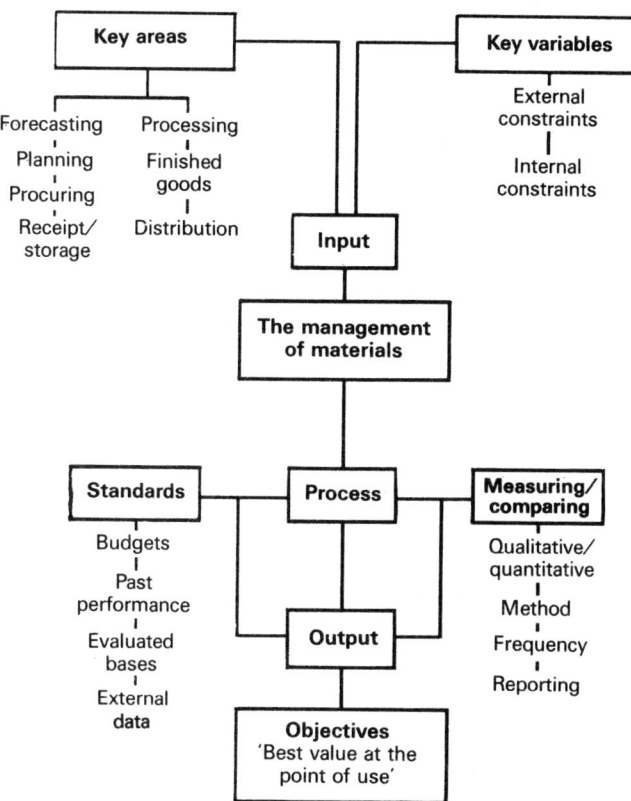

Figure 1.7 Measuring materials management performance

1. What is the annual operating cost of each function? What is the nature of the individual function's contribution to corporate objectives?
2. What is the extent of each function's shortfall in performance against objectives, expressed in cost terms?
3. Can we measure this shortfall and how realistic will the figures be?

These are important but difficult questions requiring much thought to answer them. Armed with such information, consideration can then be given to a realistic reappraisal of the use of existing resources. Should one function be strengthened at the expense of another? Would investment in additional resources yield the required improvement in overall performance within target cost?

While such analysis was being undertaken, the total cost figures would be compared with those of other major functions such as marketing, sales, finance, production and engineering, as appropriate. The degree of success achieved in meeting corporate objectives will depend very much on how well resources have been deployed and utilized. There must be no obvious imbalance.

Materials management is a key area for investigation and application. The following chapters deal with the sequence of functional activities on which the success of the management of materials depends. The sequencing of chapters is related to the material cycle and not to the relative importance of functions. For example, the two key functions of inventory control and production control are discussed in the later chapters.

MATERIALS MANAGEMENT MANUAL

A comprehensive operating manual is essential, which covers all relevant policies, systems, procedures and documentation. The manual would be sectionalized to facilitate updating, which should be done when amendments become necessary. In preparing such a manual, care must be taken to avoid over-elaboration. It must be a working document to which all staff have access to data of particular relevance to them. The manual would thus be a reference document, which would not only be value to existing staff but also be invaluable to new staff and staff under training. Particular sections dealing with relevant aspects of supply commitments would be available to key suppliers.

2

Demand, supply, resource management

Introduction
Materials management requires a sound foundation of knowledge, appraisal and analysis of probable customer demand, supply market input and internal resources available and required. The good health of an organization is very much dependent on sufficient effort being directed to long-term analysis and planning. Planning periods vary up to 10 years or more depending on the nature of the organization and its products. For example, in the aeronautical industry, the time-scale for design and development work for a new plane and the subsequent production of the prototype could take a decade or more. In the case of a garden mower or washing machine, the time-scale would be considerably shorter, probably under two years. All organizations have customers and suppliers and most will also have competitors. A common objective will be to achieve profitability or financial viability. Consider Fig.2.1. This shows a fairly basic situation where an organization deals with two suppliers, has two customers and has a single competitor.

Externally, the organization also has to operate within the constraints of economic, political, industrial and social pressures. It has to respond to demands of changing legislation introduced by home or foreign governments. Quality, availability and price of an organizations's product(s) or service(s) may be significantly affected by external events or trends. This could result in the deteriorating quality, extended delivery or increased prices of bought-in materials. Thus, an organization has not only to respond promptly to change but seek to anticipate change. Materials management has therefore to be very much geared into this process of anticipation by close liaison with other key functions and by good planning.

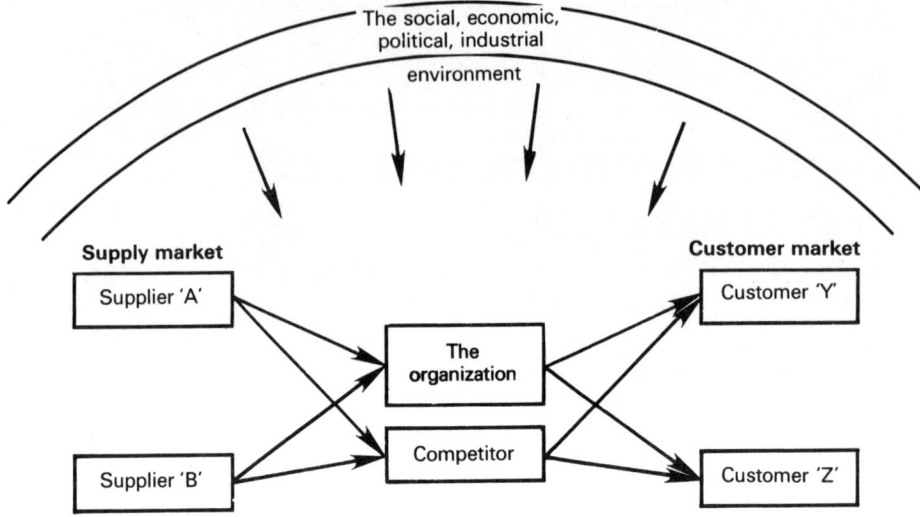

Figure 2.1   The organization and its markets

Corporate planning

Managements have overall objectives they wish to achieve. Resulting from changing internal or external circumstances, objectives often have to change. This response may be related to internal considerations, e.g. financial difficulties, or to external considerations, e.g. customer market demand. In recent years many companies have had to redeploy resources and find new customers in new markets. Because of a greatly reduced demand for shipping, shipbuilders became involved in oil-rig construction. Now there is a decline in the offshore oil industry, new markets must be sought. Hi-fi is another example where compact discs are rapidly replacing LP records. It is anticipated that by 1990 very few companies will be manufacturing LPs. This change will also affect turntable, cartridge and stylus manufacturers as compact-disc players gradually replace turntables.

During the last decade or so, increased rate of change has affected most organizations. The oil crises of the years 1973 to 1980, with the resulting impact on energy, heating, lighting and transport costs, caused major problems for most organizations. This critical development had not been anticipated by most national governments or organizations and hence little or no effort was directed to planning how best to handle it. Much, however, has been learned since this period of catastrophe. Greater emphasis is now directed to forecasting. Such effort has to relate equally to supply and customer markets — such a balanced approach has not always been sought in the past, to the detriment of the performance of many organizations.

Consider Fig.2.1 again. This shows a basic setting of an organization within its operating environment. It will be one of a series of snapshots taken at irregular periods over the years, projecting forward the probable situations of supply, demand, resources, competition, with opportunities, threats and constraints. These periodic snapshots are most unlikely to be similar one with another. Significant changes will occur. All functions have a contribution to make to corporate planning, with planners, particularly, giving adequate attention to the realities of their operating environment. Management can then focus its attention on major issues. What, then, should be the role and scope of materials management in longer-term planning?

Product demand

A manufacturing company requires a market strategy. It could seek to maintain a current output or share of a market. Alternatively, as opportunities arise, it could take a larger share of the market, increasing production. Other situations might apply when it is considered uneconomic to continue producing a particular product.

Consider a manufacturing organization, Leadright Manufacturing Company, which makes four products. Assume the time is October in the current year (year −1). The organization is preparing its new annual five-year corporate plan due to commence on 1 January in the coming year (year 1). To demonstrate the possible varying demands of a mixed product range, we are considering four products each being in a different stage of its life cycle. This is illustrated in Fig.2.2.

The stages during the life cycle of any product are development, introduction or launch, growth, maturity and decline. In this example the projected demand for the four products is as assessed in October of year −1. Demand forecasts are reviewed periodically and materials management's contribution is to

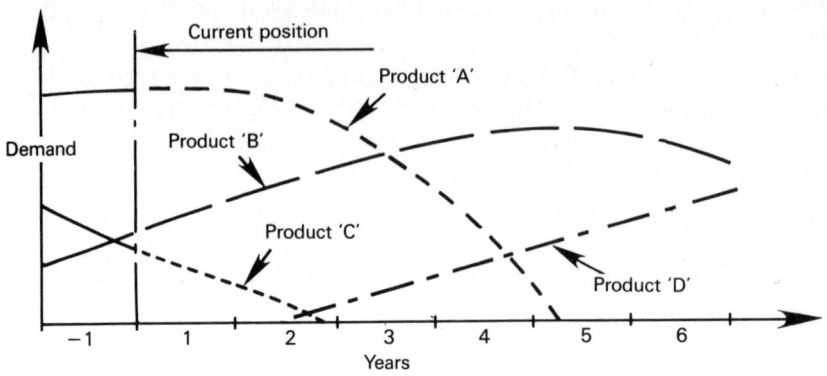

Figure 2.2   Product life cycle

support these projected varying product demands at each stage. The anticipated required flow of input materials to support production programming as viewed in October of year −1 is as follows:

- **Product 'A'**   This is in the maturity stage. Demand has peaked and is expected to remain static perhaps for one year. Subsequently, in year 2, there would be a steady decline in demand, followed later by a more rapid one.
- **Product 'B'**   This is in the growth stage. The current steady rate of increase would continue, peaking off in product maturity about year 4. A steady decline in demand would follow after year 5.
- **Product 'C'**   This is in the decline stage. The steadily reducing rate of demand would continue, falling off completely by year 2.
- **Product 'D'**   This product is in the development stage. It is planned to introduce it into the market in year 2. Steadily increasing demand would be predicted for years 3, 4 and 5.

It will be noted in the above example that forecasted product life cycles for each of the products have significantly differing time-scales. Demand patterns also vary, e.g. the peak demand for 'A' may be twice that for 'D'. Also, the life-cycle curves could be affected by seasonal and short-term market fluctuations.

Seasonal fluctuations may be predictable, e.g. the peak demand for swimsuits in the summer months. However, social changes do affect established seasonal demand, as is the case with the increasing number of people seeking holidays in the sun throughout the year. Hence, demand for swimsuits does not now peak so strongly in the summer period.

Product life cycles are reducing. Hi-fi equipment is a good example of this development. New models are being introduced by the leading manufacturers within very short time-scales. Within two or three years, spares become difficult to obtain. Increased technology and competition in the market place have influenced this trend, with many organizations being compelled to direct increased resources to developing new products to stay in business.

The projected life cycles for the four products shown in Fig.2.2 would be assessed in October of the current year as part of the corporate planning exercise. Such projections would not be static but be under regular review. By October in the following year a new corporate plan would be prepared. Year 1 in the figure then becomes year −1, year 2 becoming year 1 and so on. Actual life cycle curves may subsequently prove to be significantly different from those forecasted. Thorough market research of both customer and supply markets has to be ongoing. The means of converting material input to material/service output (i.e. resources of money, management, machines, facilities and expertise) must also be evaluated.

Manufacturing resource planning (MRPII)

Materials management cannot operate successfully unless supported by a sound foundation of MRPII. This is true for both manufacturing and non-manufacturing organizations. The extent of application will vary considerably depending on the nature and size of the enterprise. This is true, too, for computer systems application on which MRPII depends. MRPII, a development of materials requirements planning (MRPI), was introduced in the US to provide the means of overcoming production problems in major manufacturing industries. The concept takes a much wider view of manufacturing than that taken by MRPI, which we discuss in Chapter 3. Let us consider the major prerequisites for successful demand, supply, resource management.

Integration of interfacing functional activities

MRPI, with its cornerstone of a realistic, achievable master production schedule, must be integrated with inventory and work-in-progress control, procurement and quality control. Regular effective monitoring of all these activities is essential. The tight controls directed to inventories must be applied to work in progress with regular updating of workloads. Consider the following example of a large steel forged component with a machining process of an estimated 100 hours. At the end of three days machining, the hours recorded against this item is 45 hours. The balance of machining work is theoretically $100 - 45 = 55$ hours. However, problems might have been experienced during processing, incurring increased hours. The number of hours estimated might be incorrect. Hence, the balance of hours outstanding must be reassessed related to the remaining work content of the process.

Data adequacy and accuracy

The term 'level of service' is applied to the required service to customers and users and to item availability to support MRPI. Similar levels of adequacy and accuracy are essential for the data requirements from which to operate, monitor and control MRPII. Such data include item reference numbers, work order numbers, process sequences and times, specification and quality. Purchase requisition and order numbers and manufacturing lead-time data may also be required. This necessitates a regular and prompt updating of information. Production schedules too must be realistic and achievable, being related to known commitments and capacity availability.

Computer systems

Both hardware and software packages must be appropriate for the intended use, giving necessary scope for future expansion or development. The needs of all users must not be overlooked, full consideration being given to staff at shop-floor level and their working environment.

Application of techniques

Techniques can only be used successfully if applied within the framework of good systems under the right management approach. Education is an important aspect of this. If large sums are to be spent on providing first-class resources, then thought must be directed to ensure that staff are adequately trained and develop positive and constructive attitudes.

Development of new products

In a world of rapid technological change, a dynamic approach to new product development is vital. The reasons for product development are many, the main ones being to:

- Meet or create consumer demand
- Keep abreast or ahead of the competition
- Maintain or increase the volume/value of sales
- Satisfy statutory regulations
- Improve servicing of products
- Improve profitability

Consider the example of the domestic vacuum cleaner. An increasing number of new manufacturers have entered the market recently. Competition is strong. Housewives will ultimately decide which will be the best selling models. In making their choices they will consider many factors, which include:

- Price
- Style, appearance, colour, workmanship and finish
- Size and weight
- Ease of control and handling
- Effectiveness and adaptability (inc. tools and fitments)
- Safety
- Cost of running and servicing (inc. spares availability)
- Noise
- Durability

The designer must therefore be mindful of consumer requirements. He must also consider developments being made by competitors that may influence buying choice. For example, a number of new models are designed to suck up water as well as dust. The consumer will be influenced by the impact of advertising, including sales campaigns, company reputation and recommendations from vacuum-cleaner owners. We have mentioned the impact on all organizations of the oil crises of the period 1973 to

1980. The impact on the US motor-car industry is a good example. A drastic reappraisal of its previous marketing strategy was vital. It had to change its long-established policy of producing a large volume of models with high-capacity 'gas-guzzling' engines of 15 to 25 miles per gallon (m.p.g.) to compete with Japanese and European manufacturers of smaller cars with their more economic fuel consumptions of 35 to 50 m.p.g.

Capital plan

The 'capital plan', which deals with plant and equipment requirements, is an important element of the 'corporate plan'. The marketing and sales departments make their long- and short-term forecasts of probable product demand. Production management's task is to determine how it may best make its contribution. This is undertaken in close consultation with the engineering function concerned in the design, development, installation and maintenance of plant and equipment. Resources required to support planned production programmes include plant and equipment categorized as additional, modified or replacement. Purchasing is responsible for issuing enquiries and obtaining quotations. An estimating or cost engineering department could be concerned in determining total project costs. In a large organization, a number of differing schemes may be submitted from the various divisions, regions or departments. Board approval and authorization would be sought for such expenditure to be included in the capital plan to meet one or more of the following objectives:

- Return on capital employed
- Increase in production output
- Improvement in product quality
- Reduced product cost
- Compliance with factory legislation
- Maintaining current production levels

The Board would be responsible for examining the various schemes submitted in relation to the relevance and needs of the above objectives. It would consider financial outlays, expenditure phasing and the extent and timing of probable return on investment. It would also consider alternative investment opportunities. Discussions would follow with scheme originators, and some schemes may be deleted, others modified by reducing or increasing capability. The phasing of financial expenditure over the five years of the capital plan could also require adjustment i.e. advancing or deferring). Ultimately, the Board would agree on a final plan and give approval for its introduction on 1 January of year 1.

The capital plan would, however, be subject to change during its life. A brief outline five-year capital plan is shown in Fig.2.3.

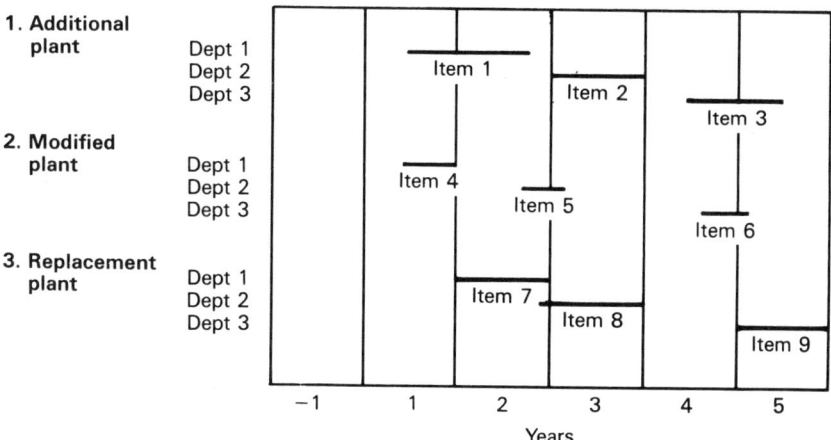

Figure 2.3 Five-year capital plan

RETURN ON CAPITAL EMPLOYED
This is evaluated by estimating the total return projected annual cash inflows v. investment outlay. The annual cash inflows over the payback period would be related to the present value of money (discounted cash flow). Consider the following example, where a decision has to be made between two proposals, i.e. projects 'A' and 'B':

Investment	Project 'A' £180 000		Project 'B' £165 000	
Period of operation	5 years		5 years	
Budgeted cash inflow	(£ 000)		(£ 000)	
	Actual	Cumulative	Actual	Cumulative
Year 1	100	100	40	40
2	100	200	40	80
3	80	280	60	140
4	60	340	100	240
5	20	360	120	360
Total payback		£360 000		£360 000

It will be noted that the projected cash inflow from project 'B' is the same as for project 'A' but for a lower investment, i.e. £15 000 less. No consideration has been given to the relative value of money over the five years.

Payback period
It will be noted that the investment is recovered during the second year for project 'A' and during the fourth year for project 'B'. The cash inflow predicted for project 'A' during the fifth year is only £20 000.

Discounted cash flow
The above figures exclude consideration of probable relative value of money over the five years. Let us assume for ease of calculation that money can be invested at 10 per cent per annum over that period. This means that the present value of £1 over the five years of project operation would be as follows:

End of year	Value related to present level (1.00)
1	0.91*
2	0.83*
3	0.75*
4	0.68*
5	0.62*

* It will be noted that 10 per cent is deducted from each related value in turn.

To determine the relative value of payback for each of the projects these discounted cashflow factors must be included as follows:

	Project 'A' £180 000 5 years (£ 000)	Project 'B' £165 000 5 years (£ 000)
Investment	£180 000	£165 000
Period of operation	5 years	5 years
Budgeted cash inflow	(£ 000)	(£ 000)
Year 1	$100 \times 0.91 = 91.0$	$40 \times 0.91 = 36.4$
2	$100 \times 0.83 = 83.0$	$40 \times 0.83 = 33.2$
3	$80 \times 0.75 = 60.0$	$60 \times 0.75 = 45.0$
4	$60 \times 0.68 = 40.8$	$100 \times 0.68 = 68.0$
5	$20 \times 0.62 = 13.2$	$120 \times 0.62 = 74.4$
Total payback	£288 000	£257 000

Project 'A' thus has an estimated higher level of return compared with project 'B', i.e. £31 000 higher, against the higher initial investment, i.e. £15 000 higher. Current and projected total annual company cash flows would also be considered, together with estimated future annual rates of inflation and the impact of probable future tax proposals. The projects may take greatly differing time-scales to complete, with greatly differing phasings of expenditure. In one case, expenditure may be spread fairly evenly over the project period. In the other, a very high proportion of the investment may be incurred during the early months. Loss of probable investment opportunity related to expenditure phasing would, therefore, be evaluated as part of total project evaluation.

Engineering spares

A logical extension to the capital plan is a company's policy on the types and levels of spares to buy and stock. Such spares are required to:

- Achieve planned levels of plant utilization
- Maintain product quality
- Extend the product range
- Give flexibility to plant operation
- Ensure safe operation of plant
- Give the required return on capital employed

Investment in spares is considered when applying for capital expenditure. Annual investment in such spares can represent up to 10 per cent or more of the purchased value of the plant/ equipment, such additional expenditure being allocated to revenue or to capital.

The value of the required investment in spares is normally determined from experience with similar plant or by obtaining recommendations from the suppliers of the plant. The determination of the value by other means is difficult. A scientific approach that facilitates precise evaluation of the lifing of all spares is an ideal. Consider steel rolling-mill bearings as an example. Rates of wear will be influenced by variations in quality of material, loading, temperature and flow of lubricating oil and ingress of dust or other abrasive material. The rate of metal fatigue in a driving shaft developing through increasing operation can be more readily determined on a test bench than in the production environment. Basic factors to consider that influence spares inventory levels and usage rates include:

- Type, age and condition of the plant and equipment
- Operating conditions and vulnerability to breakdowns
- Degree of planned maintenance carried out
- Operating hours, i.e. single-, double- or three-shift working
- Levels of production, mechanical and electrical stoppages expressed as percentages of standard period operating hours; down-time costs
- Cost of maintenance

The value of spares inventory and annual usage expenditure can be expressed as percentages of the replacement value of the plant and equipment. An empirical formula might be developed, including all the influencing aspects given above, enabling actual percentages to be compared with budget. An important point not to be overlooked is that, as a result of efforts directed to minimize spares usage, modifications are embodied that would affect the formula.

Purchasing analysis and research
Purchasing's role within materials management's contribution to corporate planning is purchasing analysis and research. Purchasing analysis and research has been defined as 'a sys-

tematic investigation of any area influencing purchasing (and hence, materials management) performance'. The foundation for purchasing research is knowledge of the key materials, energy and services required to support the corporate plan. Purchasing research and analysis is thus not concerned with day-to-day buying activities but with the longer term. It deals with the following key areas.

Economic analysis
This is concerned with forecasting probable longer-term price trends and the resulting influences on suppliers and competitors and their probable effects.

Commodity studies
Efforts are directed here to technological developments in the supply market and their probable impact on the organization's product(s) or service(s) provided. Consideration is given, too, to developing substitutes, alternative materials, value analysis, standardization and variety reduction.

Supplier analysis
Obtainable capacity in the supply market for key materials has to match forecasted future demand. This requires knowledge of key suppliers and their possible future intentions for expansion, contraction, specialization or diversification. Knowledge of an existing supplier's current performance (vendor rating) and analysis of his financial status and trends form a sound basis for pursuing such analysis. Where there is or will be a shortfall between supply and demand, attention must be given to this. A new supplier might have to be located and developed if an existing one lacks potential.

The above-mentioned areas for investigation are very much concerned with long-term or strategic purchasing. Other areas relate more to the short term but obviously have longer-term implications. These include value analysis, administrative analysis, cost analysis and life-cycle costing.

STRATEGIC PURCHASING
Purchasing analysis and research relates to longer-term planning. It is a completely different activity from day-to-day

buying. These two functions are sometimes handled by one group of purchasing staff, but this depends on the size of an organization and the nature, volume and value of its expenditure on purchased materials. The three traditional approaches to allocating work to a buyer are as follows.

Commodity oriented
In the larger organizations, where there are more than one buyer, this approach tends to be the one most generally favoured. Each buyer has responsibility for a range of commodities and is thus able to specialize to some degree in the supply market.

User department oriented
This is not so widely adopted as the above. Each buyer is assigned to provide a service to a particular department (or departments) within the organization. Each department thus has its own direct link with the supply market through one individual in purchasing.

Project/contract oriented
This approach is restricted to organizations engaged in major projects or contracts. The buyer is assigned to work directly under the project/contract manager.

In each of the above cases, purchasing analysis and research is used to great advantage to plan ahead and to anticipate probable future supply problems. Hence, efforts can be directed in consultation with all interested parties to consider the best actions to take. Deliveries of key materials can be advanced, alternatives or substitutes sought or manufacturing methods and processes modified. How best may time and effort be devoted to key materials? One approach is expounded by Steele and Elliott-Shircore in an article in *Purchasing and Supply Management* journal entitled 'Procurement positioning overview' (December 1985). This categorizes all bought-in materials into four groupings, which are strategic (security), strategic (critical value), tactical (acquisition) and tactical (profit).

Figure 2.4 shows how these categories are placed on horizontal and vertical scales of 'profit potential' and 'supply /vulnerability' respectively.

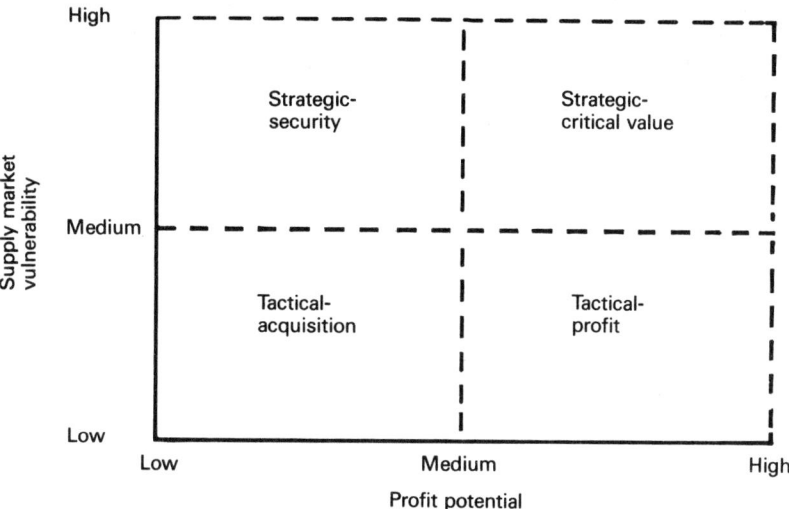

Figure 2.4 Procurement positioning overview

Steele and Elliott-Shircore comment on the two 'strategic' blocks in this scenario, which are related to long-term planning as follows:

1. Strategic–Security
   Every manufacturing operation has its critical materials, the availability of which are imperative to continuing production and sales of its products. This category covers those materials which will stop production dead in its tracks if they are not available. The major activity-characteristics for these items relate to ensuring continuity of supply under all circumstances.
2. Strategic–Value
   These items are critical to the company's profitability and must be kept under close value management scrutiny at all times. Since this block constitutes a 'survival' area it will demand considerable time, attention and effort and may involve careful, hard and protracted negotiation. Time must be made and value must be maximised.

It is particularly important to relate staff quality and capability input to the highly rated materials. The figure (Fig.2.4) can be redrawn as shown in Fig.2.5.

The nature and extent of the purchasing manager's involvement in order placing and contract involvement are related to

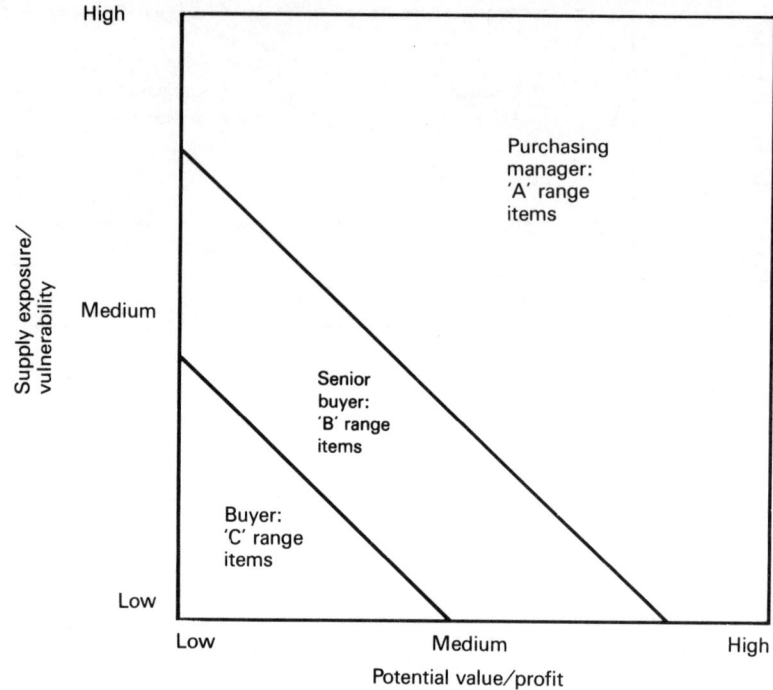

Figure 2.5 Staff involvement in procurement

strategic and tactical considerations of a purchase and the experience and competence of his staff. It should be noted that the degree of the manager's involvement is not related to scale on the figure. On an ABC or Pareto analysis evaluation he might be concerned personally with 10 per cent or less of items, which could constitute 70 per cent or more of important work content that demands his attention.

Capacity planning
Medium- and long-term capacity planning is undertaken with consideration to a number of factors.

Forecast of probable demand
Demand might currently be maintained at its present level, be growing or reducing with fluctuations in trend curves. Consider the situation where at the end of year 1 demand has been

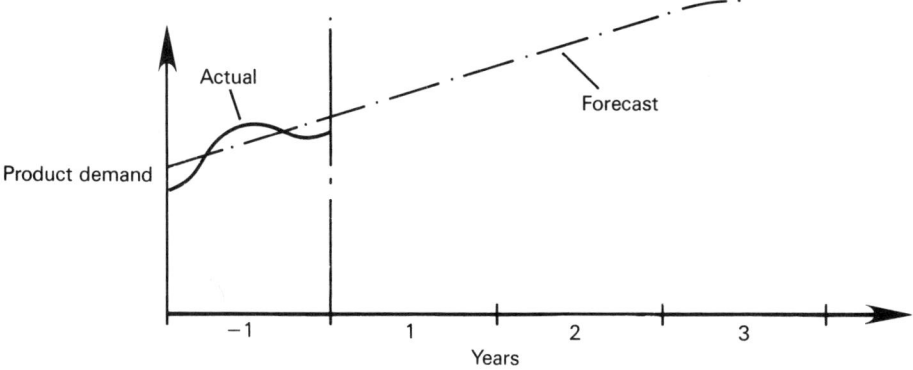

Figure 2.6   Fluctuations in demand

growing with seasonal fluctuations and the forecast future demand within the next four years is as shown in Fig.2.6.

Demand variation
Capacity planning can proceed once final consideration has been given to the forecast projected demand line. Are there likely to be any significant variations below or above the line? If so, of what probable magnitude and duration? Can realistic upper and lower limits be set?

Capacity
Current capacity may be related to the projected upper and lower demand limits. An organization can have a number of options or strategies to consider. One could be to maintain the present capacity levels and accept that there will be some degree of under- and over-utilization of capacity. Where capacity falls short of demand, can the overload be sub-let at short notice to capable subcontractors? Alternatively, can the overload be absorbed by additional shift working (when possible and desirable), over an acceptable time-scale?

In some manufacturing companies, flexibility in the utilization of equipment is possible as the production line is adaptable to handle a number of different products. The short-, medium- and long-term cost implications of the various options would be considered. Problems of under-utilization of production facilities relate not only to reduced return on capital employed but can affect management/labour relationships. For example, short-time working or lay-offs would affect the morale of employees, with work tempo being adversely affected.

Conclusions

All organizations are concerned with where they are now and where they want to be in the short, medium and long term. The long term for some may be five years. For others working on, for example, aircraft development, long term may mean a period of 10 to 20 years or more. A high standard of forecasting and planning will then be required to ensure that supply market and internal resource capabilities can be developed and harnessed to meet customer market demand. The shortfall between the two is known as the strategic gap. The probability of its existence must be determined and analysed at the earliest possible stage and appropriate corrective action taken. Subsequently, continuous monitoring is essential. Realistic resource and material planning can then proceed within the framework of good materials management.

3

Materials planning management

Introduction
As materials grow increasingly in importance, good materials planning is essential. Planning depends on regular realistic evaluations and re-evaluations of rapid and significant changes in demand. These assessments have to be related to probable material input flow, material handling and processing resources availability, with good forecasting being the basis of good planning. Which department or section should be responsible for materials planning? In supply-type organizations, i.e. education, health and local authorities, inventory control working closely with users would probably take responsibility for planning material flow. In public utilities, such as the National Coal Board and London Transport, where repairs and overhauls are carried out in central engineering workshops, materials planning sections similar to those operating in manufacturing organizations may be responsible.

Ultimately, efforts must be directed to minimizing the total cost of:

1. Inventories
2. Non-availability of materials
3. Manufacturing
4. Administration

These cannot always be readily evaluated, as there are many variables affecting materials, such as modifications, defects, market price fluctuations, delivery lead-time variations, flexibility in the production line and in maintenance requirements.

Production planning
Production planning seeks to determine, and offer, realistic achievable dates to customers, which means that the right product has to be produced to time to meet the needs of cus-

tomers. Planning has to operate within the constraints of acceptable cost and available or obtainable resources. The base point for production planning of material requirements is dependent on the nature of the demand commitment. This might relate to the sales forecast, order book or production capacity. Characteristics vary between production and customer oriented organizations. Production may be geared to replenishing warehouse finished-goods stocks or to batch or single customer contracts. The permutations are many.

Whatever the nature of its commitment, production planning is concerned with five key areas:

1. The product to be manufactured—specification/quality/quantities
2. The time-scale/target date
3. The nature/size/quantity/quality of the input material
4. Resources required and how best the commitment can be achieved
5. Cost budget constraints

Commitments fall into two main groups, planned and unplanned. Unplanned demand results from a number of reasons. For example, a number of serious complaints are reported by a company's customers. These have been caused by failure of a particular component and urgent action is required to manufacture replacement parts. In a different but familiar situation, stock records show a required item to be in stock, but this is not available through a recording error. Unplanned demand can vary significantly and rapidly and its nature and probable impact on the planned programme must be evaluated promptly. The highest incidence of unplanned demand is found in engineering companies, particularly those concerned with maintenance and servicing commitments.

Production planning must be involved in the design and development stage of new products, its contribution being to ensure that design requirements are translated into manufacturing achievement. Customer expectations are fuelled by what competitors have to offer. Material lead times, including those required to acquire new plant or equipment, new tooling or changes in production practices and layouts, must be considered. Training of new personnel or the acquisition of new skills by existing manpower may be necessary.

Production planning faces many problems, particularly those resulting from the complexity of requirements. A large number and variety of items could be handled or processed each day, including materials, components and assemblies.

Planning material flow

Planning material flow is an important aspect of the work of materials planning. There are a number of objectives to achieve, and how planning is tackled will relate very much to the method of manufacture.

PLANT LAYOUT OBJECTIVES
There are a number of layout objectives, the main ones being:

1. Minimum cost of handling and movement. Both these elements add cost but do not add value.
2. Shortest throughput times. The longer materials take to be processed, the greater the costs they attract. Individual process and inter-process queuing times must be reduced to a minimum.
3. Most efficient use of all facilities including buildings, plant, equipment and manpower.
4. Flexibility of the production line.
5. Safety considerations.
6. Cost of the layout and the return on capital employed.

METHODS OF MANUFACTURE
Methods of manufacture are classified in a number of ways, of which there are four basic forms:

1. Flow production
2. Batch production
3. Unit or job production
4. Jobbing production

Flow production
There are two basic variants to flow production. One is a continuous flow process, examples being the manufacture of chemicals or paper. Such materials are then used for a wide variety of products. In the second case, individual products pass from one operation to the next. Separate specialist work is done independently at each stage. Two differing examples are motor

cars and washing machines. In this type of production, stoppage costs are high. A delay in the volume-car production line at one point delays the whole line. In seeking to achieve the best possible prospects of continuous flow, management will be looking at the following aspects:

- Continuity of demand
- Standardization of product
- Material deliveries to quality and to time
- Balancing of all operations
- Standardization of methods, tools and equipment
- High standard of preventive maintenance
- High standard of tools and equipment in a planned layout

A key area of materials management involvement is delivery of the required material to quality and to time.

Batch production
Quantities are lower than for flow production. Generally, each operation is completed on the whole batch before the batch is passed on to the next operation. This is probably the most common type of production. The main features of this type of production are:

1. Economic batches of work
2. Grouping of general-purpose machines
3. Expensive tooling to cater for a wide variety of parts
4. Efficient planning and control to cater for changes to programme
5. Facility to move work from one machine to another

How are economic batch sizes determined? From the production viewpoint, long runs are desirable, as setting-up costs can be absorbed over larger numbers of items being processed. The initial benefits of learning gained through longer runs may, however, be offset by reduced work interest, i.e. boredom. Higher stocks at increased holding cost are required to support longer runs unless just-in-time buying (i.e. a zero stock policy) can be effectively applied to provide continuity of material flow from suppliers. The needs of many customers also have to be considered, so batch sizing becomes a form of rationing, enabling these requirements to be met.

What is an optimum batch size? A number of formulae have been produced over the years, e.g. by Raymond and Lehoczky, which are based on a basic formula developed by Harris in 1915. Some of the formulae include many variables and yet results obtained from some worked examples differ marginally from results obtained using less complex formulae. Raymond included an element A, i.e. time factor for the first operation in the batch divided by total batch time. Lehoczky included an element m, i.e. cost of finished product divided by cost of raw product. However, the four important production costs per item generally used for batch size determination are:

- Unit cost, which is considered to be constant, i.e. material, labour and overheads.
- Setting-up costs, which include all preparatory work for the batch, including planning.
- Loss of investment opportunity costs, i.e. interest on items in stock.
- Stores carrying costs, i.e. space, administration and losses.

The relationship between these elements is shown in Fig.3.1, which plots the total production cost per item against batch size.

Determination of the optimum batch size by this method does, however, exclude consideration of the profit element in the sales price, i.e. the degree of return for costs incurred.

Unit or job production

This is a one-off operation where a complete unit is manufactured to meet customer requirements. The whole product is considered as one operation normally taking place at one site location. Examples include a power station or a ship. The characteristics of this type of production are:

1. Major part of the work including design is performed separately for each order. There are variations. For example, an aeroplane manufacturer has a contract to build three similar planes. While modifications to design may be incorporated during their construction, the basic design is used.
2. Work normally commences after receipt of the customer's order. Where the product is to a standard design, work might

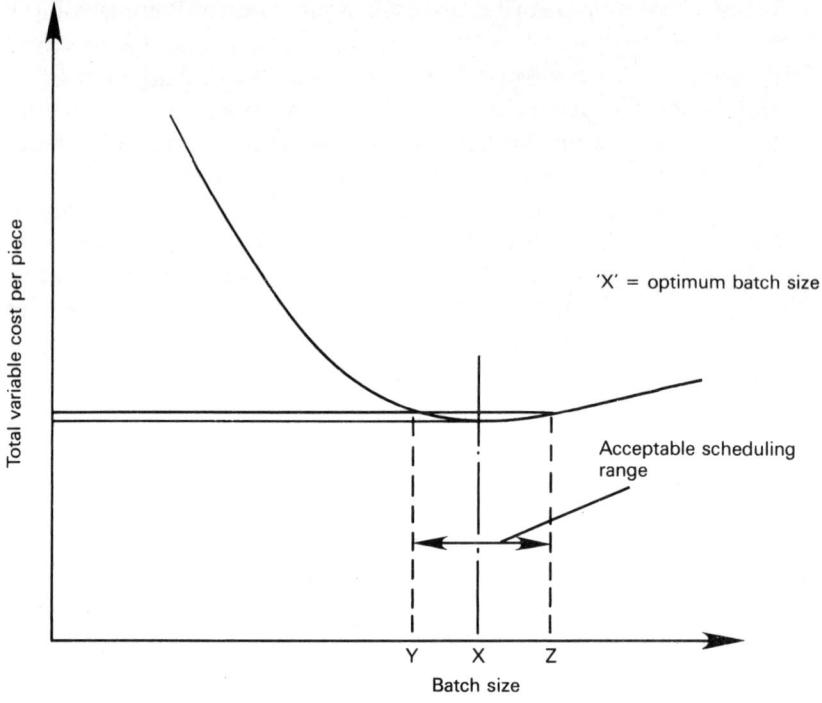

Figure 3.1 Optimum production batch size

proceed pending an order. However, customer progress payments are normally required to fund such work.
3. Impossibility to stock majority of parts.
4. Capital investment for a wide range of tools and equipment may be high.
5. Highly skilled and versatile labour required.
6. Individual planning and progress necessary for each job.
7. Longer delivery dates normally apply because of individual job planning and non-standard materials/components/ equipment deliveries.

Planning the utilization of resources is complex for this type of production where a number of projects are in process. The projects may be at different stages of completion. Manpower deployment levels for the various key trades vary greatly during the construction periods, with large peaks and troughs in demand for each trade. In the building of diesel locomotives, for example, initial work is concentrated on steel fabrication. Painters would be involved at the final stage. The planners' efforts would be directed to planning the total programme to smooth out the peaks and troughs across all projects under construction.

Jobbing production

A typical example is a maintenance engineering workshop, which produces a wide range of spares, undertakes overhaul work and deals with emergency breakdowns of plant and equipment necessitating repairs or provision of replacement parts. Work undertaken in such workshops often includes combinations of one-off orders and small batch production. A characteristic of jobbing production is the generally high percentage of unplanned urgent work that is undertaken, particularly in connection with the maintenance/servicing of plant and equipment.

The different forms of production discussed above have variations, with some degree of overlapping. Many factors need to be considered in deciding the form of production style. These include cost, flexibility, specialization, cost of down time, calibre, skills and availability of the workforce, dependability of input material flow and the degree of planning and control necessary.

OPERATING SEQUENCING

Whatever the type of production, the best use of all resources cannot be achieved without first analysing the nature, volume, speed and direction of the anticipated work flow. In the case of continuous flow production, relative location of each work station in the line and individual facilities and resources can be determined readily. The line may be set up to run for one, two or more years dependent on the forecasted product life cycle. For other types of production, an analysis is required of probable varying workloads.

COMPONENT FAMILIES

The first stage in planning the layout of manufacturing facilities is the examination of component families. The nature and magnitude of the breakdown of the sales forecast provides the starting point. In an engineering workshop, for example, component types might be divided initially for coding between those involving rotational processes, e.g. turning and boring, and non-rotational, e.g. planing and shaping. Size and complexity are also other factors for consideration in coding components into distinct families (see Fig.3.2).

GROUP TECHNOLOGY
This was introduced to lay out facilities into distinct cells, which is a fundamental change from the previous practice of grouping machines by function, e.g. locating all lathes together. Note the two approaches in Fig.3.3.

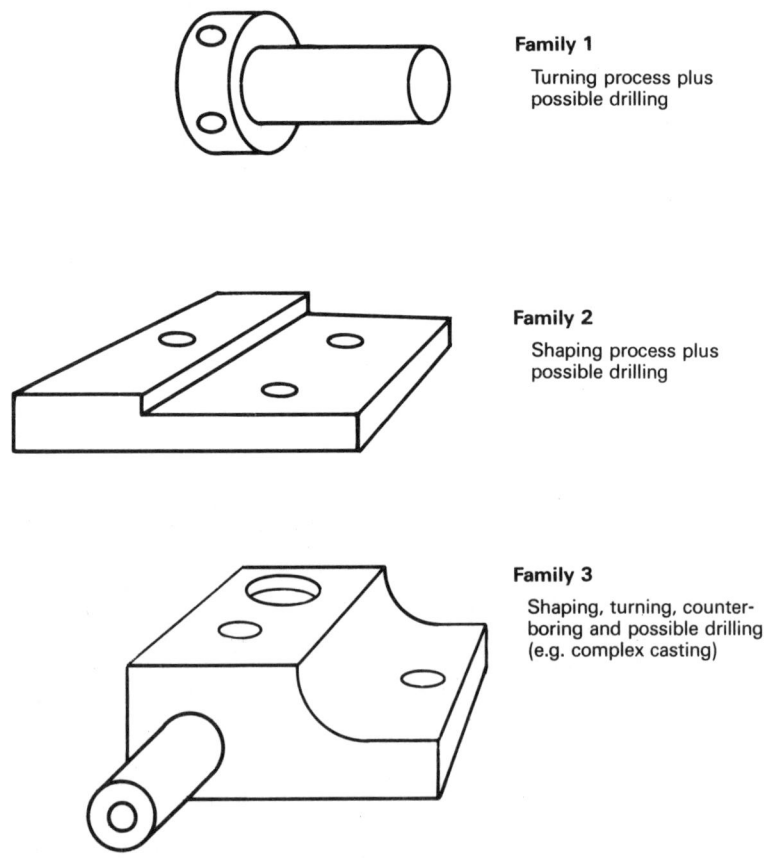

Family 1
  Turning process plus
  possible drilling

Family 2
  Shaping process plus
  possible drilling

Family 3
  Shaping, turning, counter-
  boring and possible drilling
  (e.g. complex casting)

Figure 3.2 Component families

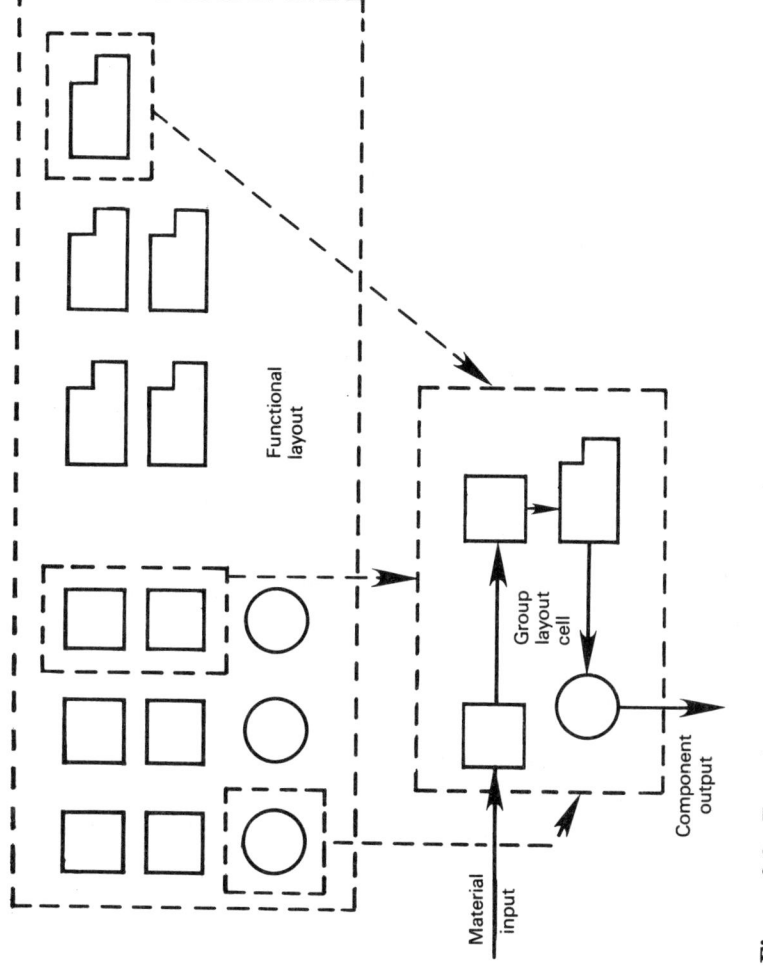

Figure 3.3 Function v. group technology layouts

Group technology layout is preferred to an existing functional one where there is a high level of work in progress with excessive manufacturing lead times and delays in input cash flow from customers. Team responsibility is encouraged and stimulated within a cell, resulting in increased work rates and reductions in inspection and reject costs. Cell members feel less strongly that they are small cogs in a wheel. A beneficial spin-off from this change of attitude means that supervision is reduced. The fostered desire by individual cell members to ensure a speedy work flow to and from their cells assists in reducing queue lengths and hence reducing progressing costs. Group technology has also been introduced by some manufacturing organizations, e.g. in the car industry, to improve productivity through reduced boredom. An operative previously restricted to one activity in a flow production line, e.g. fitting car wheels, now works with a number of people in a cell and becomes involved in many activities.

A group technology approach can result in problems as well as benefits. Increased flexibility of a higher-calibre workforce could mean a demand for higher wage rates. New machines could be required and some existing ones modified with the provision of special tooling to give greater adaptability. Machines are often less fully utilized. Desired machine groupings might not be possible because of environmental factors. For example, it is counter-productive to group some operations together if operators are subject to unacceptable levels of noise and fumes.

Materials requirements planning (MRPI)

Materials requirements planning is concerned with the scheduling and stockholding of items required for assemblies and sub-assemblies. Except in circumstances where just-in-time buying can be successfully operated, the majority of manufacturing organizations interpose stock reservoirs between the supply market and the point of production. Items held in inventories fall into one of two classifications, namely independent and dependent demand. In the first case the demand for the item is unrelated to the demand for other items, e.g. an individual spares requirement. Such demand must be forecast. Order point techniques can be used which allow for forecast errors in calculating safety stock levels. Dependent demand means that demand for an item is directly related to demand for related items. This applies where there is demand for, say, car engine assemblies, which automatically have a spin-off demand for constituent parts such as pistons and valves. Requirements can be calculated using MRPI techniques. Finished products, service parts, production supplies and office supplies are independent. Raw materials, semi-finished materials, component parts and sub-assemblies are dependent.

Demand for the finished product must be forecast. Components and sub-assemblies required for it would be subject to precise calculation. A major problem faced by many manufacturing companies is the building up of large stocks of semi-completed sub-assemblies and assemblies. Consider the situation where there is a 95 per cent chance of having in stock one specific item required for a sub-assembly. The possibilities of having two related items available at the same time in stock would be (95 × 95) = 90 per cent. Where the sub-assembly comprised, say, eight items, the possibilities of simultaneous availability would be 65 per cent (see Fig.3.4).

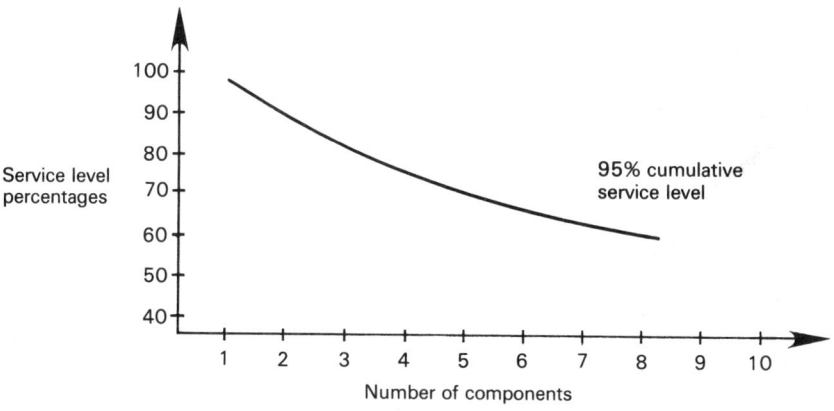

Figure 3.4 Levels of availability

Seeking a 96, 93 or 90 per cent availability could be costly. Such levels may be achieved by dual sourcing items (at higher item prices) and incurring high administrative costs through greater emphasis on delivery management.

MRPI was developed so that planning techniques could be applied to coordinating deliveries of related items for component assemblies. The aim is to make all items available at the target assembly start time. Consider Fig.3.5.

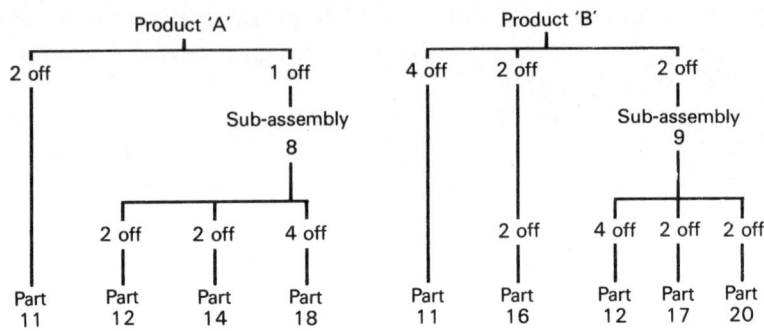

Figure 3.5   Explosion of component assemblies

Planners face a number of problems when operating MRPI. These result mainly from unplanned demand, which takes many forms. A major customer may be experiencing difficulties that require urgent programme changes. Materials drawn from stores are found to be defective during subsequent processing, resulting in other work being brought forward at short notice. Indeed, every material rejection represents an unplanned demand. A supplier's failure to meet scheduled deliveries results in non-availability of material. Design engineers constantly seek to improve products to reduce costs or satisfy complaining customers. This includes modifying or changing bought-out materials or changing the production method, with the result that demand on inventory is not met. Errors within the inventory control system, too, can result in stock-out creating unplanned demand. Management's unwitting contribution to unplanned demand is caused by advancing job completion to meet a favoured customer's request.

The fundamental problem planners frequently face is answering the question 'What are the probable future unplanned demands, particularly on key items?' As the nature, timing and volume of unplanned demand is unpredictable, this becomes a difficult task.

Net requirements planning

Consider the tabulation example below, which shows gross requirement of 20 items per week for weeks 1 to 11, available stock of 60, net requirements and work in progress of 15, from which is determined the weekly quantities to make. Given that an economic batching size of 60 items is required, we determine when processing will commence and at what weekly intervals it should be continued.

		Week number										
Assembly level		1	2	3	4	5	6	7	8	9	10	11
Gross requirements schedule (GRS)		20	20	20	20	20	20	20	20	20	20	20
Less stock	(60)											
Net requirements schedule		0	0	0	20	20	20	20	20	20	20	20
Less work in progress	(15)											
Quantities to make		0	0	0	5	20	20	20	20	20	20	20
Batching size	(60)											
Programme schedule					60			60			60	

Short-term capacity planning

In a successful system, resource capacity must match demand commitments. Resource capacity will include assigned manpower to work centres and machines. Optimum utilization of machines is also important. Production flexibility, including overtime or additional shift working, might be necessary to handle overloads on some machines or cost centres. Throughput times must be minimized to reduce work in progress. Early completion reduces costs and assists input cash flow from customers. Demand often tends to be variable rather than static; hence, resource capacity is under- or over-used, with resulting problems.

Basic steps

Determination of throughput or manufacturing lead time. This is the total time, which includes processing, queuing at each work station and transporting. Consider the following machined casting example:

	Patterns orders pending	Making patterns	Completed patterns	Casting orders pending	Making castings	Fettling castings	Machining orders pending	Machining processing
Weeks	3	1	1	3	1	1	3	6

The total manufacturing lead time is 19 weeks. The machining process is similarly broken down into separate stages such as planing, slotting and boring, with work reservoirs at each work station. Non-productive time is frequently far greater than actual processing time and so must be reduced to an achievable minimum. Short-term capacity planning must cater for realistic throughput times. Transportation, an element of time not included in the above example, will also be included as appropriate.

Planned start dates for each operation are estimated by subtracting all the subsequent processing and non-productive times from the planned job completion date.

Capacity balancing

Work will normally be planned to be processed in the most economical way, but this could result, however, in weekly or period under- and overloads as is shown in Fig.3.6.

Normally there will be capacity flexibility between a normal and a maximum level. The latter level would be accommodated by overtime working, increased shift working or allocating additional manpower. Subcontracting might be an option to consider, so orders suitable for sub-letting need to be identified at the earliest possible stage.

The projected loading on work centre 10 in the example in Fig.3.6 relates to the situation as it is seen at period 1. Subsequently, the loading levels could vary for each period, necessitating further planning adjustments.

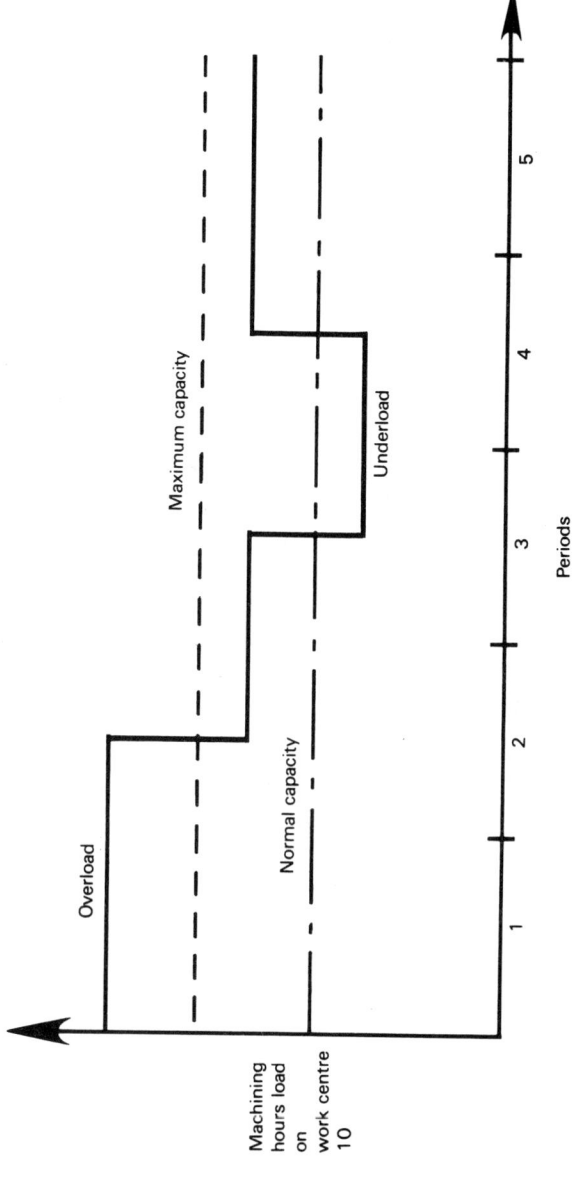

Figure 3.6 Capacity balancing

Inter-operation time

Reference was made above to manufacturing lead time with its two distinct elements of processing and non-productive times. Consider the example of two processes (planing and boring on a hydraulic valve block). The initial sequence of events is as follows:

Stage	Preparatory work	Process work	Non-productive work
1.			Receipt of block at marking-out table
2.			Pending workload for marking out
3.	Marking out for planing process		
4.			Transfer to planer
5.			Pending workload for planer
6.	Setting-up for planing		
7.		Planing process	
8.			Removal of block from planer
9.			Transfer to marking-out table
10.			Pending workload for marking out
11.	Marking out for boring process		
12.			Transfer to borer

A similar sequence of events would then follow as per stages 5 to 8 above.

The planing process, long or short, is but one of eight stages on the production shop floor. Queuing at stages 2, 5 and 10 may be measured in hours, shifts, days or even weeks. Queue sizes between adjoining machines or work centres may vary greatly because of differing workloads, machine utilization and average process times. Except under very special conditions, e.g. just-in-time (JIT) buying, queues at work stations will exist not only for the reasons stated above (where they can be minimized) but also as an insurance against idle time. Bad planning and inefficiency also contribute to queue length. Queues do, however, absorb a number of variations such as work arriving late through deficiencies on the previous process (e.g. machine breakdown) and process errors (e.g. production of scrap).

The principle of 'first in the queue – first out' cannot then always apply. Job priorities change. For example, to satisfy the urgent requirements of a valued customer, it is sometimes prudent to advance his order in the programme. An item embraced within a high-value order with a short processing time could be completed quickly and despatched to a customer to obtain urgently required payment. Where a process is complex, work might have to be assigned to one particularly skilled operator due to come on a later shift.

Network analysis planning

Network techniques are used in the planning of projects of a complex character such as the building of a new factory or launching a new product. Many activities can take place simultaneously. A target date for completion may or may not have been set. Resources must be used economically. Where serious problems arise which affect progress, it will be vital to re-evaluate the plan promptly.

Prior to the mid-fifties, project planners were dependent on the use of Gantt bar charts. Such charts were developed into cascading charts to break down job stages into smaller dependent components. However, there were serious limitations to their use, particularly for the extremely complex projects embracing high technology then being planned. The demand to seek a satisfactory fundamentally different approach to major project planning did precipitate action. Two original systems were developed independently in the United States during the period 1956 to 1958. The US Navy developed PERT (programme evaluation and review technique) for the Polaris submarine programme, while Dupont developed CPM (critical path method) to reduce the time expensive capital plant was out of commission during overhauls. Subsequently, refinements to these systems have been introduced at frequent intervals to meet particular needs; the basic concepts, however, remain unchanged. Network analysis planning is ideally suited to computer application.

In planning a project or a complex job as described above, the planner may be working to one of two objectives:

1. Determine the earliest completion date (i.e. assess the overall duration of the project).
2. Work within the constraints of a set target date for completion to determine the weighting, timing and sequencing of resources required.

To achieve 1 or 2 the planner has to determine:

- Separate individual activities within the project/job, which includes administrative ones
- Duration and sequence of each such activity
- Sequential or parallel activities
- Maximum time that can be allowed for each activity
- Earliest and latest completion dates for each activity
- Resources required for each activity, the impact if any of varying the weight of such resources and hence, the effect on the completion date and the cost economics of meeting different completion date options

Once a plan has been put into operation, there is some probability it will be affected by shortages of materials, e.g. extended deliveries, under-deliveries or rejects. Problems arise during production or site installation work caused by breakdown of equipment, damage or absence of the labour force. The planner requires scope, therefore, to re-evaluate the plan promptly if significant variations occur which affect activity duration times and hence the planned completion date. Computer application to networks provides the planner with the speedy facility to look at a number of possible options for replanning to achieve the earliest possible revised completion date or the lowest cost of plan execution, or both.

Network diagrams are so constructed that all activities can be drawn in logical order. The various terms used in networks are as follows:

Activity
This is a task, represented by an arrowed line pointing to the right (Fig.3.7).

Figure 3.7

Event
This is an instantaneous point in time representing the commencement or completion of an activity, and is generally represented as a circle (Fig.3.8).

Figure 3.8

Path
A sequence of events is a path (Fig. 3.9).

Figure 3.9

Duration
Each activity has a time-scale, which can be expressed in hours, days, weeks or months depending on the job or project. It may be dependent on resources available or used but is not normally drawn to scale (Fig.3.10).

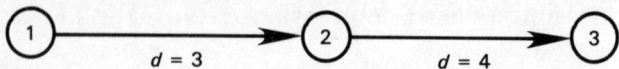

Figure 3.10

Sequential activities
Activities can be drawn sequentially in a single path (Fig.3.11).
An example could be forging followed by machining followed by
heat treatment.

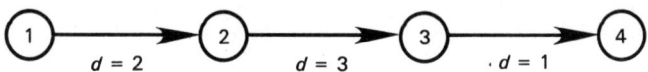

Figure 3.11

Parallel activities
Activities can be drawn in parallel, e.g. in two or more paths
(Fig.3.12).

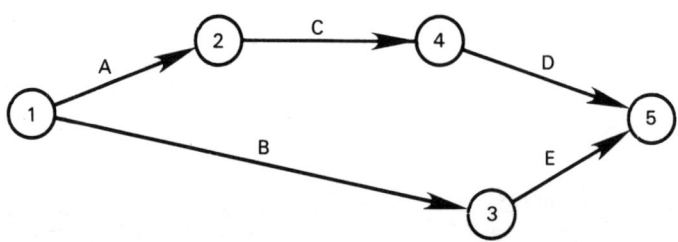

Figure 3.12

Example:
A = purchased materials   D = assembling materials

B = purchased equipment   E = fitting equipment

C = processing materials

Sequential and parallel activities
Diagrams can be constructed to cater for both parallel and
sequential activities (Fig. 3.13).

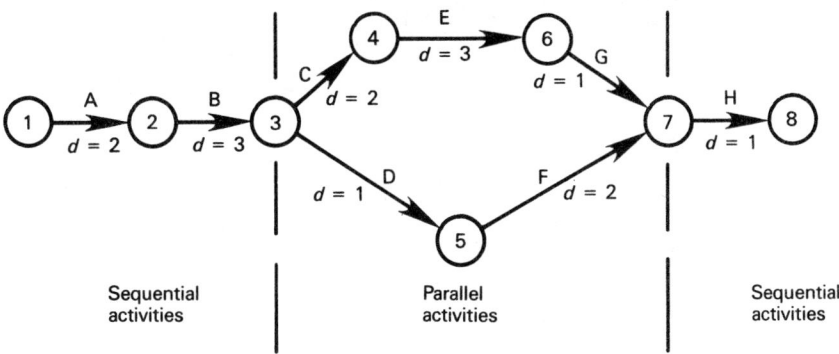

Figure 3.13

Commencement and completion of activities
Some activities cannot commence until other activities are completed, e.g. activity in B in Fig.3.13 cannot commence until activity A has been completed. Note, however, the special situation of activity H. This cannot commence until the two immediate activities (F and G) have been completed.

Earliest start date
The earliest start date is determined for each activity by working across the network diagram from left to right and adding the duration times. The earliest start date is then inserted in the upper segment of the modified event circle as shown in Fig.3.14 (a modified Fig.3.13).

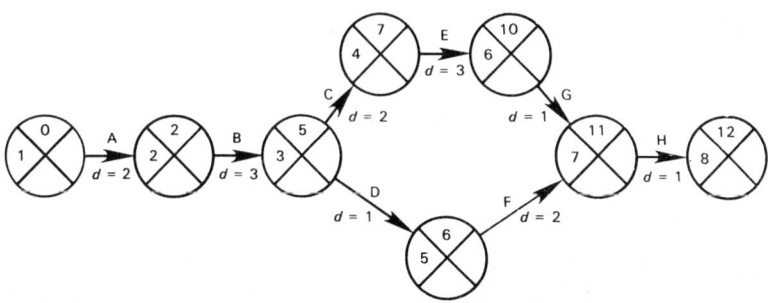

Figure 3.14

No complication arises until event 7 is reached when the rule that the largest duration time (or increments of duration times) has to be applied. In this example the duration time is 11 (determined from the upper path), i.e. 2 + 3 + 2 + 3 + 1 = 11. It will be noted that the sum of activity durations in the lower path preceding event 7 is 2 + 3 + 1 + 2 = 8 (which is a lower figure).

Latest completion date
The latest completion date for each activity can be determined by working backwards from right to left across the network diagram, using the smallest number at each junction. The latest completion dates are entered in the lower segments of the event circles (Fig.3.15).

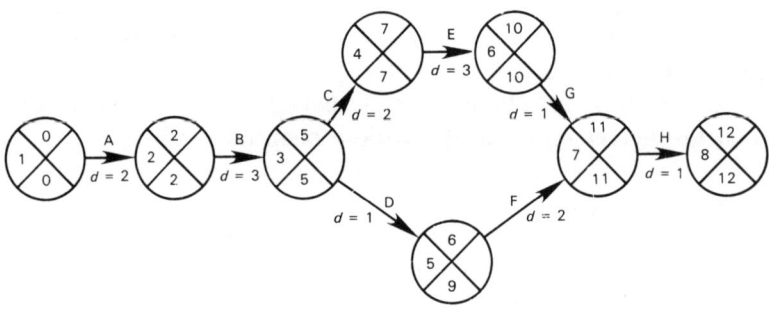

Figure 3.15

By working backwards along the two paths it will be noted that the latest date for completing activity C is 7 and for activity D is 9. What, then, should be the latest date for completing activity B? Taking the upper path first and subtracting the duration time of C (2), the answer would be 5. However, from inspection of the lower path, subtracting the duration time of 1 from 9 gives 8. Hence the latest date for completing activity B is 5.

Float
It will be noted that there is some flexibility for commencing or completing parallel activities in the lower path. Consider activity D (Fig.3.16). This can commence as late as 8 for completion by 9. It may also commence as early as 5 for completion by 6. In each case there is a maximum float of 3.

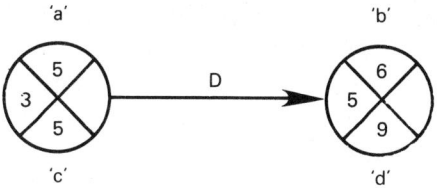

Figure 3.16

Similarly, activity F has float. If D commences at 5 for completion at 6, F can commence as early as 5 or as late as 9 for completion by 11, giving a maximum float of 2. The latest commencement date for activity H is 11.

Critical path

The network planner seeks to determine the total duration time for a project or job or has to work within the constraints of a set target date. In both cases he has to determine the path or sequences of activities running through the entire network in which no float occurs. This path or sequence is called the critical path. The earliest possible job completion date is determined by adding the durations of all the activities that lay on this critical path.

Consider Fig.3.15 as an example, where the critical path is the upper path. A serious situation might arise affecting activity D in the lower path. The duration for this activity might increase from $d=1$ to $d=5$. The earliest possible job completion date would now be dependent on completing all the activities on the lower path. This would be $2 + 3 + 5 + 2 + 1 = 13$. This total duration time is greater than the overall duration time of the upper path. The critical path now follows the lower path.

Dummy activities

Dummy activities are shown as broken arrows in network diagrams to preserve dependence and logical sequence. As they do not represent work they have no duration.

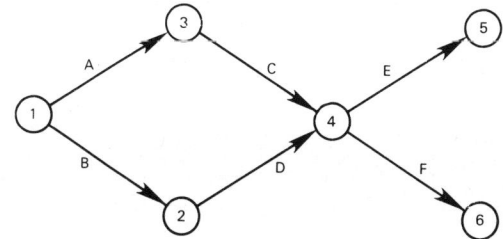

Figure 3.17

From the way this diagram is drawn, both activities E and F cannot commence until activities C and D are completed. If, however, F only requires D to be completed, the diagram would be re-drawn to include a dummy inserted between events 4 and 5 to represent the logic as shown below in Fig.3.18.

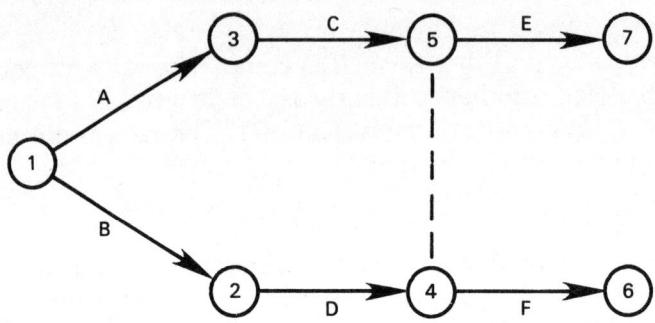

Figure 3.18

Only one activity can have the same beginning and end events. Consider the following diagram, which has been incorrectly constructed to include two activities drawn between events 2 and 3:

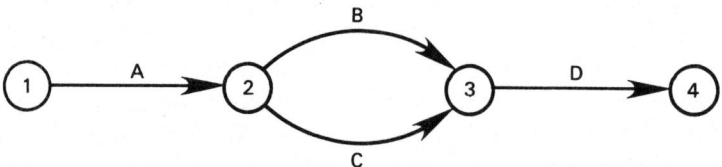

Figure 3.19

This figure would be modified as in Fig.3.20.

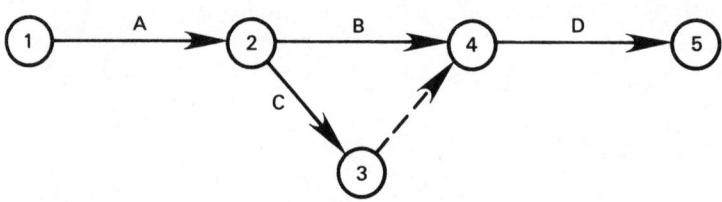

Figure 3.20

It should be noted that float could be shown for either activity B or C.

Laddering
Activities can be dependent but overlap. A good example concerns the foundry and pattern shop. In the example shown in Fig.3.21, casting work does not commence until all patterns are completed, which would be unsound practice.

Figure 3.21

Work on the first casting could start once the first pattern had been completed, the sequences thus being stepped as shown in a 'ladder diagram' (Fig.3.22).

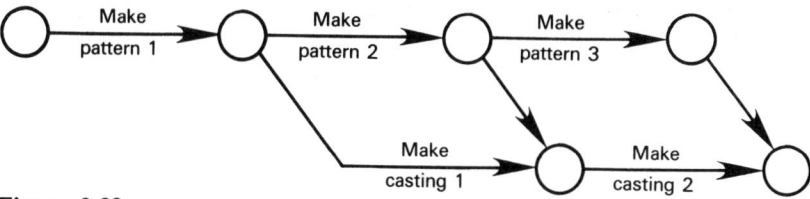

Figure 3.22

Network completion date
A completed network, which shows the nature of the construction including a number of the elements discussed above, is shown in Fig. 3.23. The critical path is emphasized.

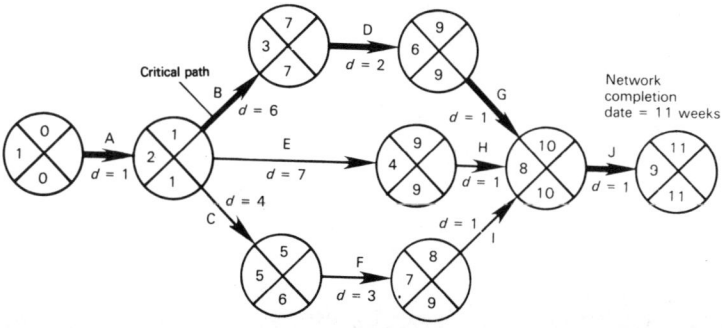

Figure 3.23

Bar charts

It is sometimes desirable to simplify particulars of a network by converting small parcels of work into bar-chart presentations for use by foremen and their working groups.

Maintenance materials planning

Maintenance commitments vary greatly in nature from product commitments. To achieve optimum production, output plant and equipment must be maintained in an economically good condition. Maintenance planning seeks the optimum balance between minimizing plant down time, spares or engineering materials stocks, engineering administration and manpower costs. Many different maintenance strategies are adopted by different organizations to minimize the cost of maintenance operations. Comprehensive planned maintenance schemes were introduced in the UK in the period 1945 to 1955 by many large organizations in heavy industry. The emphasis at that time was on production output, with much less emphasis being given to cost. Such an approach is now totally unacceptable. The modern concept of maintenance views it as an integral part of production, which has resulted in very detailed studies being undertaken to determine the probable true total costs of alternative maintenance strategies related to the nature of the operating environment. Indeed, the Japanese have developed total productive maintenance (TPM) to bring together plant management and maintenance functions with quality control on the shop floor. Three key objectives are:

- Improve plant availability
- Improve product quality
- Improve resource utilization

It is now appreciated that a diagnostic approach is required with the use of expert systems, particularly for the maintenance of complex plant and equipment.

Economic planned maintenance is embraced within terotechnology, which is a combination of engineering, management and financial practices applied to physical assets in pursuit of economic life-cycle costs. Optimum resource utilization is a key element within this. Successful application depends very much on the collection, storing and analysis of data, from which the probability and consequences of plant failure can be evaluated. Current approaches to maintenance planning include the following.

Breakdown maintenance
Carrying out no preventive maintenance but allowing plant to break down. Necessary repairs or replacement of defective parts can then be carried out. This approach is made where it would be costly to take plant out of production and where remedial action following breakdown would generally be of short duration and the repairs done were not costly.

Planned maintenance
Operating a comprehensive planned inspection system. Plant is examined at prescribed intervals for signs of abnormal wear or damage. This allows the plant to continue to operate for a limited period while remedial action is planned. Spares are drawn from stores or ordered and a suitable down-time period allocated, e.g. weekend shutdown.

Lifting of parts
Parts are lifted and replaced when they have been in service for a prescribed period of time or when they have produced a given output. An example of the latter could be a main driveshaft fitted to a steelworks rolling mill. It might be planned to replace it after 1000 000 tons throughput because of the estimated degree of fatigue sustained from that workload. This method has limitations because an item is sometimes discarded with a high residual life. Improved inspection and testing equipment is now being used to determine more accurate evaluations of metal fatigue.

There are many examples of common, relatively low-cost parts, components or items that are installed together at the same time. Will all items have the same life and thus be replaced at the same time? Maintenance strategies vary, there being a number of options to consider:

- Replace the items individually as they fail
- Replace all items on a predetermined life basis
- Replace all items when the first one fails

A classic example of the use of these options is electric light bulbs used for factory lighting. Because of the difficulties and cost of access to replace bulbs situated at some height above floor level, the first option given above would be an unacceptable one. A choice might be made between the second and third options. A variant might be to change bulbs individually as they fail up to a relatively low number, e.g. three or four, then change all the remaining bulbs. This would assume a high probability that residual life was very low and frequent failures could now be anticipated. The probable cost of loss of residual life in the bulbs would be evaluated against the cost of changing. This approach is applicable to a whole range of plant components, e.g. bearings and seals.

Replacement modules
With the ever-increasing cost of maintenance and servicing of plant and equipment work, complete assemblies or sub-assemblies are bought or built up off site for replacing on a planned or un-planned basis. This approach greatly reduces plant or equipment down time and cost. A good early example is the TV set. When these were first rented out, faulty sets were often repaired in the renter's home, a lengthy and costly operation. Today, a service engineer quickly diagnoses the fault, removes the defective module and fits a replacement in a very small percentage of the time previously taken and at a much reduced cost.

Major overhauls
The major overhauling of plant and equipment is another approach to consider. The cost of overhauling existing plant or equipment must be evaluated and compared with the cost of replacement. Probable residual life of the existing item and the comparative potential performance capabilities of the over-hauled v. replacement items would also be considered. A further comparison would be maintenance v. depreciation costs for the two options.

What level of spares and engineering materials need to be held to support each maintenance strategy? Taking lifed parts as an example, a main driveshaft might have been manufactured from defective material. Alternatively, it might have absorbed abnormal stresses during operation. Under these two circumstances the shaft might fail well below specified life expectancy. Hence, to cater for such an emergency, insurance spares must be carried in stock. Such items could be slow-moving items, some being held in stock for very lengthy periods.

Conclusions

Material planning covers a wide spectrum of requirements. Many bought out materials do not form part of a saleable product but, nevertheless, some are of high importance. Hence, material planning is a key activity applicable to all types of organizations. The higher the quality of input at the material planning stage, the lower will be subsequent handling, storage and processing problems, with lower resulting cost. Many organizations do not have material planning departments or sections as such. Inventory control, often with the loosely co-ordinated support of other departments, assists in planning requirements. Results achieved can be commendable but often they do not meet expectations because of the lack of a professional approach. Where material planning has been wrongly graded as a part-time or subordinate activity, reappraisal will yield positive results.

Material planning has been a fruitful area for the application of many new techniques. Success achieved depends on the philosophical approach taken and also on whether the emphasis is to 'push' into or 'pull' out of the production process. Finally, let us consider a technique recently introduced.

OPTIMIZED PRODUCTION TECHNOLOGY (OPT)

A particularly special feature of flow line production is that the time-scale for each stage of the process is the same. This is achieved by balancing out the work content at each stage. This facilitates JIT input flow and the full utilization of manpower and equipment resources. Failure to achieve this balance creates bottlenecks, a fundamental problem of batch production, the commonest type of production.

OPT views the total picture. This requires making a close analysis of all elements, i.e. the manufacturing process and equipment, return on investment, the nature of the manufacturing commitment, inventory levels, output levels and related profitability. What is demanded from the manufacturing profit centre is not necessarily maximum output, but maximum profit, which can be achieved from a lower but optimum level of output. OPT concentrates, therefore, on achieving the optimum solution of balanced inputs and utilization of resources.

4

Requisitioning management

Introduction

An organization cannot operate effectively unless there are clear divisions of responsibility between the various departments or functions. The procurement cycle provides a particularly good example to illustrate the need for such division of responsibility, i.e. between requisitioning and buying functions to authorize the acquisition of materials. Very few purchase orders are initiated by purchasing. Buyers generally place orders following receipt of requisitions issued by other departments. Procurement considered in simple terms (i.e. to obtain the right quality and quantity from the right source for delivery to the right place at the right time at the right price) requires that sound procurement procedures are operated to meet these objectives. Failure to meet these basic requirements can be costly; hence, adequate control over all elements of expenditure related to bought-out goods and services is necessary.

Determination of need

The procurement cycle commences with the determination of need, including, in addition to the basic item requirements of description, reference number, specification, quality and quantity, the following details:

- Delivery/completion date(s)
- Place of delivery
- Consigning instructions
- Identification method
- Budget/estimated price
- Documentation requirements (as applicable)
- Cost allocation to stock, works order, project or contract
- Special requirements, e.g. QC, QA, inspection, test samples
- Requisitioner's name and department
- Authorization for requisition release

Requisitioning responsibilities

Many requisitioners have direct interest in the use to which requisitioned materials are put, as they are concerned about successful application at economic cost. They can assist buyers to provide the service required from purchasing by giving them:

1. Adequate information, as described under 'Determination of need' above
2. Full scope to seek satisfactory alternative materials through competitive quotations and negotiating of the best contracts

This places responsibility on the requisitioner to:

1. Plan work, giving purchasing adequate time to place purchase orders
2. Consider the use of all possible satisfactory alternatives
3. Cooperate with buyers to harness purchasing and supplier expertise
4. Avoid involvement in purchasing activities

Problems of involvement in buying activities

Problems arise when requisitioners with an interest in materials usage become involved in buying activities. The requisitioner/buyer interface is of special importance and criticality, and substantial loss can result unless there are clear divisions of responsibility, which are adhered to. Involvement includes requisitioners dealing directly with suppliers on commercial aspects instead of working through the buyers concerned. Some of the more important aspects for consideration are as follows:

Overloading of suppliers

Buyers seek to avoid overloading suppliers. A supplier may not have capacity or capability to undertake contracts beyond a certain volume and value. A supplier may have a number of existing orders that are overdue. Hence, purchasing's policy will be adversely affected by ill-advised intervention of non-purchasing staff.

Order priorities

Priorities may be affected. A requisitioner dealing directly with a supplier urging speedy completion of his work could delay work of a second requisitioner who has greater need (a fact recognized and being acted upon by the buyer).

Suspension of business
A policy decision may have been taken to suspend business with a supplier because of inadequate performance or through payment problems involving financial accounts.

Erosion of buyer's negotiating position
The buyer's scope to negotiate the best prices, terms and conditions is eroded when a supplier receives clear indications from the requisitioner that he can expect an order.

Conflicting instructions
This can result in additional cost being incurred and lost time. For example, an intervening requisitioner asks the supplier to work overtime to complete an order or for delivery to be made to a location different from that stated in the order.

Inadequate contractual safeguards
Adequate contractual safeguards might not have been negotiated before the commitment is entered into. A typical example is where work commences against a verbal order but material guarantees have not been discussed and agreed.

Duplication of orders
This results because instructions are given by different individuals to different supplier representatives. One is accepted as a verbal order from the requisitioner and is not cross-referred to the written order being issued by the buyer.

Rationalization, standardization or variety reduction
Such programmes might be adversely affected. In this type of situation, the requisitioner, who is not a member of the committee involved in such programmes, issues a verbal order for non-standard material instead of dealing by requisition through the buyer.

Authorization procedures
These are circumvented as the required requisition has not been

raised and routed through the appropriate channels. This results in expenditure being incurred (sometimes high), without the approval of the person having cost centre accountability. Additionally, the expenditure may not be covered by budgeted funds.

Control
Loss of centralized control can result, with reduced awareness of actions taken. The supplier will be confused as he does not have one clear central point of contact. For example, the expediter informs the supplier to deliver items 'A' first but the requisitioner urges completion of item 'B'.

Sourcing policies
Carefully considered sourcing policies established by purchasing relating to the selection, loading and development of suppliers may be adversely affected. One situation is where the buyer has decided that a new supplier is to be given, initially, a token quantity of an item. His workload over the year will be gradually built up. The requisitioner presses for double quantities to be produced.

Reciprocal trading
Such trading arrangements made by management may be adversely affected, with serious consequences, as agreed take-off quantities of materials may no longer be required, having been obtained elsewhere by verbal arrangements.

Reasons for involvement
Why are non-purchasing staff attracted to becoming involved in buying activities? Many organizations clearly lay down and strictly observe policies that preclude such involvement. Offenders are reprimanded and discontinue such involvement. However, not all organizations lay down strict procedures and so this type of problem continues to exist. This problem is best tackled when the reasons for involvement are understood, thus enabling corrective action to be considered and applied. There are legitimate situations where technical staff are involved in commercial activities, i.e. it is within their terms of reference. For example, a works engineer could have responsibility and

accountability for maintaining plant and equipment. This could include determining what spares to buy, when to buy and from which sources. This responsibility may have been delegated by his director, who could resist its suggested transfer to the purchasing department. In such a situation there would be a need for the purchasing director and works director to re-examine divisions of responsibility between their two departments. Workloads can then be evaluated and equitably allocated so that the works engineer and chief buyer can deploy their complementary expertise and resources to the work they are best equipped to do.

Non-legitimate involvement in purchasing activities often develops over a period of time through custom and practice and has been condoned by purchasing management. Let us consider why such involvement occurs.

Qualifications
Staff consider they are better qualified to deal with suppliers for particular commodities. This raises the question: 'Should a buyer be technically qualified?' Technical and commodity knowledge will be of importance to the purchase of some items. However, specialism can be taken too far. Purchasing is primarily a commercially oriented function. Commercial v. technical expertise or professionalism in purchasing is illustrated in Fig.4.1.

How a particular buyer's job is rated on a commercial v. technical scale is shown in Fig.4.1. Many points need to be considered in the decision on whether or not a particular buying job requires a technically qualified person. These points are included in Fig.4.2.

Vested interest
Some staff do have a legitimate vested interest in achieving the best end result. Hence, they consider they have the right to work closely with particular suppliers on some or all aspects of commercial work entailed. This is understandable in some cases. A maintenance engineer requires special roller bearings. The buyer has a number of good sources of supply, with one supplier offering the best deal. However, the engineer favours one of the other suppliers, i.e. one with a proven record. He will be loath to change.

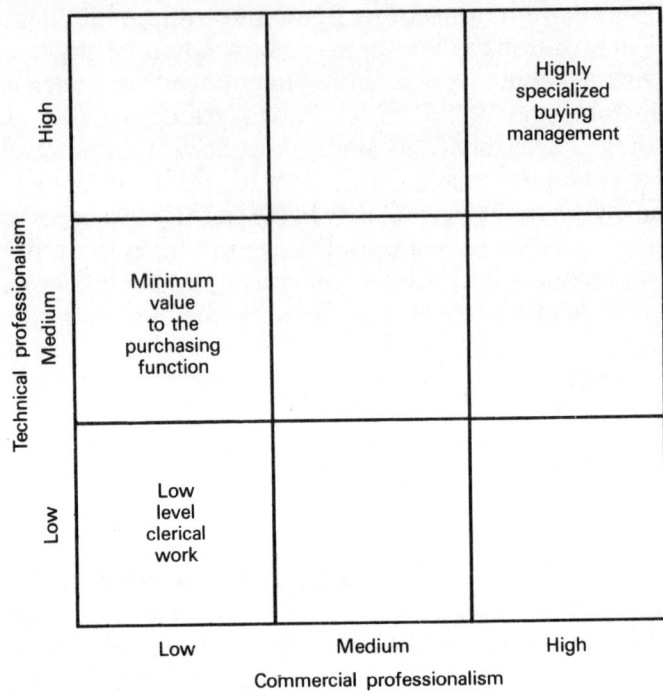

Figure 4.1 Buying orientation — commercial v. technical

For example, if a breakdown occurred during a night shift he (and not the buyer) is called out to repair the plant and get it back into production. Similarly, a designer requires a component to be supplied from his nominated supplier, possibly justifying this to his head of department.

Lack of confidence in purchasing
Has purchasing the ability to deal competently or expeditiously with requirements? This relates not only to a buyer's qualifications but to his degree of awareness or sense of urgency. A buyer may favour particular requisitioners or users, to the disadvantage of others.

Economic operation
Requisitioning staff consider that it makes economic sense for technical staff to handle both the technical and commercial

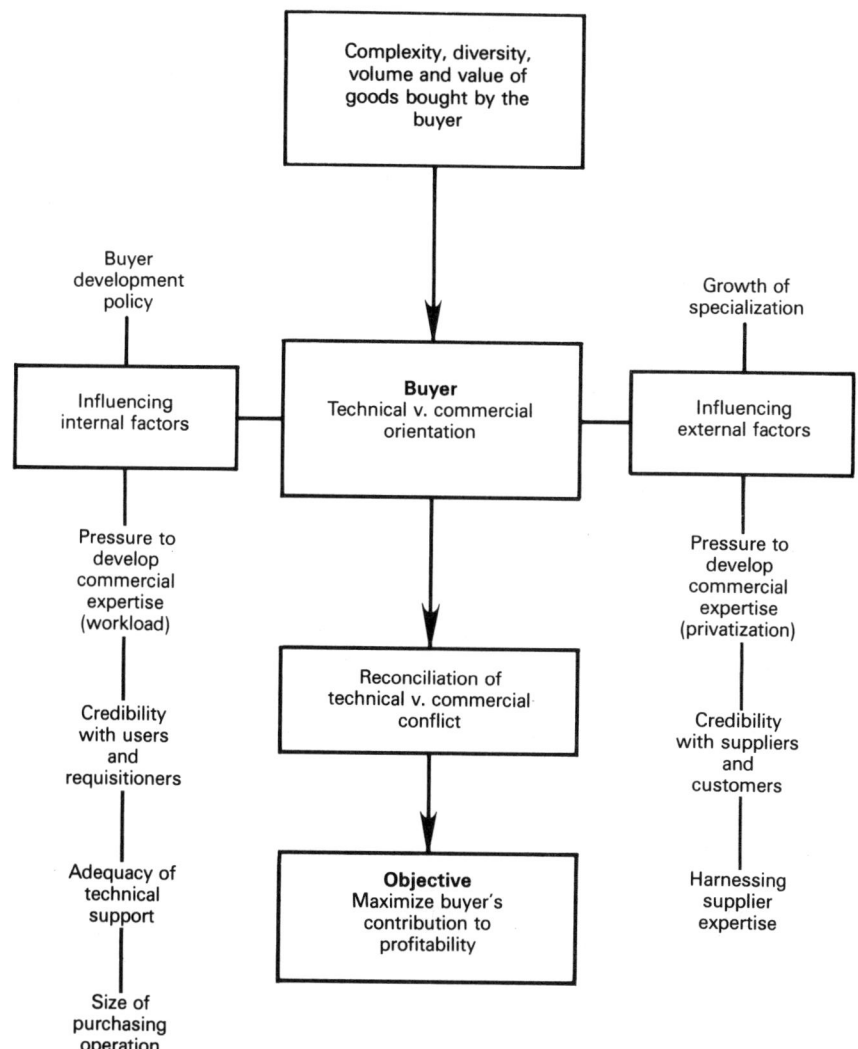

Figure 4.2 Buying orientation — points for consideration

aspects together. A strong case might be made where it was necessary, for example, to make a lengthy, time-consuming visit to a supplier's works to negotiate a contract. A buyer heavily committed at the time is then freed to deal with other important work.

Priorities

A typical example is where a requisitioner's particular requirements deserve a high priority. At the time, purchasing are
dealing with several commitments to which they (purchasing)
have given higher priority. This is an ever-present situation that
most purchasing departments face. They deal with a number of
important user departments, each having their own special
needs. A not untypical example is where the heads of two
departments phone purchasing one morning to demand urgent
attention being given to their requirements. The buyer may only
be capable of handling one within the time given. Under these
circumstances, the persons concerned want their own staff to
deal promptly and directly with the suppliers. Such staff are not
always overloaded and so could be released from other tasks to
deal direct with suppliers.

Work variety

Some requisitioning and user staff find involvement in another
department's work attractive. Purchasing, particularly, is a
function where such staff consider they can enjoy wider scope
and interest, being able to broaden horizons and deal with people
outside the organization.

Avoidance of the middle-man

This often appears to be an attractive proposition. By dealing
direct with a supplier, communications are speeded up and an
unnecessary middle-man eliminated. This point is often made as
justification for involvement.

Decision maker

Some non-purchasing staff are gratified by being able to inform a
supplier 'I am sending you an order'. They enjoy the power of
being the commercial decision makers.

Resolving problems

Problems arise at the key requisitioning/purchasing interface
for the reasons we have discussed. Some will be more difficult
than others to resolve because of their nature and the operating

situation. The purchasing manager needs to be aware that such problems exist so that he can take corrective action.

Important points requiring attention include:

- Adequacy of specification and requisitioning instructions
- Adequacy of planning at the pre-requisition stage
- Validity of the case for involvement, i.e. related to purchasing's deficiencies
- Benefits to be gained by the organization from soundly based divisions of responsibility
- Purchasing's adequacy to handle its workload

From the foregoing points it will be appreciated that buyers must earn credibility. This is important, as they are responsible for dealing with a very high proportion of an organization's expenditure. Credibility can be equated to capability plus commitment. This means that buyers must deal expeditiously with requisitioners' requirements and keep them informed on progress, particularly when delays arise. Achievement of these objectives will provide a good basis from which to develop a sound policy on requisitioning management. Requisitioners can then concentrate wholly on their own particular specialisms.

5

Source management

Introduction

It has been estimated that the average cost incurred in buying goods and services is approximately 50 to 65 per cent of an organization's total annual expenditure. More manufacturing companies are specializing in design, assembly and testing and buy high quantities of finished components, spending up to a figure of 75 per cent or more in the supply market. It is important, therefore, that buyers manage their key suppliers. This applies to buyers in all types of organizations because of high expenditure incurred and needs. Goods or services demanded by their customers cannot be provided without continuity of material supplies from key suppliers. For manufacturing companies it becomes increasingly important that they view such suppliers as an extension of their own facilities. Source management seeks to match supply with demand with resource capability. It is concerned with seeking, appraising, negotiating with, selecting and developing key suppliers and allocating requirements. This is a dynamic activity, which responds promptly and effectively to emergency situations but at the same time takes a long-term planned approach. Source management anticipates possible supply problems, and watches for and responds to early warning signals from the supply market and from users. Note is taken of industrial, economic or political developments. The degree of probability and possible extent of disruption to supplies may then be assessed more realistically, enabling appropriate preventive or precautionary measures to be taken.

Sourcing policy

Achieving continuity and security of supplies is a key purchasing objective. Planning the long-term flow of materials and dealing with emergency commitments are equally important. This is of particular relevance to key materials required to support corporate objectives. Purchasing managers should actively encourage their buyers to organize their workloads, looking beyond today's commitments. Effective forward planning and preparation significantly reduce the incidence and severity of tomorrow's material supply problems. Emergency commitments often take up too much of a buyer's workload. Hence, there is an urgent need to investigate its nature and magnitude and to determine the reasons for such levels of short-term demand. With this knowledge, action can be taken to reduce them significantly, providing the buyer with more time to concentrate on achieving continuity and security of supplies.

The word 'sourcing' is used in two contexts in purchasing. Firstly, sourcing means to seek potential suppliers in the market. It is specifically a searching activity. The second context, particularly relevant to this chapter, is the combining of the word with 'policy', i.e. sourcing policy, which relates to parameters, constraints and strategies employed to meet supply requirements. This is the framework within which the buyer seeks continuity and security of supplies. Situations frequently arise where it is vital that a quantity of a key material be supplied within a given period. Should all the requirement be placed with one supplier? There are a number of very good reasons for doing so, one of the most important ones being price, the lowest unit prices often being obtained through aggregation of quantities. For many commodities, the larger the quantity bought the higher are the discount terms offered. The decision to be made is one of risk management. The known price advantage to be gained by placing all one's business with one supplier has to be evaluated against the greater risk of not achieving continuity and security of supplies by 'putting all one's eggs in one basket'. There is no single correct approach to making this sort of decision. Each situation must be viewed and evaluated in the light of prevailing circumstances. The decision to single, dual or multiple source may require consideration of the following points.

SOLE-SOURCE SUPPLIER
In the case of a sole-source supplier the decision has already been made as a result of external factors. Therefore, the advantages

and disadvantages of placing business with one or more suppliers cannot be evaluated. The whole of an order's quantity requirements must be placed with one particular supplier. This situation arises for a number of reasons.

Monopoly supplier
This applies where there is only one supplier in the market for a particular item. It may be important to ensure that an alternative economic source does not exist. A virtual monopoly situation sometimes exists when there are two suppliers. Consider the case of special liquids or gases, where their suppliers must also provide appropriate storage and internal distribution plant and equipment. Once a supplier has been selected to install such plant and equipment, the buyer is virtually committed to him for all future supplies. In this supply situation, a supplier would only guarantee quality (with freedom from contamination), safety and performance where his full liability for problems arising could be clearly established. This stipulation dictates that the buyer has only one option, that of dealing with one supplier. Careful appraisal is required of competing potential suppliers before long-term commitments are made with one selected supplier.

Original manufacturing supplier
Where spares are required to maintain plant or equipment, these are often only obtainable from the original supplier of that plant or equipment. The manufacturer's drawing copyright, his withholding of detailed specification for spares manufacture or his special expertise are the main reasons why buyers face this type of constraint. Many suppliers claim to make their profits from the supply of spares and not from the sale of plant and equipment. Suppliers should be made aware during negotiations for plant and equipment that selection of the supplier takes life-cycle costing into consideration. Key elements in this evaluation are cost and ready availability of spares.

Spares must be obtained at keen prices, often at short notice. There must be scope, therefore, to seek competitive free capacity for spares manufacture. Some suppliers of plant and equipment do not yield to the persuasive logic of such a case. They might release drawings for some spares, giving limited scope for competitive buying. Buyers must press for the provision of all spares drawings with the right to arrange the manufacture of spares elsewhere. They have maximum bargaining power prior to placing the initial order for plant or equipment.

Customer-nominated supplier

The purchaser's customers often have their own preferred choice of suppliers and insist that these must be used for their contracts. A customer dictates this choice because he considers a particular supplier's items give best value, or their incorporation in his product enhances prestige. The supplier's vendor appraisal systems and quality certification procedures are other aspects that determine choice.

Patent, licensing restrictions and branded goods

These constraints often limit obtaining specified requirements from only one available supply source. This applies where a supplier has the patent rights or is manufacturing under a licence agreement that is not transferable. Manufacturing or processing rights might be transferable on payment of royalties. If they are, the cost incurred has to be assessed. In the case of branded goods, there might be scope to introduce competition. An equivalent open specification would, however, have to be obtained at economic cost. The advantages and disadvantages of using branded goods v. open specifications are discussed in Chapter 6.

Reciprocal or contra-trade obligations

These restrict the placing of some orders for particular specified items with a nominated trading associate in compliance with a reciprocal trading agreement. Subsequently, evidence becomes available that full compliance with this policy is resulting in loss making, i.e. relating to price, quality or delivery. In such circumstances, an acceptable revision of that policy should be sought.

Company standardization programme

Items required for the company's products or for engineering maintenance are only obtainable from selected suppliers. Such a decision would have been made by a committee on which purchasing was represented. This function provides supply market information with particular emphasis on price and availability of specified requirements and alternatives. Its task is also to harness supplier expertise. Programme implementation means that business could be placed for an extended period with a nominated single-source supplier who could leave the market. Thus, special care is essential during the initial selection of suppliers.

Government-nominated supplier

A government department concerned could direct that a specified item is obtained from a particular supplier. This type of decision often results from a supplier's previous performance or because of a policy of allocating work to particular regions. Work distribution is also sometimes restricted for reasons of confidentiality or secrecy. The supplier's vendor appraisal systems used and quality certification procedures are other aspects that determine choice. However, where a buyer has valid reasons for believing serious adverse consequences would result through dealing with a nominated supplier, he should present a good case for changing that policy.

User/designer-nominated supplier

Users and designers have vested interests in directing where orders are placed. They consider they have a legitimate right as they are ultimately accountable when material problems arise. Competition should be sought when this is possible to achieve continuity and security of supplies at economic cost. Potential suppliers must be given equal opportunities to win business, but the wishes of users and designers would prevail where they had valid cases supported by management. Purchasing should constructively seek to change a proven unsatisfactory policy.

SINGLE BUT NOT SOLE-SOURCE SUPPLIER

Total item requirements are placed with one supplier and not shared with others available in the market. This situation arises in the following circumstances.

1. The quantity involved is small, making it uneconomic to divide requirements amongst two or more suppliers.
2. Transport costs would be prohibitive by dealing with two suppliers.
3. It is uneconomic to provide two or more sets of tooling, or time constraints prevent the obtaining of a second set.
4. Development work has to be undertaken in partnership with one selected supplier.
5. The required standard of uniformity and interchangeability is not achievable by dealing with two suppliers. Pattern or colour matching are examples of this.
6. Where a machine tool such as a lathe is bought, the buyer has to deal with one supplier and is fully dependent on his capabilities, capacity and commitment.

In each of the above situations relating to the purchase of key supplies, the buyer must carefully consider the implications of being committed to a single-source supplier, particularly when that commitment will extend over a lengthy period.

CHOICE OF SINGLE, DUAL OR MULTIPLE SOURCING
Buyers often have the choice of placing business with one or more suppliers. Such choice is dependent on assessed possible advantages and disadvantages. This is risk management. Let us consider the various factors that influence sourcing policy.

Keenest price
Not all materials have differential pricing structures related to quantities bought. However, many materials do have a price break structure as shown in the example in Fig.5.1.

Single sourcing gives more scope to achieve price reductions in the form of quantity discounts. These are attractive to a buyer seeking to operate within budget or to reach savings targets. An initial price advantage is lost subsequently if the supplier has scope within the terms of the contract to apply a price increase.

The buyer negotiating a keen fixed price for his total requirement in the form of an annual contract is at a disadvantage if during the contract period other suppliers quote significantly reduced prices. However, there may be scope to negotiate for price reduction in the event of a fall in market prices.

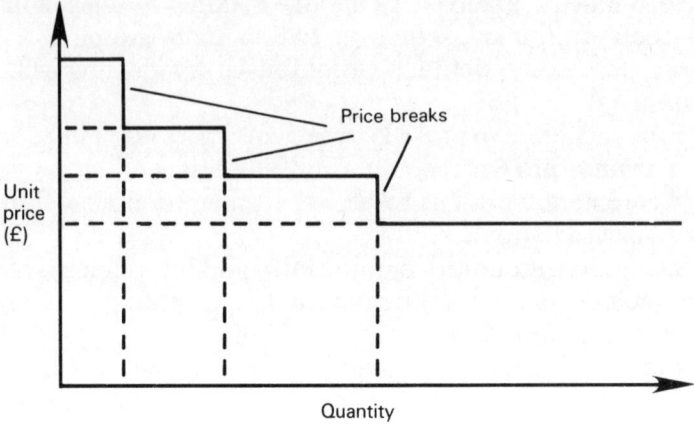

Figure 5.1 Price breaks

Quality and value
A single-sourced item is supplied initially to the specified quality. Subsequently, the supplier experiences manufacturing problems or becomes complacent. He reduces quality standards, creating serious problems for the buyer, and does not respond promptly or effectively to a demand for corrective action. It is not always possible to find an alternative supplier at short notice.

Technological developments
A single-sourcing policy limits opportunities to benefit from technological developments taking place in the supply market. However, there are benefits to be gained by placing total quantities with one supplier. Close cooperation and coordination of activities can be developed, which produces the framework within which quality problems are examined promptly and effectively. This is particularly evident on new items where joint expertise is harnessed. There is the alternative viewpoint. If a buyer deals with two suppliers, each gains from a fuller understanding of his supply needs and problems. This gives a higher degree of security for the future, as in an emergency he has two suppliers to contact for assistance.

Continuity of supplies

Where continuity of supplies is of major importance, dual or multiple sources might be necessary. If one supplier has quality problems or fails to deliver to time, supplies are obtainable from the other supplier(s). Disruption to deliveries occurs, resulting from production plant breakdowns, strikes, catastrophes such as fire, flood or storm damage, disruption to the supplier's own material flow, transport problems or bad planning or estimating.

A supplier may embark at any time on a change of policy, including leaving the market. Product diversification or rationalization policies often result from mergers or take-overs or from management's reappraisal of its market opportunities. Management changes or the loss of key personnel might also seriously impair a supplier's operations. However, in spite of these problems, which relate to single sourcing, such a policy is often successful. This might require the supplier or the purchaser carrying higher stocks as an insurance against supply failure. The additional cost incurred has to be evaluated against the savings gained from quantity discounts. However, the promotion of healthy competition is always of ultimate advantage to the buyer. Two or more suppliers in competition, each taking part quantities of his requirements, are given incentive to provide a better service to the buyer and to secure a higher percentage share of future business.

Flexibility in emergencies

The larger the contract quantity taken the greater the opportunities a supplier has to become more fully acquainted with the buyer's requirements. He will learn to anticipate some emergencies and to handle them at short notice, becoming more flexible and innovative. For example, work might commence from outline drawings, saving valuable time while detailed ones become available. A committed single-source supplier, with higher expectations of obtaining a reasonable share of the buyer's business and a steady flow of work, is a great asset to a buyer and his production and technical colleagues.

Administration costs

Administration costs should be reduced by single sourcing as only one purchase order is required with one set of documentation. Expediting is limited to dealing with one supplier and one set of invoices are handled. However, a single-source supplier is more likely to fail than two or more suppliers failing together at the same time. Savings on administration costs are reduced (or lost completely) if the buyer, expediter or QC inspector devote more time dealing with an unsatisfactory single-source supplier.

Prestige
Where a particular supplier is an established market leader in his field, the incorporation of his product in the buying organization's product enhances prestige of the latter's sales. Thus there is a definite advantage to single sourcing, providing adequate economic safeguards are applied to orders placed and their administration.

Confidentiality
Confidentiality is sometimes of high importance, demanding restriction in the circulation of design and drawing data. Single sourcing might be considered to be essential to safeguard a company's interests and hence be implemented as a management policy decision.

DECISION TO SINGLE, DUAL OR MULTIPLE SOURCE
In making the final decision to single, dual or multiple source, full consideration must be given to promoting healthy competition and to the effects that such a decision has on the longer-term continuity and security of supplies. An organization may grow and increase its requirements in terms of quantity or enhanced specifications. The case has to be made to single, dual or multiple source. Much depends on the nature and quantities of items being bought, the situation in the supply market and the reliability of particular suppliers.

When pursuing a dual- or multiple-sourcing policy, business would be shared in quantities appropriate to assessed capabilities and capacities of the selected suppliers. In the case of a smaller untried supplier, he could be given a token quantity as part of a source development strategy. The subject of supplier development is dealt with later in this chapter.

Supplier appraisal

Buyers deal with different types of suppliers, i.e. agents, distributors, wholesalers, retailers, stockholders or manufacturing companies. Purchasing has to know with whom they are dealing. Detailed supplier appraisal is normally required when dealing with manufacturing companies for key items. In companies operating to high quality standards, the main responsibility for supplier appraisal generally lies with specialist quality assurance/control staff with necessary support from purchasing and other functional staff.

Supplier appraisal may be defined as 'the evaluation of a supplier's probable capability to meet his full contract obligations'. It is carried out before there is a commitment to place a contract. As this evaluation takes place before the placing of a purchase order, it differs fundamentally from vendor rating, which evaluates actual supplier performance during execution or on completion of a contract.

Need for supplier appraisal
There are a number of objectives, which include:

1. Assessment of a supplier's probable capabilities of meeting quality, delivery and after-sales service.
2. Evaluation of one potential supplier against another prior to placing an order.
3. Determination of a supplier's possible weaknesses and hence to assess the extent to which the purchaser might need to exercise control over the contract.
4. Determination of areas of concern that can be highlighted and raised during subsequent negotiation to effect corrective action.

Method of appraisal
This includes:

1. Preparation and issue of a questionnaire to suppliers to obtain information, e.g. on capacities, numbers and types of machines, number of employees, lifting capacities, quality certification and major customers.
2. Checking returned questionnaires to reject suppliers who do

not have required capabilities to tackle the type and size of contract.

3. Verifying statements of short-listed suppliers and taking appropriate action:

- Arranging with financial accounts to check on financial status.
- Arranging for a specialist financial investigating company to undertake a thorough examination of financial capabilities.
- Checking with major customers listed on returned questionnaires if they were satisfied with a supplier.
- Checking local newspaper files if major industrial relation problems have been experienced in recent years.
- Visiting suppliers' premises to meet staff and to assess capabilities on-site.

A supplier submits an attractive quotation on price, specification, delivery and contractual terms and conditions, but will written words be translated into deeds once he wins a contract? The more critical, complex or higher the value of materials to purchase, the more important it is to have as much knowledge as possible of a potential supplier. The more serious the cost consequences of supply failure, the greater the need to undertake effective supplier appraisal.

The concept of source management views key suppliers as an extension of the purchaser's organization, so standards demanded internally must apply externally. Key areas to investigate are capability, capacity, financial viability, commitment, growth potential, constraints and systems compatibility and constraints.

CAPABILITY
Capability is the necessary attributes a supplier needs to process purchase order requirements to specification, quality, quantity, time, place, agreed price and after-sales service. Capability also includes promptness and effectiveness in dealing with problems, particularly complex ones that arise. A manufacturing company is concerned with management, money, machines, materials, men, methods and markets. Assessment of a supplier's

capabilities requires, therefore, an investigation into each of the above aspects through the functions responsible.

Management
Management's effectiveness is measured by how well it plans, organizes, delegates, motivates, coordinates and controls. One sign of possible good management is limited turnover of management and senior staff. Sound policies and procedures should be operated. The organization's structure should be appropriate to the nature and volume of work being processed, with the right numbers and calibre of staff. A good reputation will be established with customers and within the locality. Management's reputation for giving customer satisfaction is particularly important. Efficient operation also requires good housekeeping, an aspect readily determined.

Production planning and control
This function is one to which particular attention is required, as it is responsible for executing and controlling the contract. How promptly and effectively are order commitments programmed, purchasing notified of priority, long-lead materials ordered, and stocks and resources allocated? Bar charts, networks and schedules giving progress status on current orders are frequently and prominently displayed. These often reveal important information, including which major customers would be competing for the supplier's attention. Efficiency is measurable by the frequency with which documents are updated, i.e. daily, weekly, monthly or never. This indicates how the buyer's contract might be handled if received. If a major customer's order was last updated three months ago, this would not inspire confidence. Another pointer to efficiency is the value of work in progress. High quantities lying idle by each machine suggests poor planning and control and lengthy throughput times, with greater possibilities of loss, damage or misplacement.

Systems, procedures and documentation, too, are key areas for investigation. Following receipt of an order, how promptly and effectively is action taken to deal with priorities? Required answers to questions posed are not always readily determined. Supplier appraisal is very much a jig-saw puzzle where many aspects are pieced together to provide a whole picture for evaluation. This aspect of appraisal is one of value judgement.

Production

Production is responsible for machines, men, methods and supporting facilities required to handle orders effectively and efficiently. Does the supplier have adequate facilities to produce the required quality and volume of work to time? Are machines and supporting facilities suitable? Are plant and equipment modern and maintained in good condition by planned maintenance to minimize breakdowns or work spoilage? These are important questions, to which answers must be sought.

Successful completion of a contract to time is achieved by management harnessing the motivated and sustained efforts of a workforce that is competent and adequately trained to undertake specified work. Training, testing, certification and other relevant documentation must be valid and current. A visit to the factory floor gives opportunities to gauge the prevailing atmosphere and to discuss work in progress with supervisors and craftsmen. Useful information may be gained on their viewpoints. Is the workforce in serious conflict with management? Such a situation is difficult to hide. Are up-to-date methods being used to sustain or improve operating efficiency and to achieve specified standards?

Quality assurance/control

This function is responsible for ensuring that only goods to the specified quality standards are supplied to customers. Quality assurance or control must operate to established and proven levels of capability. The adequacy of staff, procedures, systems and documentation can be verified. This subject is covered in some detail in Chapter 6.

Purchasing

This is of particular interest to the buyer. He is fully aware of its importance. How efficient is the buying operation? Does it use supplier appraisal? How promptly are key sub-orders placed and how effectively are they progressed? The buyer will be keen to investigate these aspects for which his opposite number is responsible.

Stores

Whether materials are ordered direct for the buyer's contract or provided from stock, stores plays a vital part in supporting contracts. It is the responsibility of purchasing, stores and inventory control to ensure that materials are made available for production. Handling and storage facilities and methods must be efficient, adequately complemented by good systems and procedures. Materials must be released from stores fit for purpose against authorized request. Such points require investigation.

Inventory control
This function is often separate from stores. How well it operates has a decided influence on how successfully a contract is executed. A discussion with the inventory controller may reveal valuable information. The work of inventory control is dealt with in Chapter 11.

Design and development
The importance of this function to supplier appraisal depends on the nature of the work to be placed. Where complex or highly sophisticated items are being ordered, this requires investigation into design and development capabilities, particularly ability to handle serious problems that arise. Discussion with staff might reveal the sort of major problems recently experienced and how well they were handled.

CAPACITY
Can the capable and viable supplier execute a contract in the stated time? Total capacity could be inadequate. Where it is adequate, free capacity may be too small because of commitments to other customers. What proportion of the supplier's capacity would the buyer's order take? If the proportion was high the buyer could be over-committed and vulnerable. If the volume of work was very low, he could be in competition with other customers who had greater influence with the supplier. If production problems arose, whose orders would be given low priority? Consider the two diagrams in Fig.5.2.

FINANCIAL VIABILITY
Money is the life blood of a company, so a supplier's financial viability is of particular importance, covering a number of aspects.

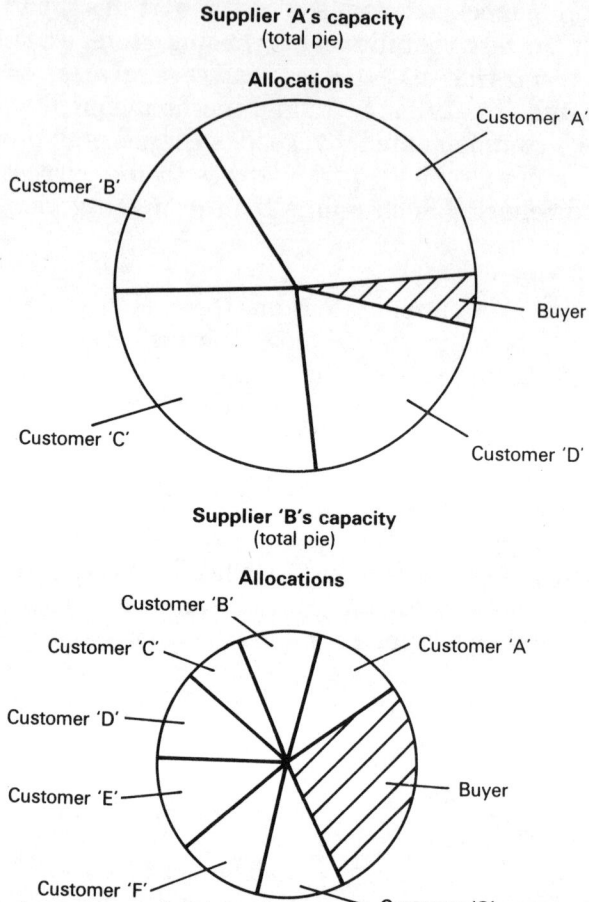

Figure 5.2 Supplier capacity considerations

Balance sheet
This gives an indication of the financial health of a company but interpretation is not always easy. Financial consultants might have to be engaged to provide a realistic appraisal. Financial ratios are aspects to which such attention is directed. These ratio figures vary greatly between different types of organizations, each having standard or target figures against which to aim. However, in any one year, unsatisfactory ratio figures revealed might have resulted from a number of causes, which include:

1. Inefficient management
2. Adverse market conditions, e.g. change from sellers' market to buyers' market
3. Cancellation of a major contract, e.g. through customer's financial difficulties
4. Abnormal extended teething problems in commissioning major new plant, resulting in greatly reduced output

Thus liquidity could be unsatisfactory, stocks levels excessively high or returns on capital employed and sales low. It will be noted that 2, 3 and 4 do not reflect inefficient management, and such problems may not affect next year's balance sheet results. Some key ratios are as follows.

Key ratios
There are a number of ratios that can be determined from the balance sheet. The first set, which are of particular importance to the assessment of supplier viability, relate to solvency and are called solvency ratios. These are:

$$\text{Current ratio} = \frac{\text{Current assets}}{\text{Current liabilities}}$$

$$\text{Liquidity ratio (or quick ratio)} = \frac{\text{Liquid assets}}{\text{Current liabilities}}$$

Vulnerability is another aspect for consideration. This is the extent to which current assets starting with cash would need to be realized to cover current liabilities.

The second set of ratios are operating ratios and give good indications of the returns being achieved by suppliers. The key ratios are:

$$\text{Stock turnover} = \frac{\text{Stocks} \times 52 \text{ weeks}}{\text{Sales}}$$

$$\text{Profit as a percentage of sales} = \frac{\text{Profit} \times 100\%}{\text{Sales}}$$

$$\text{Return on capital employed} = \frac{\text{Profit} \times 100\%}{\text{Capital employed}}$$

A specimen basic balance sheet for ABC Limited is included in Appendix 1, giving calculations for each of the above ratios and 'vulnerability'.

Balance sheet time-scale limitations
A company's balance sheet provides much useful information. However, its major limitation is that it is an historical picture of what existed in the past. This does not necessarily indicate future probable performance. The buyer's primary concern is to determine if the supplier will be financially viable during the period of the contract. This problem is illustrated in Fig.5.3.

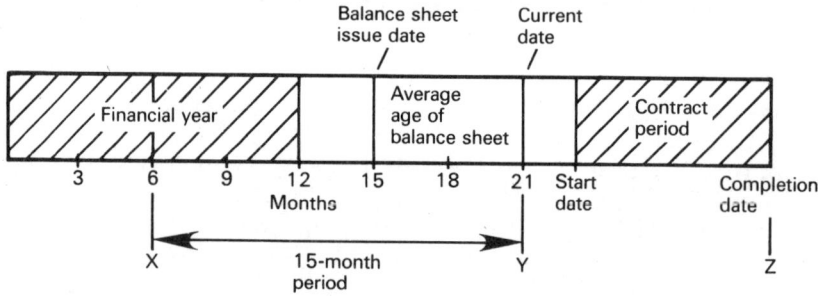

Figure 5.3 Balance sheet time-scale limitations

Company accountants sometimes produce more optimistic financial pictures than actually exist. Also, with increasing numbers of take-overs and mergers, manufacturing companies are growing into larger units or groups. Company balance sheets and profit-and-loss accounts are normally issued for the group and not for each group member. Hence, it is unlikely that financial statements are obtainable from an individual company. A number of financial situations may exist within a group. For example, it is financially sound but an individual company is not. The group may be considering selling off this company because of bad performance. The reverse could be true, where the group is in financial difficulties but the individual company is financially viable. However, where balance sheet and profit-and-loss statements are available, they do give some indication of a supplier's financial health relating to the recent past. Comparison of two or three successive years' documents could highlight significant information.

Services of financial investigators

Another important aspect of financial analysis is credit worthiness. Is a supplier able to pay his creditors? Does he pay his bills in six weeks, six months or longer? Are his material supplies likely to be cut off through non-payment for previous consignments received? Specialist financial investigators can determine such information. Some operate early warning systems to provide critical information, giving subscribers rapid reports on suppliers or customers who might be in financial difficulties. County court judgements, meetings of creditors and limited companies who have secured a mortgage or charge on their assets can all indicate financial pressures on companies. Other key data include the appointment of liquidators, winding-up orders, voluntary winding-up of companies, appointment of receivers and unsecured creditors in liquidations and bankruptcies. Subscribers make an annual charge for this type of service but would pay additionally for a special one-off assignment.

Suppliers can be assessed, too, by the maximum value of contract that they can handle. For example, a buyer wishing to place a contract valued at £50 000 may be advised not to place contracts above £25 000 with a particular supplier.

COMMITMENT

The most difficult element of supplier appraisal is assessing probable commitment. A supplier's enthusiastic, positive and constructive approach demonstrated when business is being sought is not always evident later. Personnel who have negotiated a contract generally do not handle it through to completion, as once a contract is won they concentrate efforts to winning further business. What degree of importance will the supplier give to an order? An order could be treated as low-priority fill-in work while more interesting and profitable business is sought. Assessment of probable commitment is a value judgement gained through face-to-face discussion.

A supplier's commitment to an order can be influenced by group membership where this is applicable. For example, another member of the group is a competitor to the buying company and this will influence commitment in particular situations. When purchasing key items, possible supplier connections of this nature must be checked.

CONSTRAINTS

Many internal or external factors affect supplier performance. If a supplier has embarked on a product rationalization programme, this could disrupt production if plant and equipment were being moved to another building. The situation could be more serious if plant was being moved a long distance to another site. Disruption to the flow of materials to production can also result through maintenance work such as the re-roofing of factory buildings. Supporting accident prevention measures may also restrict efforts to meet production targets.

Are any problems envisaged relating to competition for labour? Labour turnover could increase greatly if the workforce was attracted by high wages offered by a new company recently moved to the locality. Such situations exist and need investigation as part of supplier appraisal when considered to be necessary.

GROWTH POTENTIAL

Long-term commitments with selected suppliers often result when an organization plans major changes in product design and development and great increases in its volume of business. A partnership could be developed with a selected supplier with potential and the desire to grow with its customer. Hence, a key aspect of supplier appraisal is the evaluation of his growth potential, both technologically and from the capacity viewpoint. The required supplier is one who contributes fully to value engineering, component specification and design and to overall cost reduction.

This aspect of appraisal increases in importance as specialization and technology develop, i.e. in state-of-the-art buying where such a partnership could continue for many years. Assessment requires the involvement of technical, financial, production and buying specialists.

SYSTEMS COMPATIBILITY

As systems technology develops, more managements will seek integrated operations with their key suppliers, thus generating increased demand for systems compatibility. This will become of increasing importance in supplier selection in the future.

Supplier selection

The first stages in the selection process are supplier appraisal and evaluation of quotations received. Which offer best matches the requirements specified? Evaluation includes commercial and technical considerations, i.e. specification and quality, quantity, delivery, after-sales service and contractual safeguards. Is what is offered realistically achievable? Supplier appraisal seeks to provide the answer. On high-value, critical orders, supplier selection is a risk management activity requiring the obtaining of adequate data plus value judgement. It often relates to the long term as well as the short term.

What makes a good supplier? He meets the buyer requirements, clearly demonstrating commitment and achievement. He provides good documentation, including material consigning instructions, which are important aspects. Supply problems are minimized and are dealt with expeditiously when they occur. The good supplier is flexible in handling fluctuating commitments. He seeks to anticipate changes affecting supply and demand and notifies of impending and actual problems. He is selective in his choice of suppliers to ensure a good supply chain. The good supplier is often a specialist in his field, in some cases concentrating manufacture on only one product. Such a supplier is well equipped to take the initiative to guide and assist the buyer to meet his commitments and achieve best value.

Good suppliers sit at the top of the pyramid and are to be prized, nurtured and harnessed.

MAKE OR BUY

Internal departments are a possible important alternative source to consider. Capability first has to be determined. Is capacity available within the required time-scale? A make or buy decision could be a complex one. If the work is undertaken internally, would it be economic? Additional resources could be required or the work might not be in the company's main line of specialism. In an emergency situation, management may agree to making in-company, though the work may not conform with corporate planning requirements. Where it is costly to provide necessary additional resources, market research might reveal that technological developments taking place could result in the early obsolescence of the item or the manufacturing process. Licensing or patent rights restrictions might apply. Can the buyer obtain the required materials in time? If work is withdrawn from a supplier and placed internally, would goodwill be affected, as it may be necessary at a later date to place the work out again.

SUPPLIER DEVELOPMENT

A company develops a new product with special requirements that known existing suppliers cannot meet, thus requiring a new source to be developed. The need for a close working partnership between the company and supplier might mean that a local supplier with potentialities had to be developed. Buyers must anticipate and not just react to circumstances. They must plan well ahead to handle future commitments. Monopoly situations might be avoided if supplier development is pursued. Supply market capability must be matched with forecasted material demand.

When it is necessary to develop an existing source or create a new one, this can be achieved in a number of ways. Consider, first, the non-direct financial options. Expertise can be loaned or the supplier assisted with the training of staff. Work might be released on a planned basis, its complexity being gradually increased. The prospects of winning long-term lucrative contracts could provide incentive to the supplier to accept.

Financial options include taking over the supplier, but the necessary finance may not be available or the proposal is not in line with corporate plan policies. Providing a loan is another option, but this requires subsequent repayment (with interest), which may increase item prices. Where a supplier has cash-flow problems that restrict source development, advanced payments might be arranged to finance work in progress. Appropriate price reductions would be negotiated to compensate for loss of earnings on interest. Other options include seeking a financial stake in the supplying company or seeking seat(s) on the Board.

Importing

This is a particular specialist area, which can only be discussed briefly in a book of this type. Importing frequently involves dealing with trading banks, import and insurance agents and shipping departments. Foreign suppliers may have agents or distributors in the buyer's country, but it is frequently necessary to deal direct with foreign suppliers. Quotation evaluation and supplier appraisal are generally more complex than when dealing with home-based suppliers. The reasons for buying abroad include quality, price, delivery, after-sales service or because materials are unobtainable from the home market. There will be advantages, but there will also be risks. Transporting materials may be a fairly straightforward operation within the home market but not necessarily so from abroad. Handling rejects will generally be a more complicated procedure, with possible longer rectification or replacement times. Important areas for consideration include the following.

Language

A supplier cannot meet requirements unless he understands what is demanded of him. Requirements must be adequately, clearly and unambiguously stated in enquiries and purchase orders. Jargon, abbreviation and terminology likely to be misinterpreted must be avoided to prevent loss-making situations arising. When necessary, the services of language consultants should be used.

Do the supplier's representatives have language limitations that could jeopardize expeditious and efficient handling of an order? This is an aspect of supplier appraisal not to be overlooked.

Customs and Excise

This is a specialist area relating to requirements for documentation preparation and submission, with the need for accuracy of tariff and other descriptions and cost implications, i.e. customs duty where this is applicable. Many major organizations have specialist departments dealing with importing and shipping requirements. In smaller organizations, it is necessary to engage the services of competent import and insurance agents, the buyer acquiring from them an appreciation of what is entailed.

Custom and practice

The customs and practices of foreign suppliers often differ from those of home-based suppliers. They normally work to their own national specifications but do offer British Standards or equivalents. Operating periods are another point, as some foreign suppliers close their factories for a month in the summer. Deliveries quoted in weeks need, therefore, to be related to calendar weeks and not working ones.

Currency

The buyer will be guided by his manager, financial accounts manager or the company's foreign trading bank on currency buying requirements. Progress payments could apply, which include a high percentage to be paid on submission of shipping documents. Consideration might be required to exchange rates and probable future fluctuations. Currency bought forward incurring premium payments is an additional element of cost to bear.

Price-basing point

There is generally a choice of price-basing points when placing orders direct with foreign suppliers. An 'ex-works' price includes all charges incurred by the supplier up to the point of making materials available on his premises for collection. The buyer would be responsible for all further costs entailed, such as freight, handling and insurance costs incurred in transporting the materials to the specified destination. 'FOB' (free on board) buying requires the supplier to make materials available within the order price at a named foreign airport, docks or border town. All subsequent costs would be to the buying company's account. Another option is 'CIF' (cost, insurance, freight). Here materials are delivered to a named airport or docks in the buyer's country. All subsequent costs incurred would be to the buying company's account. When buying on a 'warehouse to warehouse — all risks' basis, materials are delivered to the buyer's premises or other specified destination without incurring additional cost over the order price. Materials delivered on a 'warehouse to warehouse — all risks' basis can be sent in sealed containers and opened and examined on the buyer's premises. This avoids split insurance. Realistic dates must be set for intermediate price-basing points. For example, where receipt of materials placed on a FOB basis was 1 June, an appropriate earlier date should be agreed for the FOB date to cater for the subsequent journey to site.

Legal interpretation
Where a dispute arises between buyer and supplier which goes to litigation, judgement is made in accordance with the legal interpretation agreed in the contract. Where an English buyer places a contract with a French supplier, a dispute submitted to litigation would be judged in accordance with French law unless otherwise agreed for the contract, as normally the law of the supplier's country applies.

Satisfactory reciprocal legal agreements operate between many countries where buyers and suppliers obtain fair judgements in others' courts. This is not, however, universally applicable and buyers should be mindful of this when placing orders abroad.

Evaluation of total order cost
Evaluation of the total costs incurred by placing an order abroad includes such aspects as manufacturing, packaging, handling, transport, insurance, duties payable, airport or dock fees, import agent's fees, insurance agent's fees and currency premiums. Additional cost incurred in administration includes expediting, inspection and other expenses such as visits, telephone and telex.

Supplier (vendor) rating schemes
Actual performance of key suppliers is measurable using the technique of vendor rating. This compares actual v. planned performance in key areas such as quality, delivery, after-sales service and price. Performance on quality is assessed by the number of rejects per batch quantity, cost of reworking rejects, cost to production resulting from rejects and additional administrative costs resulting from rejects. Similarly, delivery performance is assessed by the number of items per batch delivered late and degree of lateness, consequential cost to production and resulting additional administrative cost incurred expediting late deliveries. After-sales deficiencies are measured by the promptness

and effectiveness of the service being provided. Price variation from the datum price is measured.

Supplier performance can be measured against a budget or standard, past performance against previous orders or against the performance of competing suppliers.

Benefits to be derived
The main benefits sought from vendor rating are:

- Evaluation of what it actually cost to do business with a supplier.
- Use of evaluation as an ongoing tool during the period of contract to highlight shortcomings and take corrective action.
- Demonstration of a supplier's under-performance against contract and hence to give scope to obtain improvement and price reduction or other concessions on orders currently being negotiated.
- Use of the information when evaluating quotations received against future orders to place as part of supplier's appraisal.

Vendor rating results sometimes also disclose deficiencies in the buyer's or his colleagues' actions or procedures which have contributed to unsatisfactory performance. Scope for measurement depends on the value and criticality of an order and whether it is a one-off or repeat buy. Full consideration is essential of factors outside the supplier's control that influence measured results. Methods of measurement range from the simple rule of thumb, i.e. good, fair and bad rating approach, to analytical techniques used by some major companies.

Consider the example given below, where a buyer's annual requirements for an item are divided equally between two suppliers 'A' and 'B'. Both submit quotations for next year's requirements. Details of their quoted prices and previous 'rule of thumb' ratings are:

	Supplier 'A'	Supplier 'B'
Order price	£5000	£5300
Quality	Very good	Good
Delivery	Excellent	Very good
After-sales	Good	Fair

Which supplier gave the best value for money? It would be impossible to justify the choice between the two as 'good', 'very good' and 'excellent' are not quantifiable, particularly in relation to the datum prices paid. What is required ideally is another line in the above table, giving the following information:

Total probable cost of doing business with supplier	£5000 + £X	£5300 + £Y

where £X and £Y are measurable.

Vendor rating systems seek to quantify shortcomings in performance against the aspects given above as penalties, demerits or additional costs related directly to purchase order datum prices. Quality, delivery and after-sales service have to be weighted. For example, out of a total of 100 points, quality is allocated 45, delivery 35 and after-sales 20. Each allocation is further broken down. For example, quality:

Production stoppage	15 points
Reworking costs	15 points
Admin costs	15 points

Points are deducted for substandard performance. A supplier might obtain 13, 15 and 12 points, respectively, against these elements, giving a total of 40 points. This reduction of 5 points against quality gives a 5 per cent demerit against order performance as a whole. Relating this to supplier 'A's price of £5000 means the evaluation of quality deficiencies adds 5 per cent of £5000, i.e. £250, to the cost of doing business with supplier 'A'. Deficiencies in delivery and after-sales add further sums to the datum price.

The theory of vendor rating looks logical but practical problems arise in its use. The cost of setting up a vendor rating system and operating it successfully must be economically justified. Weighting allocations are generally most difficult to assess and justify. Should quality be given 40, 45 or 50 points out of a possible 100? If a particular figure seems realistic now, will it continue to be so in, say, 12 months' time if supply and demand factors change? It is essential to ensure continuity and consistency of data used in measurement. Finally, probable savings sought from the use of vendor rating must be measured against the cost incurred in operating it.

Conclusions

We have dealt at length with the subject of source management. If the required specification and quality of materials are to be delivered to time, then sufficient efforts must be directed to dealing with capable suppliers who know precisely what is expected of them. These objectives have a better chance of being achieved if sourcing is tackled in a planned, organized manner, where the time and risk factors have been fully considered. As we have discussed, staff from a number of functions within and outside materials management have important contributions to make to source management.

6

Quality management

Introduction

Quality is conformity with requirements, adequacy of specification and quality being the sure foundation from which effective materials management may be developed. Quality is defined in BS 4778 as:

> The totality of features and characteristics of a product or service that bear on its ability to satisfy a given need.

Organizations are concerned that the products they manufacture or the services they provide satisfy customers. Hence, they must buy materials that are fit for the intended purpose, with this objective being achieved at minimum total cost. The intended purpose may be related to:

- Characteristic of process in the buyer's works
- Achieving best value at the point of use
- Achieving customer satisfaction at minimum cost

The concept of quality may be considered in three ways:

1. Degree of excellence, which should be set out in product specifications to which the product should conform.
2. Quantitative sense as used in manufacturing, product release and for technical evaluation, sometimes referred to as quality level.
3. Fitness for purpose, which relates to the evaluation of a product or service with regard to its ability to satisfy a given need.

The approach to quality varies. Highly sophisticated quality requirements would be applied to, say, construction of a nuclear power station. Limited quality control might be necessary in a small engineering company manufacturing low-priced garden equipment.

There is an increasing demand that manufacturing organizations, particularly, demonstrate their ability to conform to quality requirements, e.g. BS 5750, DEF Spec. 05/21 and 25 and ISO 9000 series, and that appropriate systems and procedures exist and are used.

Quality characteristics
Material quality characteristics take many forms:

- Shape, size, tolerance, smoothness, roughness, surface finish, hardness, strength, elasticity, stiffness, fatigue resistance, weight, specific gravity, density and chemical composition
- Resistance to flow of electrical current, corrosion, heat, cold, abrasion and water
- Colour, transparency, colour/pattern matching
- Taste

Frequently, compromise is sought between conflicting required characteristics, e.g. steel where hardness is required but not at the expense of unacceptable loss of strength or resistance to fatigue. In the aerospace industry many components require both these characteristics with heat resistance qualities also. Weight limitation is also important. Take-off speed and manoeuvrability could be seriously impaired by increased weight. The cost aspect is important too; for example, it could cost an airline £20 or more per year in fuel consumption to carry one additional kilogram on one of its aircraft.

Importance of quality
All organizations have to provide the right quality of goods or services to their customers. Deficiencies in specifications and quality standards can be serious, loss resulting from a number of reasons:

Customer dissatisfaction
This is the main area for concern. An organizations's profitability or its valued reputation depend on satisfying customers. Existing customers will not be retained or new ones won unless acceptable levels of quality are achieved and maintained. Dissatisfaction could stem from substandard performance of the

final product, resulting in rejection of the defective product, material guarantee claims or claims for damages. An order may be cancelled. The supply of substandard quality goods or services could affect future business. Defects can be latent. For example, timber is purchased for the manufacture of furniture and, subsequently, warping or cracking of the furniture occurs. Product quality is dependent on material quality and, while corrective processing is sometimes possible, it incurs additional processing and delay costs.

Finally, accidents must be avoided. Loss of life or injury to persons can result from the handling or use of unsafe products. Product liability has become increasingly important during the past decade. Because of the growth of consumer pressure, the Consumer Protection Act, 1987 (Part 1), relating to goods, came into force in March 1988. The details of this Act are included in Appendix 2.

Insurance clearance
Where a product requires insurance certification, all materials used in its manufacture must be to the specified quality levels. Material assurance certificates must be provided where required, as failure to do this will result in loss of approval by the insurance authority.

Production delays
These often result following receipt of substandard materials. Work processing may be delayed awaiting receipt of replacement material. Work transferred to higher hourly rated machines to meet programmed dates will incur additional, often heavy, cost.

Late commissioning of new plant
Delay in commissioning new plant with consequent deferment of investment earnings often results from receipt of substandard materials.

Loss or damage
Consider the situation where a substandard chemical is delivered and pumped into a tank containing existing good-

quality liquid. The entire contents then become substandard through contamination. Corrective refining may be costly or impossible.

Substandard material is likely to fail in use or have a greatly reduced life. Subsequent processing work may be abortive and costly. Secondary damage to interfacing components can also result through the use of poor-quality material.

Increased inventories
Inventory levels need to be increased to cater for the higher levels of substandard materials.

Increased quality control/inspection
QC or inspection need to be increased to deal with current or anticipated quality deficiencies.

Increased operating and maintenance costs
Increased production delays caused by breakdowns result from receipt of substandard spares and engineering materials. More frequent cleaning, inspection and corrective adjustments are required, with resulting down time and loss of production output. Energy consumption, too, is increased, incurring higher operating costs. This could result through higher friction occurring between mating parts due to incorrect tolerances.

Workforce dissatisfaction
This situation can arise through receipt of substandard tools, general and consumable materials. Typical examples include electrodes (with high fume emission), gloves (providing inadequate protection) and soap (which does not lather). Such problems must be avoided, as they may affect morale and, hence, production.

From consideration of the above points it is obviously of particular importance that all staff involved in the materials procurement cycle should consult and coordinate their efforts to minimize quality deficiencies.

Avoiding/minimizing quality deficiencies in bought-out materials

Efforts can be directed in a number of ways to reduce quality problems.

Define requirements

Quality standards, e.g. BS 5750, must be clearly and unambiguously defined in the enquiry document sent to suppliers. Such requirements must be (a) essential, (b) achievable, (c) measurable and (d) economic.

Supplier capability

Selected suppliers must be capable of meeting the quality standards specified. This includes supplier quality appraisal and quotation evaluation.

Supplier's understanding of commitments

Suppliers must fully understand the quality standards they are required to meet. This could include material assurance certification, material source certification and the test certification as appropriate. Quality control and the buyer concerned must satisfy themselves that there is a closed-loop communication with the supplier on this point.

Placing of purchase order

An adequate purchase order document must be sent to the supplier specifying that he acknowledges receipt by a stated date. The acknowledgement should be progressed to ensure receipt to time and the supplier's confirmation checked that he intends to meet specified quality requirements.

Quality control

Approved procedures and techniques to be used including 100 per cent inspection, testing or statistical sampling by attributes or variables during or on completion of manufacture or at inward goods inspection.

Product quality engineering

Product quality engineering embraces four aspects of quality, which are as follows:

1. **Product quality** The quality of a product is the degree to which it satisfies customer requirements. This quality is influenced in turn by the following.
2. **Product design quality** This is the degree to which the design specification of the product satisfies customer design requirements.
3. **Product manufacture quality**   This is the degree to which the product, on delivery to the customer, conforms to the design specification. The objective of manufacture quality is to ensure that product specification is met during manufacture. There are three separate stages to achieving this end:
   - Ensuring defective materials or items are not used
   - Ensuring substandard work is rejected and uncompleted processed items are not passed on to the next stage of manufacture
   - Ensuring defective final products are not passed on to customers

These three stages can involve extremely tightly controlled quality control or inspection procedures depending on the degree of sophistication of the product or problems experienced with materials, machines or operators.

4. **Product reliability** This is the ability of the product to function as required, when and where required and for the time required. A second definition given is 'the probability of performing without failure, a specified function under given conditions for a specified period of time, if prescribed maintenance is carried out at specified intervals'.

In the case of one-off operations, such as the firing of spacecraft, reliability relates to the probability of performing without failure first time when called upon to do so. Quality therefore relates to and is very much concerned with design, materials, manufacture and the use and extent to which the product is put. Cost is an important factor. Customer requirements must be satisfied at prices they are prepared to pay. The relationship between cost and value of quality is shown in Fig.6.1.

Quality, reliability and cost are related. A company can manufacture a wide range of products each to different quality levels. This in turn results in differential product pricing. All

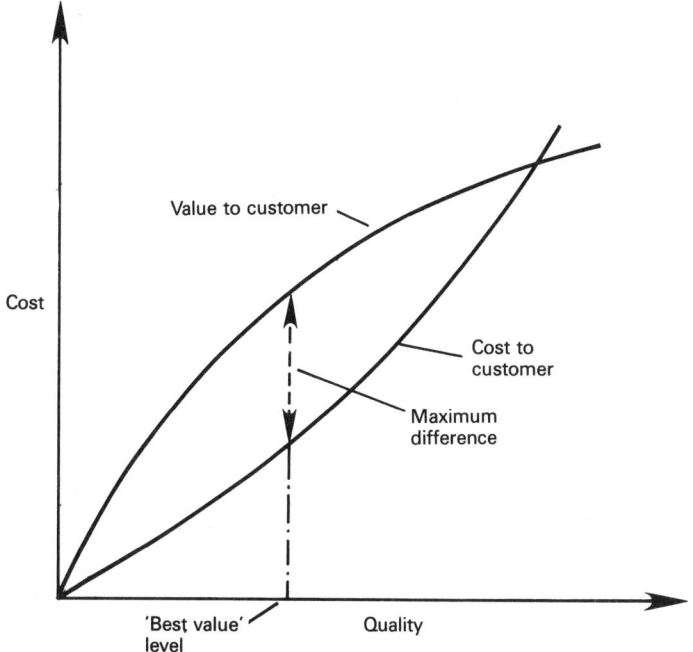

Figure 6.1 The cost and value of quality

products, no matter how well produced, are liable to limitations and failures. Ultimately, product reliability may be the most important characteristic. This is particularly true of aircraft components and equipment where quality relates equally to performance and safety. Motor-car tyres are another example. Mileages claimed by manufacturers for their high-quality tyres will generally be much higher than for the lower-quality ones. However, substandard tyres of whatever quality sometimes slip through stringent quality control or inspection, even if this situation is extremely rare. Both qualities of tyres may fail under similar operating conditions. The relationship between cost and reliability is illustrated in Fig.6.2.

The original cost of reliability relates to all costs incurred in providing a product with a particular quality level. This includes:

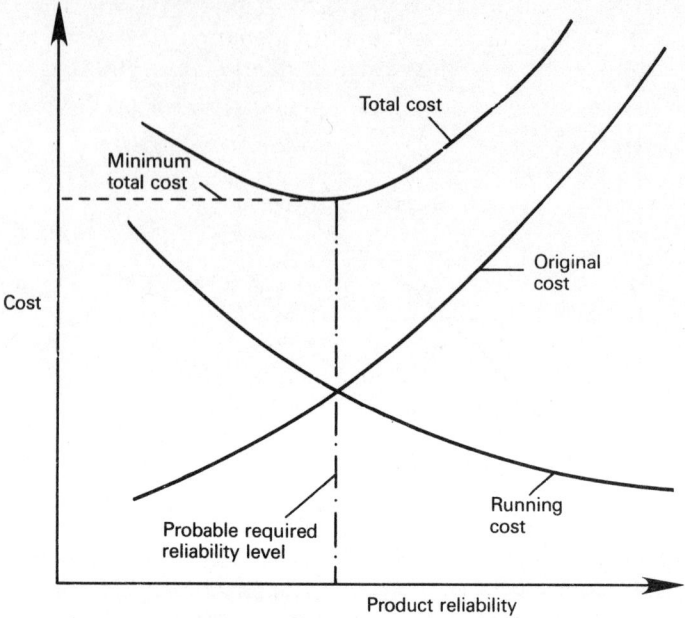

Figure 6.2   Cost v. reliability

- Product design
- Specification of the manufacturing process
- Quality control, inspection and test systems
- Rejection, scrapping and rectification during manufacture
- Producer's costs, i.e. cost of repairs, replacements and spares service
- User's costs, i.e. cost of breakdowns, repairs and replacements

Value at the point of use

The level of quality requirement will relate to whether the materials, components or equipment are being purchased for inclusion in the company's product(s) or are required for internal use, e.g. the operation or maintenance of manufacturing plant and equipment. In the former case, items have to satisfy the customer at minimum cost to the manufacturing company. In the second case, it would be economically viable to pay two or three times the price previously paid for a purchased item to obtain a better alternative giving four or five times the life in operation. Additional benefits could also include saving on down time cost through replacing worn or defective items less frequently. Maintenance expenditure would also be reduced on dismantling, removing and refitting operations.

British Standards quality systems

BS 5750 was introduced in 1979 to specify requirements for three basic levels of system for the assurance of material and/or services. These are presented in three parts as follows:

- Part 1. Specification for design, manufacture and installation
- Part 2. Specification for manufacture and installation
- Part 3. Specification for final inspection and test

Included within these three parts are the following aspects:

- Quality systems and their review, completed item inspection and test, control and status of inspection, measuring and test equipment, control of non-conforming material and sampling procedures
- Organization, planning, work instruction and manufacturing control
- Design control
- Purchaser supply material
- Protection and preservation of product quality
- Records and documentation change control

BS 5750 also deals with the inspection of purchased material, requiring a supplier to conform to specified requirements, providing evidence of conformity when required to do so and maintaining appropriate records for scrutiny. He is also required to ensure that all material that he acquires for the purchaser's order conforms to the specified requirements. Urgent material may be released provided that it is positively identifiable to facilitate recall if substandard. The purchaser is responsible for clearly stating description and identification requirements for material and supporting specifications, drawings and other related data. Requirements for receipt inspection are to be related to control exercised at source and adequacy of conformity documentation provided. While the purchaser has the right to check materials at source or after receipt for conformity, this will not relieve the supplier of his responsibility to meet quality and specification requirements.

Quality specification

Requisitioners are responsible for defining requirements on requisitions or other order initiation documents. Purchasing should check and challenge specification and quality details when warranted and within their capability. They must buy materials that are fit for the intended purpose and no more. Specification and quality requirements are defined by:

1. Brand
2. Specification
3. Sample or pattern
4. Market grade
5. Inspection
6. Performance

or a combination of two or more of the above.

Description by brand

This relies on the manufacturer's integrity and reputation. It assumes that he will be anxious to preserve the goodwill attached to his trade name and will consequently work to maintain a consistency of quality. Description by brand is necessary in the following circumstances:

- Specification is not disclosed, e.g. it might be a patented material or the process of manufacture is a secret one.
- Specification cannot be stated accurately or the success of the manufacturing process depends on such intangible qualities as skill and workmanship.
- Quantities purchased are too small to warrant the time and cost of preparing a specification.
- Testing expenses would be too costly.
- Customers for a product insist on particular branded items being incorporated in it.
- User prejudice cannot be overcome.

The use of branded goods restricts choice of supplier, distributor or agent, reducing opportunities to seek best value or keenest prices. Scope to use unbranded goods must be developed. In evaluating annual savings potential, consideration must be given to the cost and effort of testing branded goods against unbranded substitutes.

Description by specification
The majority of organizations use this best-known method of defining their requirements for purchased items. The main advantages gained from its use are:

1. That in defining requirements, some thought and consideration is necessary. This should result in a higher probability of making a better purchase.
2. A specification does form a good basis against which received goods can be checked and measured. The buyer is not restricted in his possible source of supply and is able to buy an identical item from two or more sources.
3. Suppliers are able to compete on equal terms and submit quotations against one common specification. A supplier's failure to meet specification or performance requirements can be determined and responsibility placed contractually.

Circumstances do, however, arise where difficulties are experienced in the use of specifications, such as in the following examples:

- Colour and matching selection.
- Cost of producing a specification. There may be a tendency to produce one that is too good, i.e. over-emphasized. This would increase item cost. A second and equally important point is that this may discourage suppliers from preparing quotations.
- Buyer's minimum standard might be the maximum set by the supplier.
- Cost of measuring or testing, which is not normally incurred when buying branded items.

Purchasing against the widest possible range of specifications for items requires much time, effort and cost. However, there are advantages to be gained by extending the use of specifications for standardization or rationalization.

Types of specification

There are many types of specification — organization, association, national and international. British Standard specifications are very comprehensive specifications in universal use. Some details of the relevant BS relating to quality is included under BS 5750. Where a foreign supplier is being asked to submit a quotation against a BS specification, he should be given the opportunity to quote 'equal or better' against his own internationally accepted standards, e.g. DIN.

Description by sample or pattern

This applies where goods are unique and where a specification is not available.

Description by market grade

This applies to a wide range of primary materials such as oil, coal, wheat, cotton and timber and where the materials can be specified by a recognized market grade.

Description by inspection

Many items are bought by inspection, e.g. used or scrap items.

Description by performance

This is concerned with the achievement of a specified level of performance. Description by performance may be considered at two different levels:

1. Within the bounds of current technology
2. Beyond the bounds of current technology

Most organizations are concerned with 1. Required items can be produced from available materials using existing manufacturing equipment and methods. The required end result might be specified, not the means of achieving it. For example, a ship owner issues enquiries to selected shipbuilders for a particular type of cargo ship. He stipulates that he requires a ship of a given weight, cargo-carrying capacity, with a cruising range of X miles and a cruising speed of Y knots. A desk copier is required to produce a specified number of A4 sheets at a given rate and cost.

As these requirements are within the bounds of current technology, there are reasonable prospects that they can be met.

In the case of 2, however, the situation is what is rightly termed 'state-of-the-art' technology involving many years of development work before a contract can be processed to completion. For example, a major airline aims to be market leader in the year 2000. To achieve this it requires a fleet of aircraft to an advanced design capable of carry 500 passengers at 2000 miles per hour non-stop over a distance of 12 000 miles. Additionally, the aircraft must have a vertical take-off capability and use a revolutionary new type of fuel with very low accident fire risk. Such requirements may be well beyond the bounds of current technology. New materials have to be developed. In turn, this necessitates the use of new machines for processing the materials. Improved methods are also required for material structure analysis to measure and control quality. The expertise of many suppliers and sub-suppliers may have to be harnessed to facilitate the development of feasibility studies. Design contracts need to be placed. A network analysis will be prepared. State-of-the-art technology will be an act of faith between partners in a new venture. Commitment to a new project of this type will involve high capital outlay. Such commitment will be the product of a realistic evaluation of what is achievable within a given time-scale with a good appreciation of the probable nature and magnitude of problems to overcome.

Quality control/quality assurance
A number of terms are used in connection with the determination and control of quality, the ones in common use being:

1. **Inspection**   Determination of the quality of materials, components, assemblies, or finished products for the purpose of process control, quality audit or fault diagnosis. Inspection identifies substandard quality to prevent an item being processed further or put into use (unless corrective action is possible).
2. **Quality**   The quality of a commodity is the degree to which it meets the requirements of the customer. With manufactured products, quality is a combination of quality of design materials and quality of manufacture.

3. **Quality control**   This is a management system for programming and coordinating the quality maintenance improvement efforts of the various groups in a design/manufacturing organization so as to enable production at the most economic level which allows for full customer satisfaction.

4. **Quality assurance**   Overall supervision by the manufacturer of the quality control tasks to ensure that the quality required is attained. This approach is now rapidly developing. Buying organizations rightly demand that suppliers should have responsibility for ensuring that materials conform to specification. Onus for additional cost must not be placed on the buyer. Quality assurance has been applied to a wide range of items for many decades, branded items being a good example. Ball and roller bearings are normally supplied greased and wrapped and quality assured to the specified standards. Such items are not subject to inspection and test during manufacture by the buying organization or subsequently on receipt as inwards goods.

5. **Quality audit**   The monitoring of quality levels at any stage to provide information to management.

6. **Reliability**   The measure of the ability of a product to function successfully when required, for the period required in a specified environment. It is expressed as a probability.

7. **Value**   Value may be expressed in a number of ways — use value and esteem value being two of them. A Penny Black stamp may be worth thousands of pounds to a collector because of its rarity; but in the manufacturing context, we are concerned with use value, which may be expressed thus:

$$\text{Use value} = \frac{\text{Quality} + \text{Reliability}}{\text{Price}}$$

Grading of suppliers

The degree of sophistication required by the buyer will determine the nature of the control required to exercise over the quality of the materials handled, i.e. quality assurance, quality control, field inspection or incoming goods inspection. There may be no formal inspection on some goods, but just a superficial examination by stores personnel. This applies to the supplier's operations, too. Suppliers can be graded in three categories relating to their capabilities:

1. **Grade 'A' suppliers**   Acceptable, as their control systems in operation meet the required standards of quality.
2. **Grade 'B' suppliers**   Not immediately acceptable, as their control systems in operation do not meet all applicable minimum inspection requirements. When used in conjuction with the buyer's incoming goods control, or when necessary upgrading of standards is achieved, they will become acceptable.
3. **Grade 'C' suppliers**   Not acceptable, as his control systems are inadequate and incapable of improvement to meet required quality standards. Hence they cannot be used or developed.

With the application of appropriate quality control methods, both buyer and supplier derive many benefits, such as:

- Buyer obtains goods that meet specification.
- Supplier minimizes the manufacture of unsaleable or unacceptable products. He has full knowledge of the buyer's quality specification requirements and he has the capabilities and control mechanisms for meeting them. He thus minimizes his costs through minimizing the incidence of rejects and re-working time.

Economics of quality control

The economics of quality control relate to the cost of effort expended against the cost savings achieved. There is an optimum quality control level as shown in Fig.6.3, but data is not always readily obtainable. Also, experience, judgement and experiment may be required. Efforts directed to achieve a particular quality level are related to the cost consequences of failure to achieve it as shown in Fig.6.3.

Inspection concepts

The inspection department may be required to carry out specified technical inspection on the whole or a given sample from a batch of materials being delivered into stores. An inspection report would then be prepared giving the results of the inspection. Inspected materials may fall into three categories:

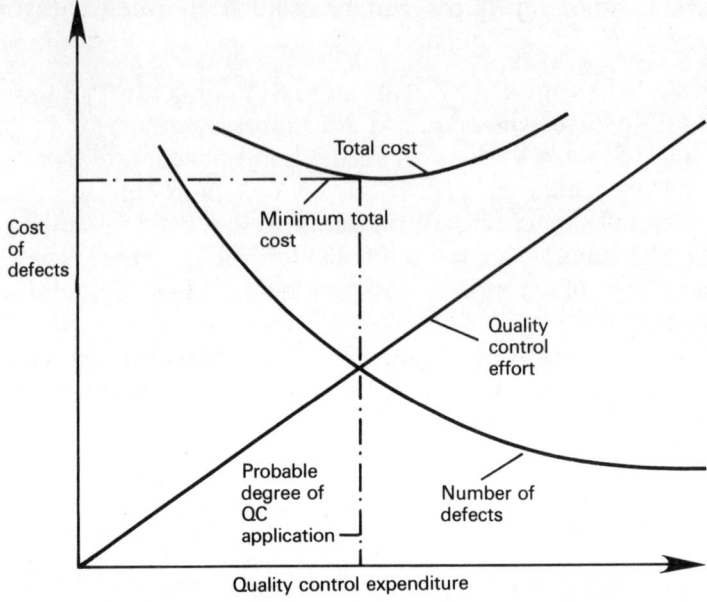

Figure 6.3 Economics of quality control

1. Acceptable, i.e. they have passed inspection.
2. Unacceptable, i.e. they have failed inspection. There may be the proviso that the whole or part of the batch is subject to the following options:
   - Return to the supplier
   - Corrective work to be done with authorization required to carry out at the supplier's expense
   - Concession to be sought where urgent and limited use is possible
3. Borderline case, where further consideration is necessary following possible transfer to quarantine area

Is the inspection of incoming materials necessary and if so should it relate to the whole or part quantities? To answer this question would require an estimation of the cost of undertaking such work against the probable cost that would be incurred if it were not. This necessitates the assessment of the degree of probability of defectives arising in a given batch quantity and the probable percentage of the whole. From such an evaluation, a decision can be taken to carry out one of three possible options:

- 100 per cent inspection
- No inspection
- Acceptance sample inspection

ACCEPTANCE SAMPLING
This is a statistical control technique of great value. Acceptance sampling may be carried out by attributes or by variables. Let us consider these in turn.

Acceptance sampling by attributes
A standard of acceptability will first have been determined against which inspected items may be grouped as acceptable or defective. For example, a manufactured part has to be produced to a particular dimensional tolerance of 10 cm + 0.01 cm. Batch parts that fall within this tolerance are acceptable, e.g. by the use of 'go/no go' gauges. Those items that do meet the tolerance specified are unacceptable, i.e. they are classified as defective.

Sample procedures will be designed so that acceptance of the sampled percentage will give a probability that the whole batch will be acceptable. Actual quality of the whole batch is plotted against probability of acceptance by the sampling plan; this is called the operating characteristic curve. See the example in Fig.6.4.

Acceptance sampling by variables
Control of outgoing quality remains, but the approach used for sampling by attributes changes. In this case, a record is made of actual measurements of samples taken for checking against an appropriate distribution pattern. Items are not accepted or rejected. For example, production uses large quantities of phosphor bronze bars of a specified tensile strength. A reliable supplier delivers regular batches to maintain stocks. A sampling plan is required to determine the size of sample to check that the tensile strength of bars received are within ± 5 per cent of the specified tensile strength. A typical distribution curve is shown in Fig.6.5.

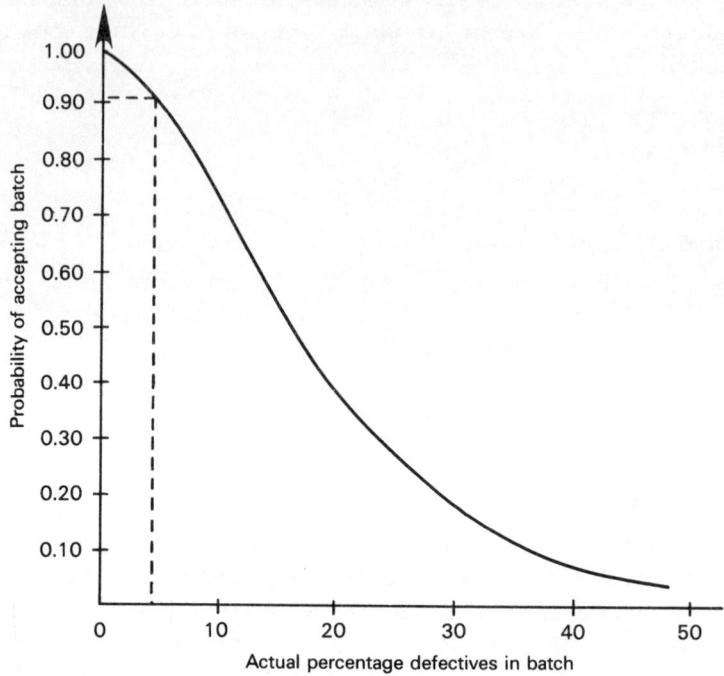

Figure 6.4 Operating characteristic curve

Sampling sizes are thus determined from cost v. probability statistical equations, with several choices of sampling being possible. A single sample could be taken from one batch, from which a decision would be made to accept or reject the batch. Alternatively, multiple sampling could be done, from which the decision to accept or reject would follow the taking of further samples. Inspection may relate to one or more attributes.

The subject of acceptance sampling is a highly specialized area of statistical analysis relating to degrees of probability of defects arising in given batch sizes. Materials management staff are not directly involved in using this QC technique, so further development is outside the scope of this book. However, an appreciation of it is useful to such staff. The reader who is particularly interested in this subject is recommended to read *Production and Operations Management* by Ray Wild (Cassell, 1984).

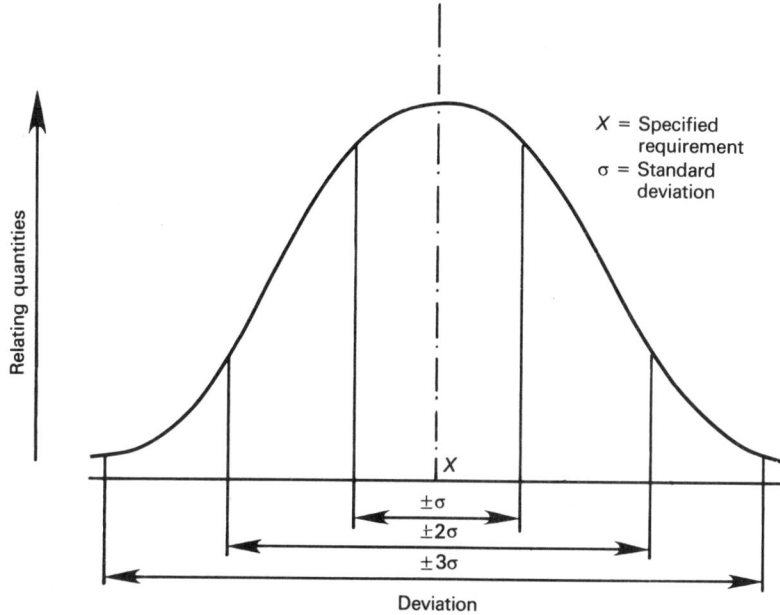

Figure 6.5   Distribution curve

Materials management contribution to quality

How best can materials management staff contribute to achieving quality standards? Firstly, staff must gain an understanding of the needs and problems of both users and suppliers relating to quality attainment on key items. Such a contribution is dependent on the degree of sophistication of items being supplied. A knowledgeable buyer can harness supplier knowledge and expertise. This does not mean that he must have a technical background, although this could be a decided advantage in a highly technical and specialized buying field. Buying is a commercially oriented function but often requires technical expertise for its successful application. The right balance must be sought between commercial and technical inputs. Technical back-up may be readily available, enabling the commercial buyer to consult with technical colleagues. Successful buying is dependent on effective coordinated contributions of a number of interdependent specialist departments.

Stores staff will become aware of quality problems at the inwards goods stage. They are responsible for ensuring that goods are fit for the intended purpose when issued. Maintaining the quality of materials in stores requires using the right methods of preservation and protection, appropriate methods of storage and handling, and rotating stock where shelf life is a limiting factor. These are important aspects where stores makes a valuable contribution to quality. Subsequently, stores receive defective items back from production or user departments for disposal action. They must ensure that these are segregated from good stock pending disposal and are adequately identified.

Production planning staff have to ensure that scheduling procedures adequately cater for quality requirements following issue from stores. Subsequently, production control staff are particularly concerned that items are identified and handled, moved and processed in a satisfactory manner to ensure quality problems are avoided on the shop floor.

All functions must work closely with the appropriate quality/inspection function to achieve this.

Value analysis

Value analysis is a technique that is very much specification and quality oriented and hence we include reference to it within this chapter. Materials and components need to be subjected to critical appraisal for a number of reasons, which include:

- Time constraints at the initial design stage
- Design considered to be innovative at the time but now made obsolete by rapid technological developments
- Materials and processes that were economical at the time but are now relatively expensive
- Originally specified materials are now in short supply
- Original design based on an attitude of resistance to change or insularity, e.g. the designer did not seek the advice of specialists or supplier expertise was not harnessed

There is therefore a need for periodic reappraisal of specifications for a very wide range of items.

It was observed during the Second World War that substitute materials often performed as well as the original materials and were often cheaper and easier to process. General Motors assigned a design engineer, L. D. Miles, to formulate a systematic method of examining products by function. Hence, the discipline of value analysis (VA) was developed in the fifties. VA commences by questioning the need for an item. What is the purpose of the function it has to perform? The analysis then works logically through many relevant aspects:

- **Function**   Are all functions essential? Are there other ways of achieving requirements?
- **Material specification**   Can a different specification of the same material or a different material be used?
- **Material content**   Can the dimensions be reduced (or increased, where a less costly material is used)?
- **Material waste**   Can this be reduced?
- **Tolerances**   Can these be relaxed? The relative costs of different machining limits are demonstrated in Fig.6.6.

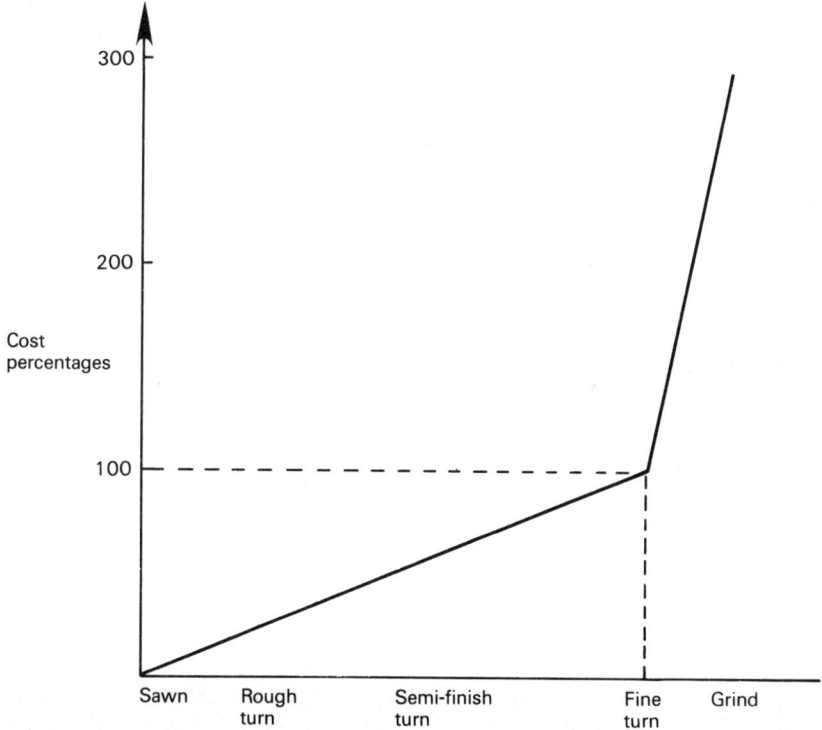

Figure 6.6   Surface finish costs (steel bar example)

- **Process of manufacture**   Can the raw material or finished component be produced by different methods?
- **Surface finish**   Can a less costly finish be used?
- **Standardization**   Can a standardized material or component be used?
- **Direct labour costs**   Can these be reduced?
- **Direct material cost**   Can these be reduced by ordering optimum quantities, more economic packaging, handling and transport, 'make or buy' analysis, or locating cheaper sources of supply?

Value analysis job plan
This follows a sequence of logical stages similar to those included in method study:

- **Information**   What does the item do? What do we want it to do? What is the cost breakdown?
- **Speculation**   What is the item really worth to us? What other ways are there of achieving required results? Would a 'brain-storming' session yield some good ideas?
- **Evaluation**   What is the lowest cost of producing the item and putting it into use? What are the costs of other alternatives? Long-term considerations must not be overlooked.
- **Planning**   What are the implications of introducing new ideas? What are likely to be the reactions of interested parties?
- **Reporting**   What do management need to know to make a decision? How best can VA be sold to interested parties? How best can cost comparisons be demonstrated?
- **Implementation**   How best can we ensure proposals are effectively implemented, controlled and monitored to ensure that anticipated benefits are realized?

Operating value analysis
The approach to VA will depend on the size and nature of an organization's operations. VA can apply equally to saleable products and engineering maintenance items. Scope to achieve the largest savings generally exists in the early years of VA application. Where anticipated savings are great, it may be advantageous to appoint a value engineer on a few years' assignment. He would call on specialisms available in the various

departments. Representatives from each department could be co-opted on one- or two-year assignments to work part-time as VA team members. The VA team approach is shown in Fig.6.7.

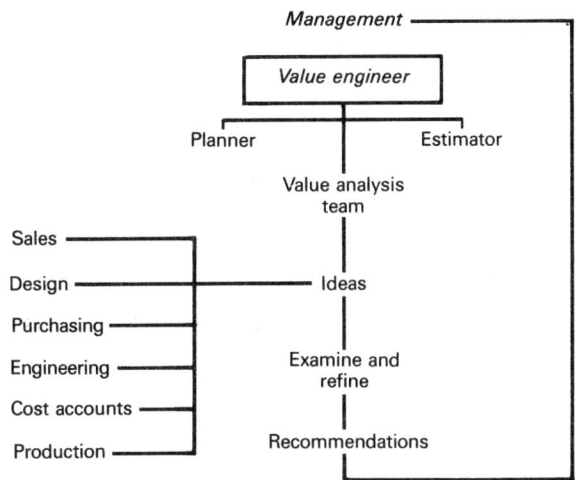

Figure 6.7 Value analysis team approach

Selection of items for analysis
Organizations have limited resources and hence priorities must be determined, e.g. using an ABC analysis technique related to item annual usage expenditure as a basis. Cost-savings potential is not always related directly to usage expenditure. Some items offer greater scope for fruitful analysis than others by nature of their material content or design and the timing of a previous analysis. Significant savings have been achieved in many areas in addition to those made in bought-out or made-in costs. The main areas are:

- Producibility
- Performance
- Reliability
- Availability
- Weight reduction

Return on expenditure can vary considerably. Returns varying from 10:1 to 30:1 were reported by major organizations during the first decade or so following the introduction of the technique in the UK. Later, as value engineers worked through priority lists and greater effort has been concentrated at the design stage, scope for value analysis has reduced. However, scope will still exist, particularly during periods of great technological change.

Own use or sale

The philosophy of value differs between the consideration given to items for own use as against for sale. The lowest priced item will be bought that satisfies product customers. However, when buying for internal use, emphasis will be on value at the point of use. For example shear blades used on the production shearing machine cost £100 per pair with a life of one month. A special new blade recently advertised may cost £1200 per pair with a guaranteed life of two years. Purchase of the new blades would halve annual purchasing expenditure, giving also bonus savings on blade removal and fitting costs.

'Zero defects' quality improvement programmes

A number of organizations, particularly in the car, electronics and aerospace industries, have developed quality improvement programmes designed to direct and motivate staff. In parallel with this, suppliers have been harnessed in an integrated approach with the common objective of achieving zero defects. Such a programme requires a clearly demonstrated management commitment, without which little progress will be made. A realistic time-scale must be set as changes in procedures, working practices and attitudes will be required, and these cannot be accomplished overnight.

A quality improvement team may need to be formed. Tasks would be selected and allocated within the team. Quality problems must be identified in key areas using an ABC analysis approach. Priorities can then be determined and efforts directed accordingly.

All staff directly involved in quality require educating and training to develop a positive approach to eliminating substandard quality. Individual contributions must be harnessed, and hence active participation must be stimulated. Finally, effective control and audit procedures are required so that the success and cost of corrective action is measured.

In a group of companies, progress would be made on a broad front by coordinating activities and bringing together representatives from the associated companies. Ideas could then be raised and considered as widely as possible, the good ones being supported and developed. Key suppliers must play a prominent part as they have important contributions to make. They should be integrated within a total team approach. Some manufacturing companies spend very high sums developing and maintaining effective quality assurance or quality control programmes in their quest for zero defects. Consequently, cost savings achieved result from the speeding of production and reducing scrap and hence re-working. The major benefit will be increased customer satisfaction evident from fewer complaints and the return of fewer defective goods for replacement or repair. This leads to increased sales through gaining an enhanced reputation for quality and reliability.

Conclusions

While the control of quality within an organization is normally independent of production or engineering departments, quality is nevertheless, the concern of all staff. This is particularly true for those engaged in materials management, whose daily efforts are directed to working to meet the needs of users and customers at total minimum cost. A good appreciation of the organization's requirements for quality and specification is, therefore, not just desirable but essential. All other important aspects such as price, delivery, inventory values and economic manufacturing are secondary to adequacy of quality and specification.

7

Price management

Introduction

What is price? In most economies it is a monetary figure. To the buyer, it represents value in terms of the utility of the item being bought. To the supplier, it is repayment for the cost of producing the item and the cost of the capital needed to finance production, plus an extra sum (profit) to ensure that the business can continue by renewing resources for the future. By far the most common element in pricing is costs, and cost-based methods of pricing are still the most universally used. It has been estimated that 70 per cent of companies relate the prices of their products directly to costs. However, increasing emphasis is being placed by suppliers on other factors such as demand, competition and marketing considerations. Pricing strategies have been developed placing differing degrees of emphasis on some, or all, of these factors. These are discussed later in the chapter under 'Pricing methods'.

Price is of particular importance as it is generally evaluated at the time of placing an order, whereas specification, quality and delivery achievement cannot be assessed until later. Purchasing has a particularly important role to play in this area to contribute to profitability. All buyers are employed to seek the lowest possible prices compatible with obtaining good value, to reduce or contain costs.

Price objectives

A supplier's target might be a particular return on the capital employed in the business or a certain percentage return on net sales. He could be concerned with preventing competition, maximizing profits or stabilizing prices. Limiting factors relating to market conditions, production and distribution might allow some of these varied objectives to be combined, but others would conflict. The supplier's objectives will determine how he establishes his selling price, e.g. 20 per cent return on capital investment, 10 per cent return on sales, 10 per cent on investment after tax, or 5 per cent increased market share.

Achieving the keenest prices

Over-specification must be avoided. Efforts can then be directed to obtaining competitive quotations from competent suppliers where scope exists, i.e. when not dealing with a monopoly supplier and time permits. However, whatever the constraints in the supply market, negotiation skill can be used to achieve the keenest prices possible.

ABC analysis of prices paid

A selective approach is required commencing with the evaluation of annual expenditure on bought-out goods and services. Efforts can then be directed to the higher-value 'A' items, where possibly 60 to 70 per cent of total purchasing expenditure is incurred. Cost savings potential is greatest in this group of items.

Measuring price

Price may be measured in a number of ways, which include evaluating against:

- Budget or standard price
- Estimated price
- Supplier's costs
- Currently achieved price
- Previous price
- Established market price
- Published indices
- Spot price v. forward buying
- Quoted price(s)
- Prices achieved by other buyers
- Fixed price v. price variation formulae

But in critical situations, as in times of scarcity or extreme urgency, there would be less emphasis on price, the main consideration being given to:

- Importance of the item to the organization

First-time, repeat or modified buy
Price assessment depends on the proposed purchase, i.e. first-time, repeat or modified buy. In the first case, less information would be available than for the second. The modified buy is concerned with changes in specification, and so is closely related to the first-time buy. There is, however, one important difference between the two, as the buyer may have choice of supplier for the first-time buy but be more likely to be committed to the existing supplier for the modified buy.

Purchase price cost analysis (PPCA)
Products can be priced in three ways:

1. Price related to cost
2. Price not related to cost
3. Price related to a combination of 1 and 2

In the case of 1 the buyer should determine the nature of the cost structure on which the supplier bases his price by using the technique of purchase price cost analysis (PPCA). Frequently, too little information is sought or is available in this area. Purchasing must devote more time to investigating the potential contribution to profit that can be achieved through applying PPCA. It must be appreciated that purchasing expenditure budgets are often greater than that of their associated manufacturing departments.

Reducing prices
Much progress has been made in recent years to improving purchasing professionalism in sourcing and negotiation to reduce prices. However, much scope still remains for purchasing to contribute to higher profits by achieving keener prices. Many factors influence price to the supplier's or to the buyer's advantage, and so buyers need to assess what scope there is for reducing or containing prices. They can then pursue the right approach and apply appropriate techniques to optimize opportunities. Consider Fig.7.1, which details these various influencing factors.

Selectivity and use of PPCA
There is no case for devoting time and money to this technique if

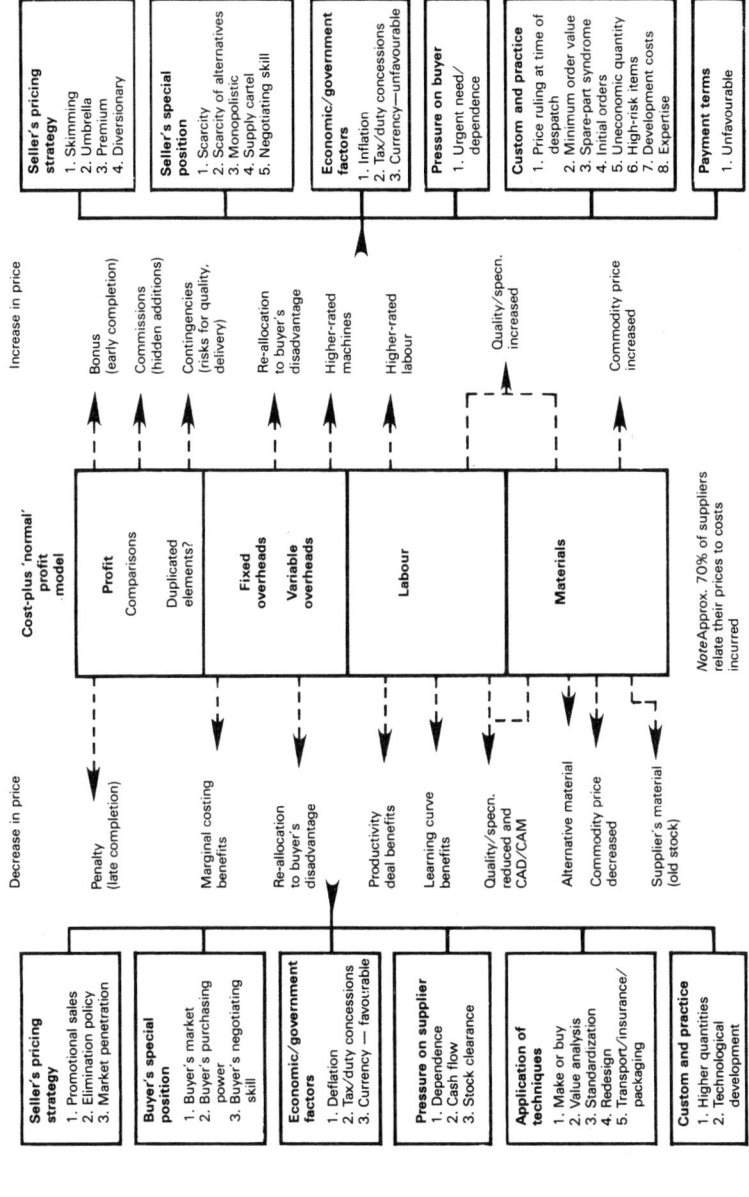

Figure 7.1 Factors that influence price

the returns do not cover the investment. Carrying out a price analysis of all of an organization's purchases would be a considerable and an unjustifiable task. In an article 'Supply positioning overview' in *Purchasing and Supply Management Journal*, December 1985, Steele and Elliott-Shircore consider the various categories of orders handled by the purchasing function and their criticality and contribution to profit potential. They write:

> Purchase price and cost analysis is used:
> * To assist in establishing effective prices with suppliers via negotiation.
> * To form the basis of a purchase control system in the form of target prices.
> * To identify variances in some or all the elements of the price which may have an adverse impact on profit.
> and finally and equally importantly,
> * To assist in selecting efficient and productive suppliers.

COST-PLUS PRICING

In this method the total variable and fixed costs are calculated and a percentage added. It is a relatively simple method in concept but relies heavily on the accurate identification and allocation of costs. Overheads are a particularly difficult area, being too frequently historical. The method ignores market forces such as demand, competition and elasticity. Prices to be paid often result from very inefficient operations and administration. Cost-plus pricing is much used for capital equipment and component types of products, but less used in continuous bulk manufacture. However, cost considerations are obviously important, particularly for indicating minimum price levels below which it is not worth while marketing a product.

Cost-plus pricing involves breaking down the selling price into distinct elements of cost, which are:

* Material
* Labour
* Overheads

Additional elements of cost frequently included are:

* Packaging
* Transport

- Less scrap (rebate or discount)

It has been estimated that over 70 per cent of suppliers determine product prices from costs incurred, adding to them an element of:

- Profit

Let us consider these elements of cost in turn.

Material

Establishing details of all the materials used, and their percentage contribution to the finished product, requires analysis of quantities, grades or qualities used. Details of market prices of most materials are readily available in trade journals and other relevant publications. However, a supplier sometimes obtains materials under contract at rates below the market price, often with significant discounts. Material is also provided ex-stock for a contract, bought at prices much lower than current ones charged to the buyer.

Are scrap and wastage rates applicable? Standards are established by custom and practice as to what is a reasonable level for a particular process, but other points should be considered, such as:

- Does the supplier have a market for seconds? If so, scrap allowances could be reduced or not be applicable.
- Do the buyer's requirements allow for a proportion of seconds?
- Are inspection procedures adequate enough to prevent delivery of substandard materials? If good procedures are being operated by both buyer and supplier, are costs being duplicated?

Labour

Analysing direct labour content requires knowledge of the types and grades of labour involved and factors such as manufacturing methods and process times. Details of wage agreements might be available but their impact on prices could be affected by productivity deals, bonus schemes and shift premiums.

Overheads

Overheads are classified as fixed or variable. They are generally expressed as a percentage of labour charges, material charges or a combination of the two. This is a difficult area in which to establish correct or realistic rates. Trade associations publish averages for particular industries. However, averages disguise variations within an industry. Methods used to account for indirect labour and materials contribute to this. It is important to establish that overheads are not being loaded unfairly to a contract. Fixed overheads include such elements as plant and building depreciation, rates, insurance, water, National Insurance, research and development and general administration charges. They do not vary with the volume of production but are fixed allocations, being the same under full or zero operating conditions. Variable overheads vary proportionally with the volume of output. Electrical power consumed by production plant and equipment is a good example of this, as it generally varies directly with volume of output. Semi-variable overheads include such examples as lighting, where power consumption generally varies with the season and day and night shift working. Lighting is also required for maintenance work and for security purposes during non-production hours. Costs are thus incurred which are not proportional to production output.

Break-even analysis

The relationship between costs, volume of output, sales revenue and rate of profit is the basis of the break-even analysis. This relationship is shown in a simplified form in Fig.7.2.

It will be noted that the break-even point occurs where the total sales income equals the total cost of the product at a given level of output. By using such an analysis, a supplier predicts the effect of a change in one or more of the factors such as price, costs or profits. Together with additional information about the pattern of demand for his products at different price levels, he has available a very useful model on which to test the effects of different prices before any commitment to the market is made.

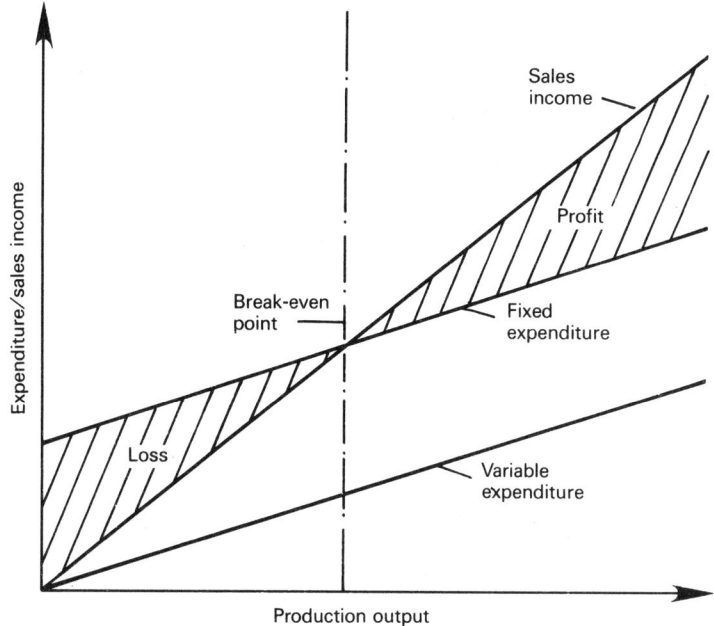

Figure 7.2   Break-even analysis

Absorption and marginal costing
Absorption costing is based on the theory that all costs incurred
by a business should be charged to production, i.e. direct labour,
direct material, variable production overheads, fixed production
overheads, administrative expenses and selling expenses. Where
fixed production overheads are allocated by cost centres, this
facilitates comparisons with cost breakdowns supplied by other
suppliers. A breakdown of direct material and labour charges
enables quantities of the various materials and individual costs,
and the various grades of labour with wage rates and numbers of
hours, to be determined. This breakdown is then assessed
against the buyer's own estimate, when provided. Where other
suppliers quoting for an order have included cost breakdown
details, these too can be compared, and significant differences
noted and investigated. Such data is invaluable to the
knowledgeable buyer at the order placing stage and later when
claims for price increases are challenged. The buyer is then able
to compare and evaluate against original cost breakdowns.

Major organizations, e.g. MOD, require by the terms of their contracts that suppliers will provide detailed cost breakdowns. While it is true that many suppliers do not provide such information, an increasing number now accept this development as standard practice.

Marginal cost pricing caters for a supplier's total fixed and variable costs to be recovered from the existing volume of production. The cost of producing an extra item will only incur the variable costs involved. This extra item could be sold at a much lower price without loss of profit to the company. If sold at a price above the cost incurred, it makes a contribution to profit. The buyer must be alive to the possibilities of placing purchase orders on a marginal costing basis.

The subjects of absorption and marginal costing are important areas of costing, and readers who are keenly interested are recommended to read *Practical Cost and Management Accounting* by G. Knott (Pan Breakthrough).

Profits
Viewpoints differ on what is a reasonable profit. A buyer needs good suppliers who are financially viable to stay in the market. Thus they must more than recover their costs in the prices they charge for their products. The percentage profit margin will vary depending on many factors. A supplier would expect a high profit where he takes a high risk, e.g. an initial order on a new line of product to the buyer's specification. He would also expect a high level of management expertise to be reflected in high profits. The efficient supplier who provides high-quality goods to time rightly requires high returns from this level of service. A supplier might also expect a higher percentage profit on a small order compared with a larger one.

The buyer prefers to see profit stated separately and not concealed within other elements of the price. Unfortunately, profit is not generally disclosed. Purchase price cost analysis should be used when it is advantageous to do so and the supplier can be persuaded to provide relevant data.

Pricing methods
Approximately 30 per cent of suppliers base their prices on factors other than cost incurred. Transport and insurance costs,

too, may require special consideration. Buyers need to be aware of the various pricing methods in use and, hence, determine what scope there is for challenging prices and how best to deal with suppliers when such methods are applied. Pricing methods not based or partially based on costs include the following.

Price to meet competition

This method is used when competition is strong between suppliers with little product differentiation. In some respects the situation reflects the perfect market in that a supplier has little control over the price. He follows the market trend or loses business. Pricing to meet competition is used in oligopoly, i.e. few suppliers and a small number of competitive firms control the market. Car tyres provide a good example. Suppliers seek to convince customers that their products are not essentially alike or produced to similar quality standards. Suppliers using this method need to control costs strictly to remain competitive.

Return-on-investment pricing

This method is used when the supplier requires a given return on capital employed. The selling price will be determined to give this return, taking into account the number of units to be sold. As this method ignores competition and elasticity of the market, it is generally not used alone but to complement other pricing methods.

Penetration pricing

This method is used when a supplier enters a new market or extends his presence significantly in an established one. A gradual increase in price then follows, the supplier calculating that some of the new buyers would remain loyal either because they like his product or through inertia. Introductory offers fall into this category. Penetration pricing is most effective when the demand for the product is elastic.

Skimming pricing

This strategy involves setting a price higher than would normally be predicted. It is usually applied to a highly distinctive product, heavily promoted in the early stages of its life cycle. This policy may be reversed at a later stage by penetration pricing to extend the product's life cycle by appealing to the lower end of the market. The advantage of this method is that it serves as a hedge against mistakes. The price can be reduced if it proves to be too high.

Geographic pricing

If transport costs form a large part of product cost, various pricing methods can be used. Examples include 'free on board' and 'ex-works', where the supplier prices his product related to a certain price-basing point. The buyer pays separately for subsequent transport and insurance costs. A development from geographic pricing is zone pricing, where the supplier divides his market into a limited number of zones and averages out delivery costs for all customers in each zone.

Base-point pricing

This is not now in common use. It involves calculating transport and insurance costs from a predetermined despatch point to the buyer's point of receipt. The base point bears no connection with the point of production but is a common point chosen arbitrarily and used by all competitors in the industry. The steel industry used to price products by this method but no longer does so.

Price variation formulae (PVF)

Many purchase orders are placed where the price has not been fixed firm for the duration of the contract but is subject to price variation. Price variation formulae (PVF) have a particular special application, and are used when a contract involves significant elements of both material and labour, is of high value and long-term, and when significant inflation might be anticipated during the contract period. Price variation formulae clauses are also known as 'contract price adjustment', 'rise and fall' and 'escalation' clauses. The elements of PVF contracts are now outlined.

Datum price

This relates to the cost of material, labour and overheads, with the profit element applying at the date of estimating.

PVF applicable

An appropriate formula needs to be agreed for a contract. It could be a standard one such as BEAMA (British Electrical and Allied Manufacturers' Association) or one modified to meet the particular needs of a contract. If the buyer seeks the use of a non-standard formula, this will incur additional administrative effort, which could be costly and time-consuming.

Indices for materials and labour
These are normally obtainable from an appropriate authorized monthly publication, e.g. the *DTI Index* (Department and Industry).

Formula 'mix'
The relative weightings of materials and labour are evaluated and agreed for the contract, together with the fixed element. The build-up of these three elements is shown later in Fig.7.3.

Supplier expenditure curves
The materials and labour expenditure curves need evaluation to determine the timing and extent of expenditure during the period of the contract. This is shown later in Fig.7.5.

Terminal date(s)
Is there one terminal date for the contract or a series of scheduled dates? For example, the target date for capital equipment could be 12 months, but aircraft components are to be delivered in specified batch quantities over a six-year period. In each case, price and payment would be escalated from datum prices related to a specific date or dates.

Mini-contracts
Where a contract involves both design and manufacturing, the two might be treated separately to advantage. For example, a contract price is £50 000, of which £10 000 is for design work. The planned contract period is 12 months, with design work scheduled for completion within one month. Obviously, the supplier should not be given scope to apply escalation to design costs over the 12-month period.

Delayed completion to contract
Where delay to completion results from the supplier's failure, escalation must relate to planned not actual completion. Extension to the contract period would increase the value of the

material and labour indices during a period of inflation and hence increase the total price.

Progress payments
Agreed progress payments should relate to the datum price, with escalation adjustment being applied at the terminal date. For example, a contract price is £90 000, with two payments to be made of £30 000 each prior to completion. Payments of those amounts should be made. If, on contract completion, the PVF increase is calculated to be £5000, the final payment would be the outstanding balance of £30 000 + £5000 = £35 000. The supplier could reject this proposal, calculate probable inflation and demand inclusion of part of the £5000 in the first two payments. The buyer should vigorously resist this.

Materials, labour and fixed elements
The material, labour, overheads and profit elements which provide the build-up of the datum price are converted into three elements for use in price variation. This is shown in Fig.7.3.

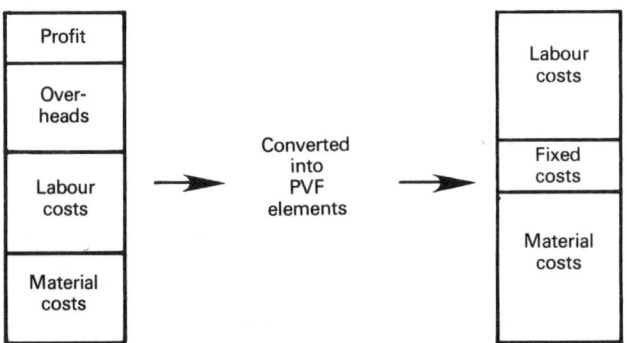

Figure 7.3   PVF formulae elements

The effects of inflation on the datum price elements are shown in Fig.7.4. It should be noted that the timing of material and labour indices will vary for different types of PVF contracts. In the example shown in Fig.7.4, we use the standard BEAMA time-scales.

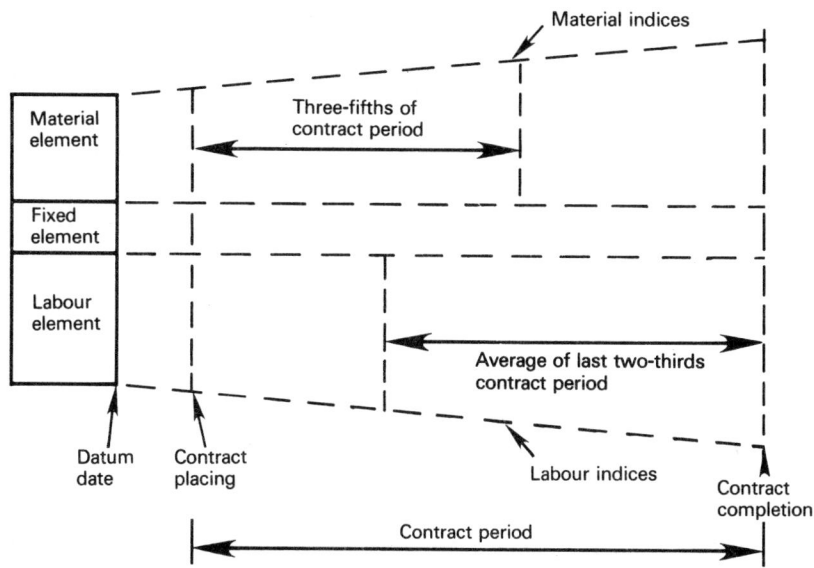

Figure 7.4   Effects of inflation on PVF

XYZ COMPANY EXAMPLE
Consider the following example. XYZ Company have placed a
PVF contract for capital plant. Details are as follows:

Date of quotation	1 August 1986
Datum price	£100 000 (effective 1 July 1986)
Completion date	31 August 1987
BEAMA 'mix'	6% fixed, 50% material, 44% labour
Datum indices for 1 July 1986	Materials — 250 Labour — 220
Application of indices (a) Materials	Datum date — index $= M_d$ Three-fifths* of contract period — index $= M_r$
(b) Labour	Datum date — index $= L_d$ Average of last two-thirds* of contract period — index $= L_r$

*BEAMA-type formulae standards

The total final price to pay for the contract is calculated using
the following formula:

$$P_t = P_d(0.06F + 0.50M_r/M_d + 0.44L_r/L_d)$$

where P_t = total price to pay and P_d = datum price.

The contract is placed on 30 August 1986.

Actual movement of the appropriate authorized published indices from June 1986 to August 1987 were:

1986	Jun.	Jul.	Aug.	Sept.	Oct.	Nov.	Dec.	
Material	250	251	254	257	258	260	263	
Labour	220	221	222	222	223	224	225	

1987	Jan.	Feb.	Mar.	Apr.	May	Jun.	Jul.	Aug.
Material	267	270	273	275	275	278	278	279
Labour	227	228	229	231	231	233	234	235

1. **Determine index M_r** The index M_r is determined at a point three-fifths of contract period (Sept. 1986 to Aug. 1987), i.e. seventh/eighth month, which is March/April 1987, giving $M_r = 275$
2. **Determine index L_r** The index L_r is determined as the average of the last three-fifths of contract period (Sept. 1986 to Aug. 1987), i.e. the months January to August 1987 inclusive, giving

$L_r = (227 + 228 + 229 + 231 + 231 + 233 + 234 + 235)/8$
$= 231$

Then

$$P_t = 100\,000 \times \left[0.06 + \left(\frac{0.50 \times 275}{250} \right) + \left(\frac{0.44 \times 231}{220} \right) \right]$$

$$= 100\,000 \times (0.06 + 0.55 + 0.46)$$

$$= 100\,000 \times 1.07$$

Total contract price (P_t) = £107 000

In the above example the PVF increase amounts to £7000. Is this justified? The timing of the application of indices M_r and L_r in the above example relates to standard calculated weighted average rates of expenditure. BEAMA-type formulae do not cater for significant stock support. The greater the proportion of material supplied ex-stock, the earlier would be the weighting and hence the material index figure would reduce, to the buyer's advantage. In the extreme case, all material is provided from stock at datum date or pre-datum date bought-in prices. In this situation there would be no escalation unless the supplier sought to charge the prices he would pay to replenish stock.

The application of the labour indices (average of the last two-thirds of the contract period) means, for example, the expenditure could commence one-third through the contract period and continue with a constant weight of manning. The earlier use of labour on a contract, or heavier manning at an early stage reducing as the contract continues, would result in the weight of manning moving earlier. Hence the value of the indices would reduce, with advantage to the buyer. He should investigate this possibility before agreeing to a proposed standard formula. Within each industry, wage rates currently increase gradually over the year. However, individual companies make their own wage awards at different times throughout the year. Current practice in most organizations is towards annual increases. Hence, once a pay increase has been made to a group of workers their wage rates would be static for 12 months. Price variation formulae conveniently ignore this, to the buyer's disadvantage. He should determine the timing of the supplier's wage awards. He may then evaluate labour increase implications during the period of the contract. For example, following negotiation with the unions a supplier gives his employees a 7 per cent wage increase on 1 April. One week later he receives an enquiry for a potential contract that has to be completed in 11 months. Obviously, labour costs should be applied at current rates and there should be no increase in wages during the next 11 months. Should the supplier win the contract under these circumstances, a BEAMA-type formula embracing labour cost escalation should not be applicable.

A typical supplier expenditure curve for materials and labour is shown in Fig.7.5.

Timing of material and labour indices can be significantly affected by inflation curves. Where inflation rises at a constant rate, it favours neither buyer nor supplier. If inflation rate is forecast to reduce, the buyer will be at a disadvantage. Consider

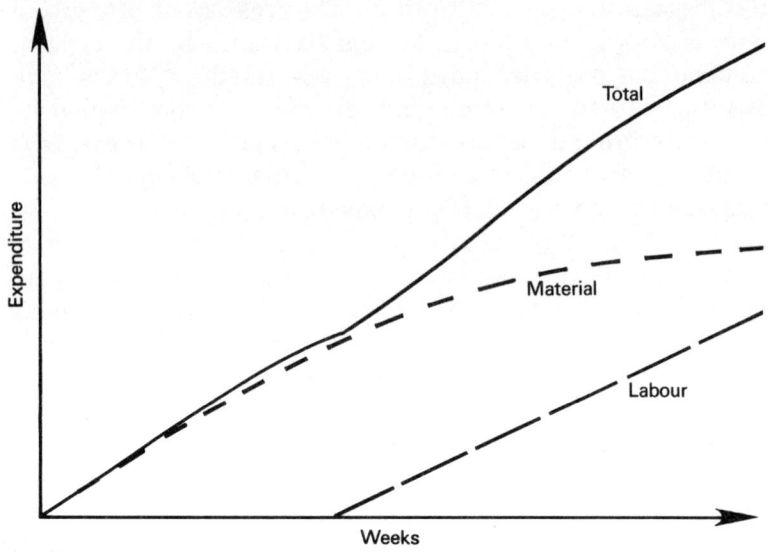

Figure 7.5 Supplier expenditure curve

Fig.7.6(a) and (b). As the inflation line flattens, the weighted effect is reduced. As the labour expenditure curve follows the material one, this effect may have a greater significance.

Learning curve
We have previously considered the labour element of a supplier's price. In its simplest form this element of cost comprises:

1. Grade(s) of labour (i.e wage rates)
2. Number of man-hours worked by each grade

Often various grades of labour, e.g. skilled, semi-skilled and unskilled, with differing wage rates, work on a contract, with each grade working different numbers of hours. For some contracts these details are obtainable together with the wage rates applicable. A PVF-type contract caters for variation in wage rates over a proposed contract period. The possible extent of such variation can be forecast. Where the number of man-hours can be determined, can they be verified and reduced? Reductions to acceptable levels are achieved by:

• Use of more suitable grades of labour

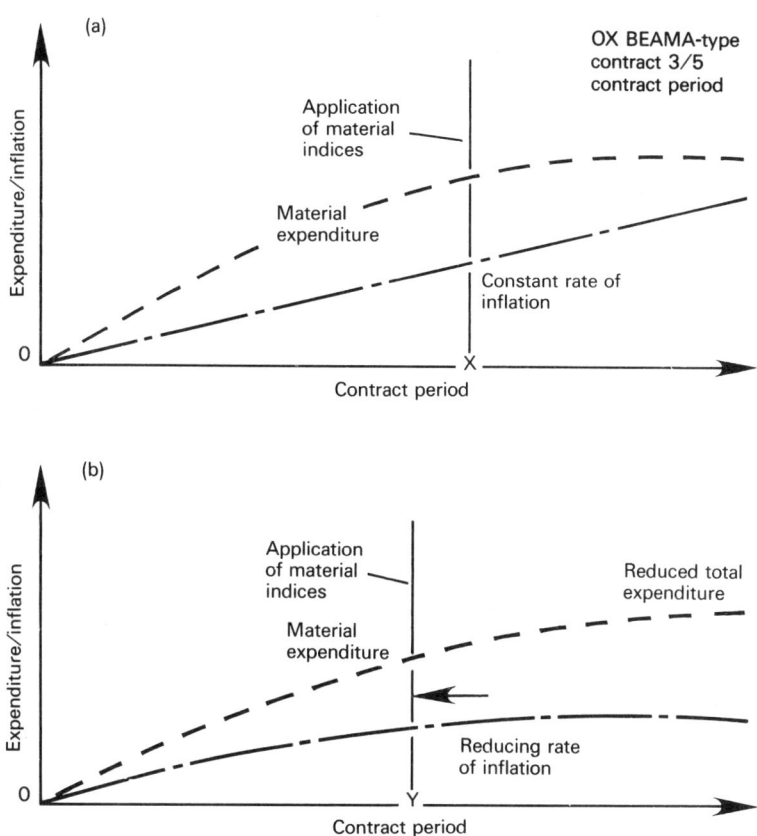

Figure 7.6 Inflation effect on expenditure curves

- Improved planning and work flow with improved methods and practices
- Application of incentives where benefits are not offset by higher hourly rates
- Application of any learning element where scope exists

Consider Fig.7.7, which shows four types of learning curves. It will be noted that, because of their nature, simple and machine-paced learning curves give little scope for learning. True learning curves relate to the labour element of manufacturing costs, specifically to the number of man-hours. They are concerned with the relationship between the number of man-hours per unit and the number of units produced. The reduction in man-hours so achieved results from operator learning.

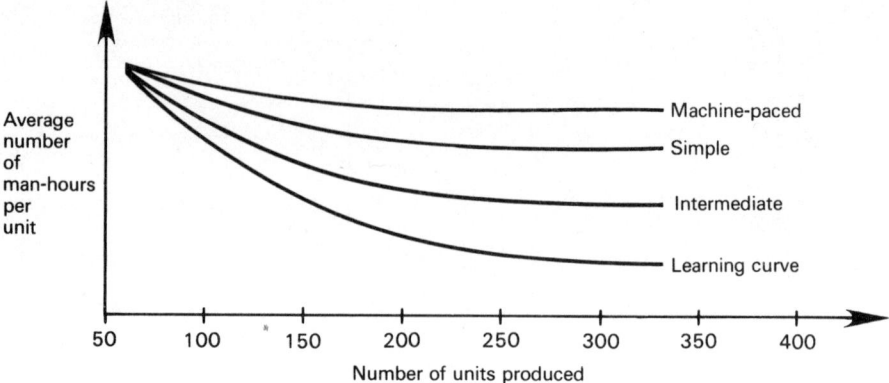

Figure 7.7 Types of learning curves

The learning curve and its everyday application
The learning curve is a specialist technique used regularly by
very few buyers, i.e. those employed mainly in aerospace,
missile, electric and electronic industries, where particular
sections of work are complex, multi-process and highly labour-
intensive. Here significant savings are made by its application.

For the majority of buyers not engaged in such work, what is
the significance of the learning curve concept to them? The work
content of many orders placed might be termed 'intermediate
curve' work. Much of what applies to the true learning curve
applies here, too, but to a lesser degree. Price reductions are
achievable and can be significant. Even where orders fall into
the category of 'machine-paced', scope for applying the concept
of learning will be greatly reduced but not necessarily zero.
Hence, its use should not be ignored.

Consider the hypothetical example of an 80 per cent learning
curve shown below and in Fig.7.8, where the reducing decrease in
average number of man-hours is plotted against the number of
units produced.

Number of units	Average man-hours per unit
10	7000
100	3100
300	2100
500	1900

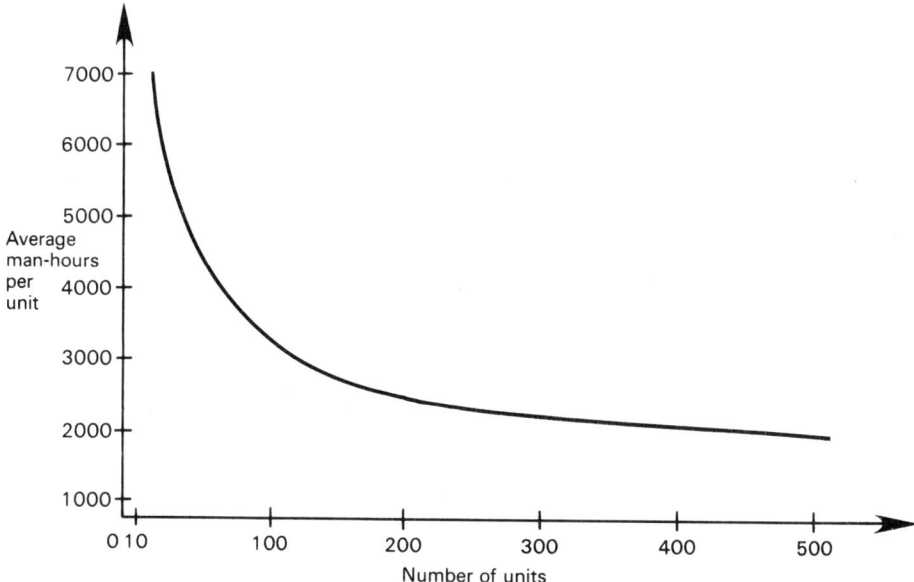

Figure 7.8 Example of 80 per cent learning curve

The theory of a 90 per cent learning curve can be shown in the following tabulation. This is an hypothetical case to facilitate understanding. In practice, observations could only be meaningful if done over much larger quantities of units or items.

Number of units	Man-hours required	Cumulative man-hours required	Average man-hours per unit
First	800	800	800
Second	640	1440	720
Third	594	2034	678
Fourth	558	2592	648

The following relationships should be noted:

1. As production doubles from 1 to 2 units, the average number of man-hours per unit reduces from 800 to 720, a reduction of 10 per cent.
2. As production further doubles from 2 to 4 units, the average number of man-hours reduces from 720 to 648 (a similar reduction of 10 per cent).

If this pattern continued at the same rate, the average number of man-hours per unit to produce 8 units would be 583 (i.e. 648 − 10 per cent).

The task of calculating projected reductions in average man-hours can be simplified by use of the hyperbolic formulae or by plotting on log–log graph paper. The curve so produced is a straight line. Using the data given in this example, we would obtain the curve shown in Fig.7.9 if the number of units was projected to 256.

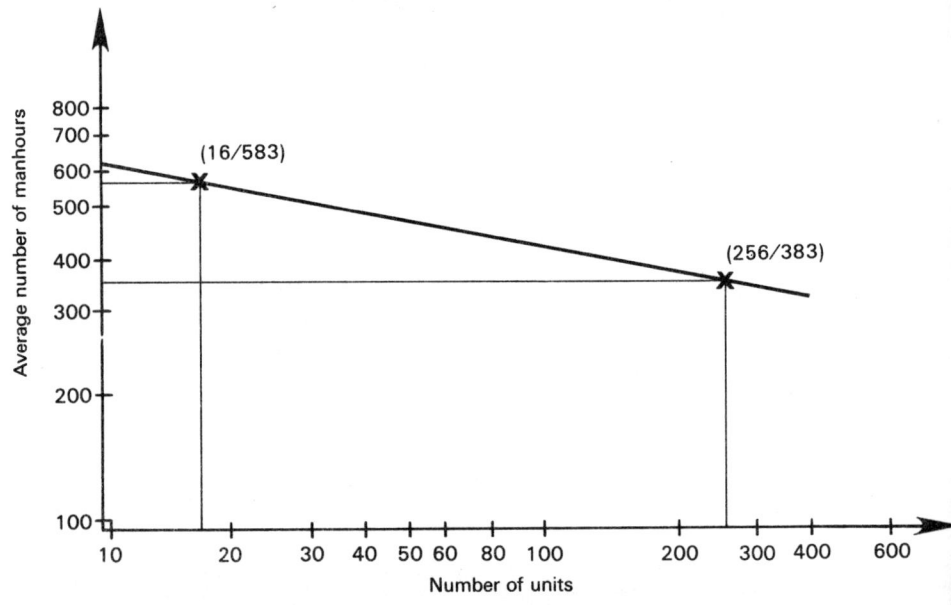

Figure 7.9   90 per cent learning curve, log-log projected

Reasons for achieving reductions

Tradesmen achieve improvement in performance by reducing the number of man-hours on repetitive work through:

- Remembering instructions and dimensions. Non-productive time referring to manuals, drawings or supervision is thus reduced. With increased familiarity with the work, less mistakes are made, reducing the need for time-consuming and costly corrective effort.

- By better organizing of the task, i.e. setting tools and materials at the right place.
- Improved planning and cooperation in a teamwork situation. This minimizes interference and increases productive time.
- Improved methods, i.e. finding more effective ways of doing the various tasks.
- Developing skills, dexterity and judgement.
- Developing stamina to work at sustained higher rates of working.

Soon after the introduction of the learning curve, it was recognized that there were many spin-off benefits resulting from the complementary effects of management innovation with operator learning. The learning curve concept was broadened and was referred to as the 'management curve', 'experience curve' or 'time-reduction curve'. These additional benefits include:

- Improved production planning. Familiarity with an operation should result in better scheduling. Material flow can be improved.
- The number of design changes can be reduced, engineering decisions being stabilized.
- Material problems can be analysed, resulting in better utilization and less scrap.
- Purchasing can be better utilized to reduce problems on incoming materials. Other spin-offs from buying repeat quantities of materials include discounts for higher quantities.

Practical problems of application
There are a number of problems that may arise in applying the learning curve. The calculated benefits sought by the buyer may not be fully achieved should the supplier experience the following problems. These will tend to modify the learning curve, as shown in Fig.7.10.

- Change of tradesman, which may result in the replacement man having to go through the learning process from the beginning.
- Delay to continuity of work. This could include the long

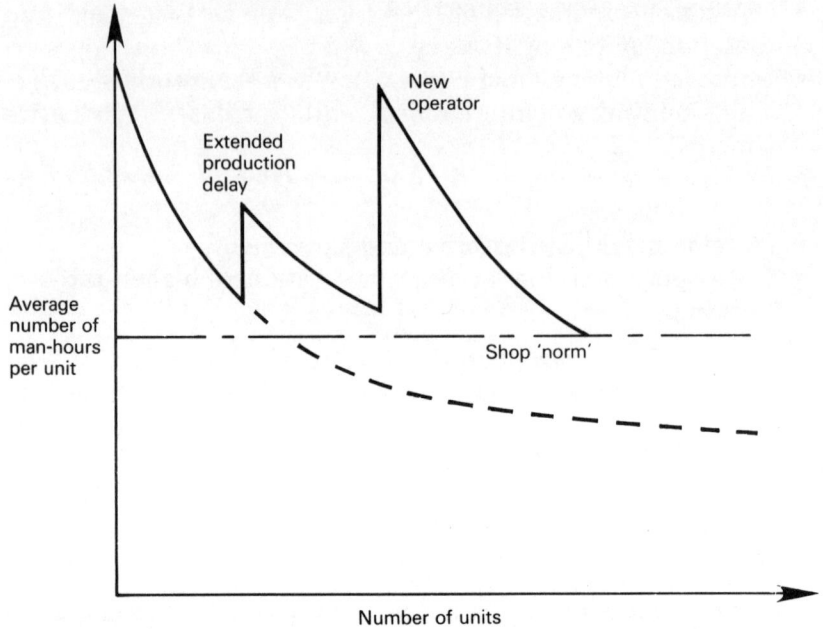

Figure 7.10   Factors limiting benefits of learning

interval of time between completing one batch and commencing the next one. It could also include interruption of work (e.g. the tradesman is ill or there is disruption to production).
- Boredom of operators. Learning may only be sustained over a limited number of units, whence the curve flattens out.
- Shop 'norms'. Here, under trade union policy, there is a restriction to payable and non-payable productivity. Hence, the learning curve will flatten out at a higher point than calculated.
- Impending termination of contract with probable laying-off of tradesmen, who could delay completion of contract by reducing their work rate and so hope to be retained longer in employment.

It will be noted, therefore, that significant reductions in price are achievable by adapting the learning curve. While there are limitations to its use, which we have discussed above, buyers should seek to take maximum benefit from its application.

Challenging price increases

In times of inflation, particularly, buyers are faced with regular price increase demands. Much time and attention is devoted to this key area and so price increases should be challenged in a systematic and logical way. There are a number of main points to be considered.

Selectivity

The time and effort devoted to challenging price increases should be related to the probable impact on annual expenditure, i.e. by ABC analysis and reasonableness of claims. The implications of agreeing to pay increases must be carefully considered to avoid setting precedents for the future.

Buyer's objectives

The buyer may have four-stage objectives, which are:

1. Not to pay any increase
2. Pay a reduced amount
3. Defer date of increase
4. Seek a combination of amount to pay and when

The buyer is influenced by the length of time an existing price has been held, the relation of the proposed increase to inflation over that period and budget constraints.

Planned action

Price increase notification may relate to existing purchase orders or to future ones. In the case of the former the first check is to determine if it is within the terms of the purchase order. Does it allow for the supplier to submit a claim for a justified price increase? The order price could be a fixed one, not subject to increase. In this case, with no amendments to order issued, the claim is not valid and should be rejected.

There may be an agreed mechanism included in an order for dealing with price increases. If so, is the claim valid? Where the supplier's stated policy is to give notice of impending price increases, has such notice been given? His policy could be one of annual price reviews. Materials involved in commodity markets might require more frequent reviews. The buyer needs to be aware of all circumstances that give a supplier scope to increase his prices so he can develop a countering strategy.

Once it is established that the supplier has a possible case, is the claim reasonable or not? On what date was the existing price introduced and was it negotiated? If so, how do the settlement v. claim figure compare? Was a price breakdown used in negotiation and is an updated one now available for checking against inflation? If the situation is urgent, can quotations be obtained quickly for comparison? It will be appreciated that claims for price increases do not necessarily relate to total order quantities and require checking.

Where a supplier does not give a breakdown of the proposed increase, is a standard 'price increase justification' form available to send to him? The use of such a form can be included in enquiry or tender documentation. Where a period contract has a break clause allowing price review, a request for a price increase could be considered if justified by a detailed breakdown of costs. The supplier must not view this provision as an end in itself but as the basis for further negotiation and agreement.

Obtaining the keenest prices by avoiding or minimizing price increases is a key area to which the buyer must direct his attention. When a claim for a significant increase is submitted, what priority does it demand? The degree of urgency of current or anticipated user/customer demand is the base point. While a buyer must deal effectively with suppliers, his first consideration is to ensure that he meets his commitments to customers, particularly important ones. Can requirements be met from existing stock? If the need arises, can part order quantities be placed with another supplier, and if so, at what price(s) and within what time-scale, and are these acceptable? Constraints such as licence and patent rights could prevent dealing with other suppliers, and such points require checking where applicable. A final piece of important information is needed. How much does the supplier value prospects for future business and hence to what extent is he likely to be reasonable in negotiation? This is a difficult area for evaluation, but the buyer's good judgement could result in a fruitful outcome.

Negotiation preparation stage
Once answers have been obtained to the above questions, preparatory work for negotiation can commence. The best results are achievable in negotiation when the buyer is fully prepared

and equipped for his task. Commodity knowledge and an appreciation of the needs, capabilities and problems of users or customers provides the base point. Complementing this is knowledge of the supplier and his representative(s); knowledge of the supply market, e.g. alternative sources of supply; knowledge of existing stocks; purchase price/cost analysis information; purchasing bargaining power related to the attractiveness of the business or future business to the supplier; time and back-up resources necessary for the task; and skill in negotiating. This provides the capability to optimize the use of knowledge, strategy and tactics to achieve buying objectives.

Negotiation is a specialized technique, which we do not develop in this book. It does, of course, relate to many aspects of business, not just price. It is a very important subject for study, and readers working in purchasing are strongly advised to study it. There are a number of good textbooks available on the market.

Payment terms

Payment is paid for most orders following receipt of goods. However, cash flow is of critical importance to all organizations and suppliers particularly require the means to fund the manufacturing of high-value contracts placed with them. Buyers must seek agreement on methods and terms of payment in accordance with management policy. Where special arrangements for payment have to be negotiated, agreement is required from financial accounts. They need information on the anticipated phasing of significant items of expenditure to facilitate cash-flow planning and adjustment. Of particular interest to them is notification of large individual items of expenditure anticipated over the coming year.

Methods of payment

These include cheque, cash, credit transfer, contra-accounting, barter for other goods and banker's draft. On major contracts for plant and equipment, it is normal practice to make progress payments. The amounts and timing of such payments should relate to the nature and magnitude of a contract, time-scale and supplier expenditure curve. Consider Fig.7.11.

The supplier's theoretical expenditure is related to the value

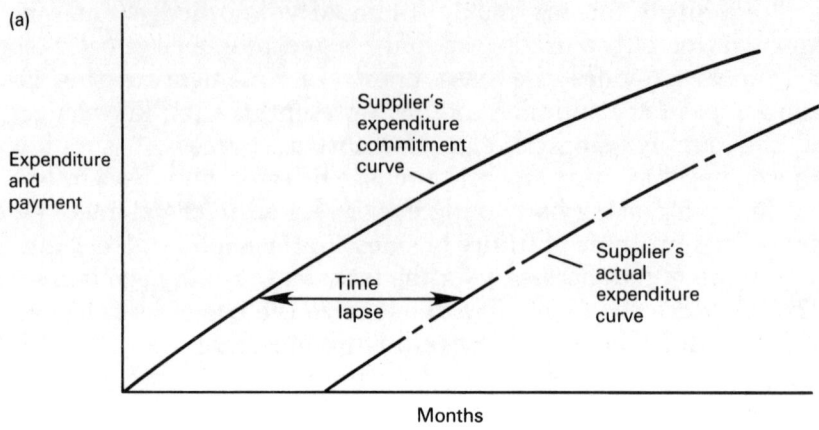

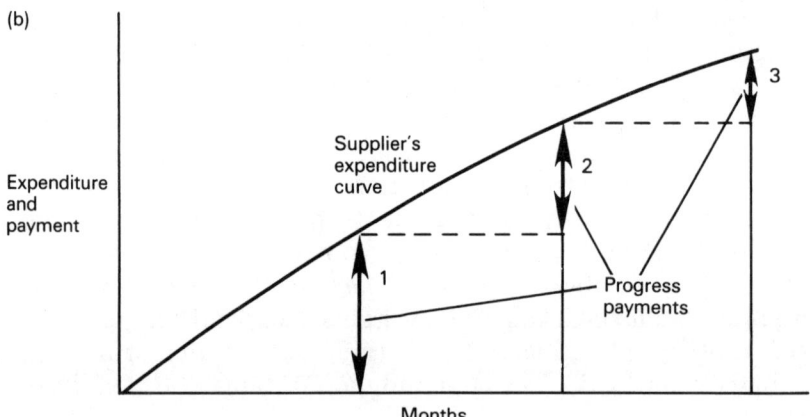

Figure 7.11   Supplier's expenditure — actual v. committed

of received material from his sub-suppliers. Payment could be deferred for several weeks (or months). Negotiated progress payments should be phased to run below the forecasted supplier's actual expenditure curve (see Fig.7.11(a)). There are special circumstances when it is advantageous to assist a reliable supplier (with temporary cash-flow problems) by advancing progress payments. This step requires a compensatory reduction in price related to loss of investment opportunities through advancing payments.

Invoice settlement terms

Periods of high interest rates result in cash-flow problems, so suppliers seek shorter payment periods from their customers. Many organizations state that they will pay invoices by, say, the middle of the month following date of receipt of goods. This means that, on average, payment is made one month following receipt of goods. A supplier, anxious for earlier payment, might offer invoice settlement terms of, say, 1 per cent discount for payment in 14 days. This means, on average, advancing payment by 16 days. If investment yielded a 15 per cent interest rate per annum, advancing delivery would result in a loss of investment opportunity to the buyer of

$$15 \times \frac{16}{365} = \frac{2}{3} \text{ per cent}$$

Receiving a 1 per cent discount thus results in a net gain of

$$1 - \frac{2}{3} \text{ per cent} = \frac{1}{3} \text{ per cent}$$

Such savings might not be acceptable. Firstly, it may not be financial acounts' policy to make advanced payments because of cash-flow problems. Secondly, the cost of making special arrangements for payment could be too high. See Chapter 8 for further details relating to payment terms.

Conclusions

We have emphasized that direct expenditure on bought-out goods and services often represents 50 to 65 per cent of an organization's total annual expenditure. Also, price cannot be considered in isolation from other elements of cost (which it may influence significantly). Nevertheless, it is an element of cost where prompt, quantitative and, in many cases, valid measurement can be made. An organization's future depends on its ability to contain costs. Hence, price is a particularly fruitful area to direct professional expertise. A key purchasing objective is to obtain the keenest prices without adversely affecting continuity and security of supplies to achieve lowest total cost at the point of use. This demands reconciliation of commercial v. technical conflict, requiring both purchasing and non-purchasing staff to work closely to achieve this objective and avoiding a narrow, insular approach.

8

Legal aspects management

Introduction
Domestic consumers enjoy increased protection through the introduction over the years of the Sale of Goods, Trade Description and Consumer Protection Acts. This has provided a more equitable balance between buyer and supplier. The former is now much less disadvantaged than was previously the case. However, the old saying '*caveat emptor*' (let the buyer beware) still remains valid. Buyers in the industrial, public and commercial sectors are, however, in a special, privileged position. Unlike domestic buyers, they have general and special conditions of purchase, which they can negotiate and apply to contracts. By so doing they can safeguard their organizations' contractual interests by minimizing loss-making situations. Contract law is a specialized area, but it is essential that purchasing staff have a good appreciation of it.

Objectives for using purchasing conditions
The use of contractual conditions is particularly important to the purchase of high-value and critical items. These conditions must apply during the full contract period, which includes, when applicable, a maintenance guarantee period. The use of these conditions has the following objectives:

1. Providing a clear, full and unambiguous statement of the nature of the supplier's commitments and the conditions under which the purchase order/contract has been placed.
2. Preventing or reducing the probability of major problems arising.
3. Providing prompt identification of such problems should they arise.
4. Placing responsibility on the supplier to take necessary remedial action at his expense and making it unattractive for him should he fail to meet his commitments.

Suppliers seek to apply their own particular conditions of sale to safeguard their interests. Such conditions will often be in conflict with those of the buyer. The buyer's task in negotiation is to reconcile differences to best advantage. The degree of success depends on many factors such as need, urgency, value (i.e. attractiveness of business to place), criticality (i.e. cost consequences of failure), competition and, particularly, negotiating skill. Suppliers do not impose stringent conditions of sale on all customers but are selective, relating or reacting to circumstances. A supplier keen to win an order could make significant concessions, accepting some or all of the buyer's conditions.

When adequate contractual clauses have been written into important orders or contracts, representatives and principals of both parties are then fully aware of their respective commitments and obligations. Oral or 'gentlemen's agreements' are to be avoided for good reason. If disputes arise, failure to meet contractual commitments needs to be determined. Contract negotiators are not always available later when problems arise. A dispute might have to be submitted to arbitration or to litigation. A good case requires adequate documentary evidence, clearly stating the intentions and liabilities of the parties to the contract. Increasingly sophisticated specifications and complexity of contracts demand greater emphasis and specialism being directed to contractual aspects. However, a buyer is primarily employed to wear a financial hat, not a legal one. Management will rightly demand he directs his efforts to contributing to profitability. The application of contractual conditions has both preventive and remedial objectives. It is not always prudent to pursue a legitimate legal course of action as the cost consequences of taking such action sometimes offset awards made by the Courts. Another important point is that many organizations are loath to gain the reputation for a readiness to take disputes to the Courts.

Forms of conditions of purchase
Different forms of conditions of purchase are used in particular circumstances. These are listed below in order of general usage.

General conditions
These are normally written on the obverse side of enquiry forms

and purchase orders and are used for the procurement of a wide variety of lower-value, less complex and less critical materials and components. The number of clauses usually varies from 5 to 20 and include such aspects as delivery, right to reject, price, terms of payment and packaging. See specimen general conditions of purchase in Appendix 3.

Special conditions
These are normally included in a separate cross-referenced document attached to the order. They are used where there are major orders for materials, components, plant and equipment and for site work. The number of and types of clauses vary greatly between organizations. Many of these clauses are dealt with later in this chapter. The extent of their application will relate to the magnitude, value, complexity and criticality of the contracts or purchase orders placed.

The two following sets of conditions relate mainly to plant/equipment and site work.

Model conditions
These are used by such bodies as the mechanical, electrical, structural, civil, welding and engineering institutes and associations to provide an equitable basis to cater for the respective needs of buyers and suppliers/contractors who are normally named in the documents as 'purchaser' and 'contractor'. They include conditions for manufacture, erection, installation, at home or overseas. There is much similarity between the clauses used by the various bodies, particularly in relation to site work requirements.

Site conditions
These relate to the particular conditions on sites where contractors are engaged to work and cover many aspects. One clause of particular relevance to materials management is security, which includes for the provision, use, safeguarding, removal and disposal of materials. Unless adequately covered, this can be a major loss-making area.

Particular special conditions are sometimes incorporated within the body of the purchase order to assist staff who receive copies of orders for action. A typical example is where liquidated damages apply for late delivery. Financial accounts and expediting staff need to be aware of this aspect when a supplier defaults on delivery.

Order of precedence
It is sometimes necessary to apply two or more different forms of conditions to contracts. Conflict in the wording can arise between, say, a clause in the special conditions and wording written in the body of the order. Which should take precedence? Discrepancies between drawing and specification details is an example of differing contractual requirements. Good communication is essential between buyer and supplier to eliminate possible points of doubt, and the careful wording of contract documents should reflect this philosophy. The order of precedence should be stated in the contract document.

'Battle of the forms'
We have discussed the possible conflict between buyer's and supplier's conditions. The buyer has to satisfy himself whose conditions of contract will prevail. Consider the following sequence of events in an order placing cycle:

Stage	Buyer	Supplies
1. Enquiry issued		
2. Quotation issued		
3. Discussion/negotiation		
4. Purchase order issued		
5. Acknowledgement to order issued		

A contract comprises two essential elements, an 'offer' and an 'acceptance'. At what stages above are these made? Many buyers would wrongly select the supplier's quotation as being the offer. The purchase order is, in fact, the offer, but the acknowledgement is not always an acceptance. This document can take one of three forms. If the supplier confirms acceptance of all the conditions of purchase without qualification, it is an acceptance of the offer on the buyer's terms. However, the supplier could seek to impose some or all of his own conflicting terms and conditions, i.e. modification to specification without prior agreement, change to delivery date or price increase. These are counter-offers, which give the buyer the choice of acceptance or rejection. He has to reconcile areas of conflict to best possible advantage in prevailing circumstances. The supplier could have taken a third course of action and rejected the offer and returned the purchase order. Serious production problems might have developed since he submitted his quotation, making it impossible for him to accept the buyer's offer. All acknowledgements of significance should be hastened and, on receipt, scrutinized promptly. Disputes do arise relating to what had actually been offered and accepted within a contract. An arbitrator or the Courts would scrutinize the last document issued and check action taken against it. Many buyers have experienced major problems in the past in the aptly named 'battle of the forms', so it is essential that they verify, and not assume, whose conditions of contract will prevail.

Contractual commitments to customers

When an organization undertakes a customer contract, purchasing needs to be aware of the contractual obligations to that customer. The buyer can then ensure that similar obligations are passed down the supply chain. For example, it has been agreed to pay liquidated damages to a customer of 1 per cent of the total contract price for each week of delay. The buyer, therefore, may wish to negotiate a liquidated damages clause with his main suppliers. Where there is a commitment to give a customer a 12-month materials guarantee, major suppliers should be asked to give a similar guarantee for the materials they are providing. Purchasing must therefore work closely with the customer contracts department from an early stage and be mindful of what clauses have to be included in enquiry and tender documentation being prepared for issue to suppliers.

Product liability

The subject of product liability has become of increasing importance in recent years. The fundamental problem has been that a claim for negligence could not succeed unless the claimant proved that he was owed a duty of care, that there has been a breach of that duty, and that damages resulting from that breach have occurred which were a foreseeable consequence. Breach of duty means that something has been done (or not done) which is not considered to be the act of a reasonable person. Many claimants have failed in the past to obtain compensation for injury or other damages suffered. The onus was on them to prove negligence, on the balance of probabilities. This they were not able to do to the satisfaction of the courts. As a direct consequence of growing consumer dissatisfaction and pressure, the EC issued a directive in 1985 relating to product liability; the directive was implemented in the Consumer Protection Act, 1987. The main provisions of the Act are included in Appendix 2.

Specification and quality
Contractual clauses relating to quality and specification include the following.

Approval of subcontractors/placing of major sub-orders
This enables necessary supplier appraisal to be carried out down the supply chain. An appropriate clause requires the supplier to submit his list of intended sub-suppliers for approval and copies of major orders placed for information.

Approval of design and drawings
This gives scope to find discrepancies between the two at the earliest stage. An appropriate clause would require the supplier, on finding discrepancies, to refer immediately to the purchaser before proceeding with that portion of the work.

Submission of samples
Where applicable, samples are to be submitted for approval before allowing the supplier to proceed further with the order.

Inspection/test procedures
The nature, timing and documentation requirements are to be defined to ensure both parties operate to one fully comprehensive procedure.

Rejection of substandard material
The appropriate clause gives the purchaser the right to reject, by reference to the applicable standard against which decisions will be made. It will include material returned for rectification or replacement, or rectification work to be undertaken by the purchaser at the supplier's expense.

Material guarantees
Materials or components can fail for various reasons within the prescribed 6, 12, 18 or 24 months' guarantee period through:

- Fair wear and tear (useful life expired)
- Design fault
- Substandard material
- Faulty assembly (in the case of a component)
- Incorrect application
- Abuse or misuse
- Failure of a subcontracted part (component)

Many aspects are covered by material guarantees. Normally a supplier states that his material is guaranteed for 12 months (or lesser or greater period) against failure under fair wear and tear conditions. What are the main limitations to guarantee cover which some suppliers apply? Buyers need to be aware of these when negotiating this clause for inclusion in a contract. The main points for consideration are:

- Timing of the guarantee, i.e. does it operate from date of receipt, putting into use or processing? A component may be in storage for, say, 12 months before issue. Its period of guarantee may then have expired.
- Replacement or rectification, i.e. some suppliers state that they 'reserve the right to rectify or replace defective material'. Rectification of substandard materials may not be acceptable to the buyer and an appropriate clause should specify this.
- Passing on of a lesser guarantee, i.e. it is necessary to establish clearly if any subcontracted parts are subject to this limitation. For example, television sets used to be guaranteed for 12 months except for one component, the tube, which was only guaranteed for 3 months. However, with improved technology

and customer pressure, this constraint has now been removed.

Visits for inspection/test
These may be essential to ensure that manufacture or assembly proceeds correctly and hence minimizes the probability of defects arising later. This requires that the purchaser, giving reasonable notice, should be given right of inspection or to witness tests. The clause should clearly state, however, that final responsibility and liability for meeting specified requirements still rests with the supplier.

Material assurance and test certificates
These are of particular importance where such certification is required. Where material source documentation is an essential requirement, this should be clearly stated.

Plant and equipment performance
Full and adequate specifications and the application of acceptable material guarantees do not always fully protect the purchaser's interests. Performance of plant, equipment or components needs to be adequately covered contractually. Let us consider a number of examples of appropriate clauses relating to unsatisfactory performance.

Right to reject for under-performance
Where performance proves to be significantly below that specified, there must be the right to reject and reclaim all monies paid. For example, valves may require to operate at a specified working pressure. A batch of delivered valves fail under test at a much lower figure and is unacceptable, being unfit for the intended purpose. In this situation the buyer has the right to reject the components and to be supplied with replacements. However, the clause must specify the figure below which the purchaser has the right to reject. If, for example, the valves were to fail 3 per cent below the figure specified, the purchaser (and the Courts) might consider this acceptable with qualification. Financially, it could be disadvantageous to reject the valves and face a long period awaiting replacements. Payment of some form

of compensation might be the best solution to the problem. See the 'liquidated damages' clause below.

Methods and standards for measuring performance
These must be clearly and adequately specified so that both parties work to common, agreed ones. This reduces the possibility of disputes arising. The valve example given above is measurable, but this is not always the case. Hence the need for an agreed defining of the methods(s), the equipment to be used and the conditions under which measuring is done.

Liquidated damages for under-performance
Sometimes performance is only marginally below specification, so the buyer does not have the right to reject the equipment or component. A sliding scale of liquidated damages could be negotiated related to probable consequential loss suffered by the purchaser resulting from shortfalls against specified performance. Consider the example of components with a required operating life of 10 000 hours which achieve 9700 hours in service. This reduced life might be acceptable provided the purchaser receives reasonable compensation for the shortfall in the form of liquidated damages. Payment could be calculated on, say, 1 per cent of the contract price for each ½ per cent shortfall in performance. If, in this example, the contract price is £50 000, the supplier is liable to pay liquidated damages of

$$(1\% \text{ of } £50\,000) \times \frac{(10\,000 - 9700 \text{ h})}{\frac{1}{2}\% \text{ of } 10\,000} = \frac{£5000 \times 300}{50}$$

$$= £3000$$

Theoretically, liquidated damages should be a realistic pre-assessment of probable loss that the purchaser would suffer through the supplier's failure to meet specified performance. In practice, this is difficult to apply, and a formula of the type given above related to percentages of the contract price and performance achievement is normally used.

Performance bond
This type of clause is sometimes negotiated, particularly when

dealing with a new major supplier. To demonstrate his confidence in achieving specified performance, the supplier would
be required to deposit an appropriate substantial sum or bond
into the bank. This sum would be paid to the purchaser should
the supplier fail to meet his commitments.

Delivery
The main clauses include the following.

'Time is of the essence'
Used in limited special cases where the supplier/contractor is
very keen to win business. He fully appreciates and accepts the
high cost of failing to meet specified delivery date(s). A special
example of the use of this clause was reported in 1987. A West
German shipyard tendered to refit the British liner, the QE2.
They contracted to meet a completion target date which
commited them to paying £2m to the owners, Cunard Company,
if delivery was delayed, even by one day. The liner sailed by the
due date.

A supplier would carefully consider the degree of probability
and cost consequences of failing to meet a specified delivery
date. The possibility of winning lucrative business does influence
suppliers to accept such an onerous clause.

Liquidated damages
The purchaser could incur consequential loss through produc
tion delays if material deliveries are extended. The Courts do not
favour 'penalty clauses' unless combined with bonuses for early
delivery. Accepted practice in the use of liquidated damages
clauses follows that discussed above under 'Plant and equipment performance'. These clauses normally require defaulting
suppliers to make sliding-scale payments for each day, week or
month (as specified) of delay. Liquidated damages are defined
as a realistic pre-estimated cost of consequential loss which
would stem from extended delivery, but they are now normally
expressed as a percentage of the contract price for each day,
week or month of delay (both the percentage and the period
being specified).

Force majeure
Extended deliveries result from many causes, which are not

always within a supplier's reasonable control. Consider the following:

- Inadequate control by supplier (e.g. bad planning or late release of sub-orders)
- Purchaser's deficiencies (e.g. late release of information or 'purchaser supply' material)
- Failure of the supplier's sub-supplier(s) to deliver to time
- Failure of other third parties (e.g. haulier or subcontractor)
- Industrial, political and other factors (e.g. war) which are outside the control of the two contracting parties
- 'Acts of God' such as storms, freeze-ups and epidemics

When liquidated damages are being applied, a satisfactory, complementary *'force majeure'* clause must also be negotiated. Failure to do this could negate a valid claim for liquidated damages. Suppliers should be denied scope to avoid meeting their commitments. They must accept liability for extended deliveries which result through failure to exercise reasonable control over a contract.

Approval of sub-suppliers
This requires the supplier to submit the names of his proposed major sub-suppliers for approval before releasing his orders. The use of capable sub-suppliers greatly assists in achieving deliveries to time.

Copies of major sub-orders placed
This requires the supplier to provide copies of major sub-orders placed. The buyer thus has information of what sub-orders have been placed, with whom, when and on what basis.

Submission of progress reports
The submission of regular updated progress reports also assists the achievement of improved deliveries. Some problems that arise are disclosed before they become critical, giving more scope to take corrective action.

Price
Contractual clauses relating to price include the following.

Price fixed for duration
Where this has been negotiated, the price is fixed for the duration of the contract and is not subject to increase unless the buyer amends order requirements which incur additional cost.

Price variation formulae
Used where the datum price has been determined from current actual or estimated costs of labour and material. The variation in price is determined from movement of agreed official published indices for labour and materials which occur during the contract period. PVF requirements must be established and written into the contract.

Variations to contract
This is required to deal with price increases or decreases that result from agreed variations requested by the buyer. Such variations include specification, quality, method and timing of delivery, purchaser supply materials, tooling or storage requirements.

Currency
Applicable when payment in a foreign currency has been negotiated for the contract. The basis for calculation must be stated to cater for possible fluctuating rates of exchange, where this is not fixed.

Payment
Many contracts are placed where part-payment is agreed prior to delivery. Making such prior payments earlier than could have been negotiated results in loss of investment opportunities for the purchaser. For example, an £18 000 payment paid early on 1 March instead of on 1 April could result in the loss of £225 to the purchaser, i.e. if the £18 000 had been invested at 15 per cent for one month). Important objectives are to negotiate the best payment terms and to apply appropriate contractual safeguards to orders. Some of the main points are now discussed.

Payment terms
The agreed terms for payment should be stated. The timing of

payment should be related to supplier achievement. Hence the need to specify the method to be used to validate claims for payment. This could include submission of progress reports to support the claim, which would then be verified. The circumstances under which payments can be legitimately deferred must be stated clearly.

Transfer of title
Where payments are to be made prior to receipt of materials, the buyer requires 'title to the goods' to protect his organization's interests should the supplier go into liquidation. Failure to obtain title would result in loss of these payments should such a situation arise.

Insurance in joint names
This is a complementary clause to transfer of title and is required to safeguard against a catastrophe occurring on the supplier's premises. Without this clause, there would be no insurance cover if the goods were damaged or lost.

Access to design and drawings
A supplier might be unable to complete a contract through going into liquidation or some other cause. The purchaser may have the contractual right to take the material but cannot arrange completion of the work elsewhere through lack of necessary design and drawings. The benefits obtained from the use of 'transfer of title' and 'insurance in joint names' clauses could be nullified without the inclusion of an 'access to drawings and design' clause. This would only apply where transfer was possible (see next subsection).

Manufacturing licencees
A supplier might be manufacturing under licence. Such a licence may not be transferable if a contract cannot be completed. Where a third party has ownership of design and drawings, permission for their use must be sought. The buyer has to be mindful of this contractual point when placing orders. Transferability can be an important factor to consider when selecting a supplier.

Bank guarantees
A large down-payment with order is sometimes agreed. Situations do arise where a supplier becomes bankrupt immediately following payment of the cheque into the bank. Title to the goods might give no benefit to the buyer in such circumstances, as there might not be any goods in existence to which title is granted. Prior negotiation of a bank guarantee would prevent the loss of the down-payment. An appropriate clause would require the supplier to deposit the down-payment with the bank.

Deferment for early delivery
Early delivery is not always desirable for many reasons. An appropriate clause would state that early deliveries will not be accepted without prior agreement. If material is delivered too early, a decision might be made to accept to ensure availability providing payment can be deferred until the due date (to avoid loss of investment opportunity).

Site work indemnities
Some contracts placed for capital plant and equipment require the supplier to install and commission on the purchaser's premises. Buyers have to ensure in such cases that suppliers take out adequate insurances to safeguard the purchaser's interests. The aspects relating to materials are as follows.

Plant or equipment being supplied
The supplier is to insure fully against loss or damage from the time it is delivered to the purchaser's premises to completion of work by the supplier's employees on site. The type of cover required is 'contract works, all risks' insurance. The amount of cover required is the full replacement value of the plant or equipment (i.e. contract price plus an agreed percentage to cater for inflation).

Purchaser's existing plant, equipment and materials
The supplier is to insure fully against loss or damage to these existing items caused by his employees for the period that they are on the purchaser's premises. The buyer must state the 'public liability and third party' insurance cover required, con-

sulting as necessary with his manager or his organization's legal adviser. He must verify that insurance premiums have been paid and cover the period that the supplier's employees will be working on the purchaser's premises. Where the purchaser is a large organization with high-value production, it may be company policy to take out the necessary insurance cover, particularly when dealing with relatively small suppliers who cannot arrange such high-value cover.

Insurance premiums for work carried out by suppliers are elements of cost which the purchaser has ultimately to pay.

Patent infringement

Substantial claims are sometimes made by designers of equipment, components and processes and for material specification against organizations who infringe their patent rights or registered designs. Suppliers do not always obtain from such people full manufacturing rights, and hence they and their customers could be sued for unlawful use. To avoid claims of this type arising, the buyer should ensure that suppliers accept a suitable patent infringement or registered design clause in contracts placed with them. This requires the supplier to indemnify the purchaser fully against any claims, costs, damages and expenses in respect of infringement to patent or registered design resulting from the sale or use of any goods covered by the contract. The buyer's obligation is to notify the supplier immediately of claims for infringement and to cooperate fully with him in his negotiation of litigation which he, the supplier, would conduct.

Such indemnity does not apply to goods supplied that have been manufactured in accordance with the purchaser's specification or instruction.

Packaging and preservation

Specified quality standards can be affected by inadequate packaging or preservation. Requirements need to be stated clearly to prevent damage and deterioration. For example, the specification could require the supplier to protect the materials against deterioration or damage during transit or storage. Examples include exposed machined surfaces to be coated with a specified compound, items such as instruments that are vulnerable to moisture to be sealed with sachets of silica gel enclosed, and all unexposed machined surfaces to be suitably greased or oiled before assembly as appropriate. Where applicable, the clause could include for storage at the supplier's premises and during installation. The method of crating, casing, palleting or packing for the journey to the specified delivery point is to be stated. The user, processor or customer should then receive items in a fit-for-purpose condition.

Storage

The buyer might wish to defer delivery when he does not have available space, facilities or manpower to off-load. An appropriate storage clause would state the degree of notice required and maximum period of delay which would not incur additional cost. To deal with extensions to that period, weekly rates should be agreed as a contractual commitment.

Confidentiality/secrecy

This relates particularly to purchaser- and customer-supplied designs and drawings where confidentiality must be observed. The appropriate clause would state that designs and drawings must not be reproduced or their contents communicated to third parties, without prior approval of the purchaser. In special circumstances a separate secrecy contract document would be required. This provides additional essential safeguards to the purchaser. Third parties, i.e. subcontractors, might require certain information to enable the supplier to fulfil his obligations. Hence, the clause would state that particular information can be disclosed to third parties, i.e. employees, agents or subcontractors, to the extent necessary for them to fulfil their obligations. All such persons must be bound by written agreements. Responsibility would rest with the supplier to take all necessary steps to ensure that such agreements are complied with and enforced. This requirement would not apply where the information was already in the public domain; the supplier would not be held liable if information became public knowledge if this had not resulted from a negligent or wrongful act. The word 'information' would include specifications, design and parameters of design, drawings, blueprints, sketches and flowsheets and other tangible details.

The secrecy agreement document would be prepared in

duplicate, with each copy being signed by both parties, each retaining a copy. The preamble to the agreement would generally be along the following lines:

Agreement made on this day..............................between (buying organization's name and address) (hereinafter called the Purchaser) and (supplier or contractor's name and address) (hereinafter called the Seller or Contractor).

Documentation
Successful execution of contracts can be dependent on there being a clearly stated policy relating to documentation procedures.

Documentation requirements
These are to be clearly specified, including such details as format, size, type of paper/cloth and references. This caters for identifying, handling, filing and reproducing.

Routing or distribution
The numbers of copies of required documents to be stated and their distribution, e.g. one copy to the buyer with other copies to engineering, design or QC as appropriate.

Retention period
This requirement should be stated.

Purchaser supply (free-issue) material
The purchaser sometimes provides materials. It could be normal practice to subcontract certain items for processing, e.g. machining, surface plating or surface hardening. The purchaser could have surplus material available for use on the contract. Sometimes he can obtain the materials at keener prices and on shorter delivery times than can the supplier.

The clause would state that material so provided is to remain the purchaser's property while off his premises. The processor is to undertake to safeguard the material and not to make it available for use by third parties. Ownership of any scrap produced is to be stated. If the processor finds, on receipt, that material does not correspond with specification, he is required to contact the purchaser promptly for instructions to work or return for replacement (the work content of the material supplied could be greater than specified with price adjustment implications). Additional costs that would be incurred must be agreed by the buyer before processing proceeds.

Material is to be adequately insured while it is off the purchaser's premises. Normally, the purchaser covers this requirement within his overall insurance policy. The buyer is responsible for determining if there is any supplier liability relating to the insuring of such material. Liability for cost resulting from spoilage by the processor needs to be stated. The purchaser might have supplied material valued at, say, £50 000. Subsequent spoilage by the supplier might reduce it to scrap value or incur costly corrective work and consequential loss through delay.

Tooling, jigs and fixtures
Where these are to be supplied by the purchaser for the contract, the following safeguards are to apply.

Ownership
The items are to remain the property of the purchaser and the supplier must adequately protect them at all times and allow access for inspection (with reasonable notice) to him.

Insurance
Normally the purchaser will have taken out an insurance policy, which should provide cover for all his tools, jigs and fixtures wherever they may be located. However, the buyer needs to establish that contracts which include 'purchaser supply' items are adequately covered by his organization's insurance policy. Where liability for such insurance cover is to be placed with the supplier, this is to be stated in the contract, with the amount of cover required. The insurance covers loss, deterioration and damage not resulting from normal fair wear and tear usage.

Use for or by third parties
The purchaser's materials are not to be used for or by third parties without the buyer's prior approval.

Refurbishment and replacement
Liability for maintaining the items in a satisfactory usable con-

dition needs to be established for the contract, including cost liability for refurbishment or replacement.

Patterns

Some manufacturing companies machine castings of various types such as iron, steel or phosphor bronze. They make patterns and despatch to foundries to supply castings from them. As in the case of tools, jigs and fixtures, clauses should be applied to orders covering ownership, limitations to use, safe custody, access and refurbishment or replacement cost liability. Normally, the purchaser would arrange appropriate insurance, but this needs to be determined.

Letters of authorization

Time constraints

Occasionally, time constraints prevent the prompt issue of order documents. Some suppliers will not commence work against an impending order as they consider that they do not have adequately authorized instruction. Full information is not always available to enable a purchase order to be prepared and issued by a required date. The need arises, however, when it is necessary to ask a supplier to initiate work against an impending order. Consider the three following situations.

Impending price increase

The supplier states that a price increase becomes operative in, say, two days' time. He requires a contractual undertaking from the buyer to proceed within this time-scale if he is to hold the existing price. If such written confirmation is not received, the price increase takes effect.

Release of sub-orders

The supplier states that he cannot meet requested delivery unless he receives immediate authorization to place sub-orders for (1) a long lead-time item or (2) materials urgently required for the initial stages of production.

Allocation of order in production schedule

The supplier states that he has insufficient free capacity to accomodate new orders. Other customers are already negotiating with him to take available free capacity. Unless he receives, in writing, a firm undertaking that an order will be placed, he will accept an order from a competing customer. Sometimes the delivery date given is extremely tight, the production time-scale equalling the specified delivery period with no slack.

Letters of authorization

On receiving such statements referred to above, the buyer has to check validity. He may decide that the situation warrants giving the supplier immediate instructions to proceed with specified work. As the order document cannot be released within the stated time-scale, he will send a letter of authorization. This document gives the supplier positive assurance of the buyer's intentions to place an order and on what basis. It is a legal document. Hence, the supplier's interests are safeguarded if an order is not forthcoming. The word 'authorization' is to be preferred to 'intent', being more positive in defining the nature of the proposed document. The world 'intent' is sometimes regarded as being weak, as it infers an intention that will not necessarily be acted upon.

The use of letters of authorization also protects the contractual interests of the buyer. The supplier has no cause to delay processing work or to apply an impending price increase. Letters of authorization must be fully, clearly and adequately worded to achieve these objectives. The buyer can limit his cost liability to the value of the work authorized. For example, the supplier requires to place an immediate sub-order for materials costing £1000 of the total contract price of £10 000. The letter of authorization could limit the supplier to placing the sub-order only. This would limit the buyer's initial liability to £1000 only. If, subsequently, the purchase order is not released, the letter gives a commitment to pay all justified costs incurred from issue of the letter to receipt of any subsequent cancellation instruction. Such commitment might also have to cover the supplier's inability to dispose of materials processed, or loss of capacity resulting from acceptance of the letter of authorization. Obviously, the buyer would seek the full advantages from the use of a letter of authorization but with minimum commitment.

Suppliers will not proceed against a letter of authorization if the purchaser's full commitment is not clearly and unambiguously stated. What a supplier would accept as a suitable form of authorization should be checked. Some suppliers do not accept telexed instructions, as they do not bear authorizing signatures as is the case with letters of authorization.

Suspension of contract

Circumstances arise when a contract has to be suspended, e.g. through reduced production by the purchaser, his inability to receive and store materials or cancellation of a customer contract. It is advisable to include a suitable suspension clause to cover these eventualities. This would require the supplier to accept suspension in deliveries for a stated period at no extra cost to the purchaser. The supplier would be required to resume deliveries on being given specified reasonable notice that suspension was to be ended.

Cancellation of contract

Circumstances arise when the purchaser has to cancel a contract. He could be over-stocked or his customer contract cancelled, necessitating cancelling orders down the supply chain. Such a clause should state that reasonable and justified costs incurred by the supplier up to the time of cancellation will be met by the purchaser. The supplier could claim loss of capacity. This can be a major area for dispute and the clause should deal adequately with this aspect. For example, material being supplied could be non-standard, i.e. not suitable for use on other customers' orders, and hence not readily disposable. Alternatively, the supplier has turned down other promised orders to accommodate the purchaser's order. Free capacity is thus made available, which the supplier cannot readily fill.

Arbitration

Disputes arise that cannot be resolved by the two parties to a contract. When this occurs, a procedure is required to deal satisfactorily with them without recourse to legal action through the Courts. Such a course of action is arbitration. A suitable clause for inclusion in contractual conditions might broadly state that:

> Should a dispute arise which the two parties to the contract cannot resolve then one party may, giving the other party due notice e.g. 14 days, submit the dispute to an agreed nominated arbitrator who will appoint someone to investigate the dispute, his ruling on which both parties shall accept.

The clause might also state who the arbitrator shall be. For example, where the two parties operate in, say, the engineering industry, the clause might further include that:

> The arbitrator shall be the President for the time being of the Institute of Mechanical Engineers.

Such a clause lays down the method of settling a dispute, externally. Taking a dispute to arbitration can be time-consuming and costly, but sometimes this step is considered to be the best approach to the satisfactory resolving of disputes.

Legal interpretation

Situations arise when disputes go to litigation. For all contracts of significance, the two parties must agree in which country a case taken to court would be judged. For example, where the buyer and supplier both reside and operate in England, the contract would conform to English law. If, however, a UK buyer places a contract with a West German supplier, the contract could be in accordance with West German law. The law of the supplier's country normally applies unless the buyer has successfully negotiated otherwise.

Serious problems may not arise where there are reciprocal legal arrangements existing between particular countries. Within the EC such arrangements exist. Hence a UK buyer could expect a fair hearing in a West German court. Similarly a West German buyer could expect a fair hearing in a UK court. Such agreements do not exist between all countries. Disputes can thus arise which are not always resolved to the purchaser's reasonable satisfaction, incurring considerable loss. In selecting foreign suppliers, the buyer needs to be mindful of this point. As in the case of arbitration, taking a dispute to court for settlement is not a step the purchaser willingly wishes to take. Most companies seek to resolve disputes without recourse to arbitration, with litigation being the last resort. However, the inclusion of a satisfactory legal interpretation clause provides a final safeguard for handling disputes.

Legal advice

Virtually all buyers in the public and private sectors have their own conditions of purchase. Many have comprehensive sets of conditions from which they can select appropriate clauses for inclusion in contracts. Wording of clauses is important. Many of the larger organizations employ legal specialists. Others engage the services of legal advisers to deal with queries as they arise.

The writing of contractual clauses is a specialized field. Wording must be clear, adequate and unambiguous and, hence, open to only one interpretation. The language used, therefore, must be completely acceptable to arbitrators and solicitors. Purchasing staff have, as part of their duties, to satisfy themselves on the adequacy of contractual clauses that they apply to purchase orders and contracts. Safeguarding his company's interests is one of the most important responsibilities of a buyer. He must therefore gain a good appreciation of legal aspects, seeking specialist advice as necessary.

9

Delivery management

Introduction
The concept of delivery management considers suppliers as being extensions of the purchaser's own organization. Equal emphasis is required to progress externally supplied materials as is devoted to progressing internally. Effort directed to efficient conversion or use of materials is nullified if externally supplied items are not available by required dates. This concept means that there is an essential need to manage deliveries of bought-out materials. Too often progressing such materials is considered to be a subordinate activity compared with the commercial aspects of buying (i.e. sourcing, evaluating, negotiating and placing orders). The purchaser pays an agreed price for specified goods or services. One of the supplier's commitments is to deliver to time but, unfortunately, reality too often differs from expectations.

Quality assurance is a parallel situation where much progress has been made to place fuller responsibility on suppliers to meet their obligations. Quality assurance has largely superseded quality control in many manufacturing companies, the supplier taking full responsibility to meet specified quality. His customers benefit by not having to devote costly resources assisting him to meet his obligations on quality. However, 'delivery assurance' is in rather a different category, as a buyer cannot apply similar British Standards safeguards.

In discussing delivery management we are dealing with the input flow of materials into an organization. Subsequent marshalling, storage and distribution of finished goods to customers is dealt with in Chapter 13.

Need for a sound base
To manage suppliers effectively requires active involvement, from the determination of a need, to the receipt and processing

or putting into use of material. Indeed, involvement does not end there. A supplier's actual delivery performance has to be compared with planned. Selection of good suppliers with whom to place future business depends on such appraisal. Skill and judgement exercised at the supplier selection stage significantly reduce progressing problems later. High consequential loss can result from late deliveries of materials and must be prevented.

A rapidly developing specialism and professionalism is being applied to managing deliveries. The buyer has a key role to play. He is responsible for negotiating with and selecting suppliers. He has a number of objectives, not least of which is achieving deliveries to time. Buyers are judged on their ability to select good suppliers, which we discussed in Chapter 5.

Importance of expediting

Expediting is the main activity normally associated with delivery management. The word 'expediting' describes external progress chasing, i.e. progressing suppliers as opposed to progressing internally. It is concerned with two separate aspects: (1) information seeking and (2) action taking, i.e. hastening. In both cases it should be a dynamic activity requiring the resourcefulness of competent and energetic staff. Delivery problems must be minimized. They must be anticipated and prompt action taken to resolve them by applying necessary pressure on a defaulting or dilatory supplier.

When placing an order, a buyer will have considered many aspects, particularly quality, delivery and price. Delivery, though important, is not always ranked first or second in his priorities. One supplier could have a good record on delivery. A second may be new to the buyer with no proven record. Hence, the nature and degree of expediting effort required is influenced by knowledge of suppliers and past delivery performances.

REASONS FOR EXTENDED MATERIAL DELIVERIES

Suppliers fail to meet promised delivery dates for many reasons, and staff responsible for progressing orders need to be aware of these. Effort can then be directed to anticipating delivery problems and to taking corrective action. Some of the main reasons for extended deliveries are now outlined.

Unachievable promises

A supplier gives a promised delivery date he knows to be impossible to meet. To win business, he agrees to meet a customer's delivery requirement, achievable or otherwise. Subsequently his interest in meeting his obligations is related to the degree of pressure being brought to bear on him to improve delivery (and the value of future potential business).

Choice of supplier

Where choice of an unreliable supplier is outside the buyer's control, the customer or other nominator should be notified of probable extended delivery. A change of supplier might result.

Attractive price

The supplier is known to be unreliable but is selected on price. Tight budget constraints may compel the buyer to give price top priority in supplier selection.

Genuine mistake

A supplier could make a genuine mistake in setting a delivery date from capacity shortfall, an under-estimate of work content or an incorrect assumption of material availability from stock or from his suppliers. A knowlegeable buyer might identify an error on work content assessment and be aware of current or anticipated delivery periods for particular materials. Where he doubts the supplier's ability to meet a specified date and it is not possible to change the supplier, progressing would be given higher priority.

Buyer's undue pressure

The buyer exerts undue pressure on a preferred supplier, requiring him to meet an unachievable delivery date. The supplier considers it prudent not to displease the buyer and so agrees, reluctantly, to meet an impossible date. He hopes there will be slippage in the buyer's programme which will accommodate late delivery and is prepared to take this risk.

Delay in placing purchase order

Delay occurs for various reasons, e.g. the authorizing signature cannot be obtained. However, the delivery date originally requested is still demanded by the buyer, under pressure from the requisitioner. The supplier accepts this demand, hoping that extended delivery will ultimately be accommodated.

Quotations converted into purchase orders
Suppliers forecast the percentage of quotations that should be converted into orders. For example, a supplier estimates that, for every 10 quotations submitted, he will win five orders. Results can exceed expectations and he could win too many orders to handle. In this situation he has two options: (1) be selective, decide which orders to reject and notify the buyer, and (2) accept all orders and not lose secured business. The sensible supplier would explain his dilemma to the buyer, as specified delivery dates are sometimes adjustable and extensions might be acceptable.

Staff responsible for buying and expediting need to identify at the earliest possible stage if any of the above situations exist. Knowledge of job content and process sequences and times assists in assessing if a given delivery date is realistic. A supplier's policy or bowing to pressure and agreeing unachievable dates would be quickly noted where business is on a continuing basis. Late release of purchase orders is outside a supplier's control and, where such a situation arises, weight of progress action might need to be increased. Efforts should also be directed to avoiding delayed release of future orders, including the 'education' of requisitioning and user staff. Buyer and supplier relationships are important and it is not in the best interests of the two parties that the supplier becomes overloaded. The buyer should counsel his key suppliers accordingly. Successful expediting is based on knowledge of suppliers, their capabilities, limitations and probable intentions.

The economics of late and early deliveries

We have discussed the various reasons why delivery dates are not met. Additionally, delays occur through plant breakdown, scrapping of materials and failure of a sub-supplier to meet his promised deliveries. Delays also result from shortcomings in the buyer's own organization, e.g. delay in release of information, late release of 'free-issue' material or incorrect materials dispatched. Realistic and economically viable delivery dates should be the target at which to aim, as consequential loss can be incurred through late and early deliveries as follows.

Loss resulting from late deliveries
A number of loss-making situations can result from late deliveries of materials, the main ones being:

1. Production stoppage, i.e. materials not available for processing
2. Replanning work, working overtime, or utilizing higher-rated and hence costlier machines, to minimize the effect of delays to programme
3. Payment of liquidated damages to a customer because of late completion of his order

Loss incurred in the above situations can be measured directly, financially. In the following cases, it cannot readily be measured:

4. Loss of customer goodwill, which jeopardizes prospects for future business
5. Deterioration in a public service such as transport, or a service to domestic consumers

Where materials are required for new capital plant and equipment, late delivery could result in delays in commissioning, with subsequent deferment of return on capital invested. Delay to material delivery does not always result in a loss as described above. Where material is to replenish maximum–minimum stocks, delay could result in stocks falling to a set buffer level, without causing a stock-out. The setting of maximum–minimum stock levels is dependent on many factors, not least of which is realistic estimating of probable fluctuations in delivery periods.

Loss resulting from early deliveries
High loss can result from early deliveries and there is increasing pressure to apply more scientific control in this key area of material control. The main reasons for loss are:

1. Loss of investment earning opportunities through capital being tied up in stock.

2. Deterioration through materials being held in storage for extended periods, particularly items with a limited shelf life.
3. Increased probability of loss or damage related to additional time during which material is held in storage.
4. Double handling is required because storage, handling facilities and manning requirements have not been planned. With large or high-volume items this could be costly.
5. Creation of heavy demand on limited storage space, reducing efficiency, and hence delaying subsequent location and identification of items.
6. Creation of unnecessary hazards through overcrowding stores.
7. Expiry or reduced life of a component's material guarantee. This applies where the supplier's guarantee is effective from date of receipt of goods into stores.

The longer an item is held in stock, the greater is the possibility of misplacement, loss (including theft), damage, deterioration and obsolescence.

The economics of late and early delivery are shown in Fig. 9.1. Target dates are not always realistically set. They are often subject to frequent revision and hence need to be under constant review, being advanced or retarded as necessary.

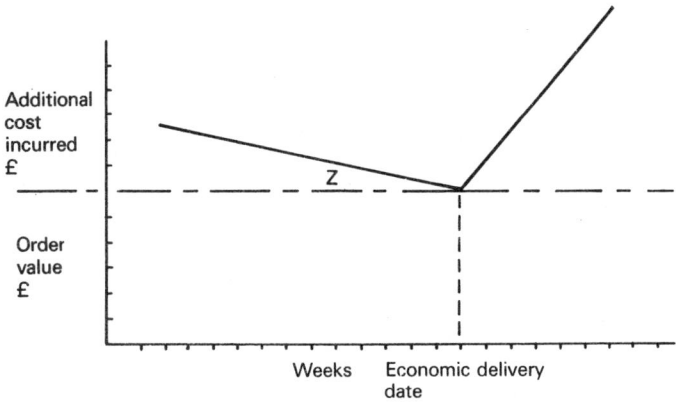

Figure 9.1 Economics of late and early delivery

Prior to the severe tightening of financial controls on inventories which most organizations introduced in recent years, expediting efforts were directed mainly to minimizing late deliveries. Consequently, expediting staff were not adequately trained in minimizing early deliveries. Production departments applied pressure on expediters to obtain deliveries to time and if an item was delivered early there would be one less problem to give cause for concern.

During economic recessions, a supplier may win fewer orders and hence have fewer commitments to meet. He will aim to complete orders quickly to obtain payment. The buyer should counter this, stating on his orders 'early delivery will not be accepted'. Consignments delivered too early would be returned, or accepted and payment deferred until the due date, as considered to be appropriate at the time. Defaulting suppliers will quickly appreciate what is unacceptable practice. The expediter's objective should be to achieve deliveries on time.

Ideally, the buyer requires all requisitioners to give realistic delivery target dates. Frequently, they do not because of bad planning, work overload or an unawareness of what are realistic dates. In the latter case, this occurs through poor communications from purchasing to requisitioning staff, i.e. a failure to inform on updates of manufacturing lead times. So, many examples of late deliveries of materials occur, incurring heavy loss, and yet inventories are excessively high against budgets. This suggests that some emphasis has been directed to progressing the wrong materials.

Responsibility for expediting

Good management of materials depends on satisfactory divisions of responsibility between the different functions it embraces and also within individual functions. Expediting is a particular case, reponsibility being allocated in various ways, as shown in Fig.9.2.

A buyer can be responsible for expediting or delegate the activity to his assistant. The latter would refer back when significant problems arose. Alternatively, expediting could be a separate activity under a section or chief buyer. Where expediting is considered to be of greater importance, the function could come directly under the purchasing manager. The reasons for

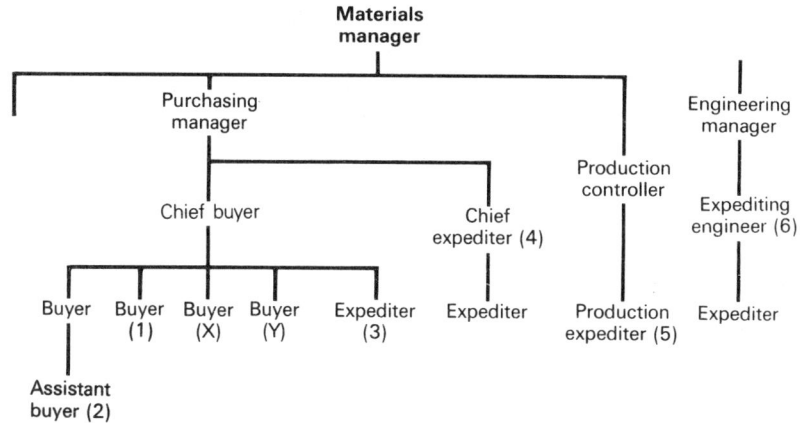

Figure 9.2   Responsibility for expediting

adopting different organizational approaches include buyer workload and his need to concentrate on such commercial aspects as sourcing, appraisal, negotiation and order placing; supplier location; frequency of supplier visits; job complexity and level of contact.

Where material input flows are critical on a day-to-day basis, i.e. flow-line production, the expediter might report directly to the production controller. This would avoid lengthier communication through purchasing. However, close liaison must be maintained with purchasing. On major contracts there may be a need to appoint an expediting engineer who reports directly to the contract manager. Here, again, close liaison must be established with purchasing. Buyer–supplier relationships, communication and contractual safeguards are aspects of importance. The engineer could also act as an agent of purchasing, e.g. when he visits a particular company or geographical location, he could undertake assignments on behalf of purchasing. The form of approach should be adopted which serves the organization's best interests. Conflict between production/technical and commercial interests must be minimized.

Aids to expediters

There are a number of documentary aids to assist expediters. The Gantt chart is one. Major purchase orders could specify that this chart is to be submitted at specified intervals, e.g. monthly, comparing actual v. planned performance (see Fig.9.3).

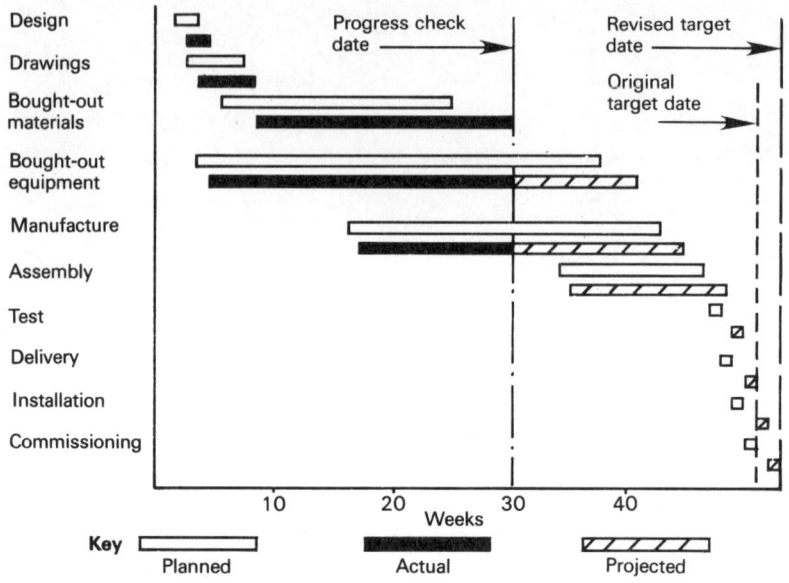

Figure 9.3 Gantt progress chart

The expediter can verify the validity of information given on the chart when visiting the supplier. Agreed progress payments should be related to identifiable stages of work completed. Invoices submitted at each stage could be checked by the expediter to ensure claims were justified. Updated charts may disclose delays to programmes, projecting probable impact on planned completion dates. From such information, action might be taken to minimize slippage to programme.

Supplier visits
What is the value of progress visits to supplier's premises? Some organizations only arrange visits when a catastrophe develops, a reactive approach. Supplier visits might then be made by an expediter or senior colleague. Some organizations employ one or more senior expediters or progress engineers, but each organization has its own particular needs. The benefits gained from progress visits are as follows.

1. Progress is determined at the place of manufacture. Investigation can be detailed, with discussions with those involved, including operatives on the factory floor. In such discussions, problems may be highlighted that otherwise could have been overlooked.
2. The supplier is less likely to give misleading information when he knows that such visits are to be made. He will also note the special importance the expediter attaches to the contract.
3. Personal relationships are developed to the mutual benefit of both organizations. In face-to-face situations a better appreciation is gained of the needs and problems of each party, which provides a sounder basis for overcoming difficulties.

Supplier visits are planned in a number of ways depending on the nature and magnitude of commitments. For example, a company located in London places major orders with suppliers located throughout the UK. Much of the routine expediting is done by telex, telephone or letter. Supplier visits are an essential, complementary element of the activity, but must be economically viable. Choice of transport includes car, train or plane. On longer journeys the time devoted by the expediter and cost will be determined by the method of transport. A return journey made by plane, on one day, avoids the cost of accommodation which could be incurred by the use of car or train. Visit costs may be budgeted as departmental overheads or charged direct to particular contracts, products or projects. The tiring effect of lengthy journeys requires consideration, particularly when travelling time is extensive. Emergency situations do arise, so good lines of communication are necessary whereby the expediter can be contacted at short notice at known locations and redirected as necessary.

Liquidated damages
Liquidated damages are discussed in Chapter 8. Expediters should be aware when this clause applies to particular orders. The buyer must be notified when material is delivered late, enabling him to consult with financial accounts regarding a possible claim on the supplier.

The expediter's organization could be liable to a customer for liquidated damages which result from a supplier failing to deliver to time. However, the customer may not impose such damages when the purchaser demonstrates to his satisfaction that he has acted effectively to meet commitments. Such competence could be demonstrated as follows:

- Work is placed with an approved competent supplier.
- Supplier is given reasonable manufacturing lead time.
- Order is progressed effectively by a person of appropriate status, dealing with appropriate level of contact.
- Customer is notified promptly when problems arise that could affect delivery, with details of action taken.
- Sequence of all actions taken is provided as documentary evidence, giving full and accurate details of all actions taken.

Expediting and quality control

Expediting and control of quality are two important and closely associated activities. Let us consider how closely the two functions might work together:

Combining of the two activities

Control of quality could be the responsibility of inspection, quality control or quality assurance departments. Departments responsible for the quality of materials, components and equipment required for the company's products are normally independent of production and report to a higher managerial level. However, a company may buy many high-value, complex, critical non-production items. A good case could be made to combine the control of quality with expediting. For example, a large company places many major contracts for plant and equipment with widely dispersed suppliers. Would it be economic to combine the two activities? An expediting/inspection engineer could undertake both functions. Visits to suppliers' works would be planned so that stage inspections and witnessing of tests were part of progress requirements. This requires the individual to wear two hats. Hastening deliveries and reducing delays must not be achieved, however, at the expense of shortfalls in specification or quality.

Liaison between expediting and QC/QA/inspection

In the majority of cases the functions are separate areas of specific interest. Staff responsible for quality must notify the expediter promptly when items due for delivery, or on receipt, have been rejected. He will then be aware of outstanding commitments. This also includes items delivered to site or to another manufacturer's premises. The inspector would act as the expediter's agent and carry out this delegated progress function.

QC, QA or other inspection documentation is another key aspect with which the expediter needs to be acquainted. Frequently, materials, components, plant or equipment are delivered but cannot be used because supporting certification is not received.

Liaison with other functions

The expediter is an essential link between internal departments and suppliers. The strength of this link depends on the quality of the two-way communication with all staff involved, including buying where this latter function does not embrace expediting.

Liaison with users and requisitioners

Users and requisitioners are those most concerned that delivery requirements are met, as they have a vested interest in the successful execution of work in which they are involved. The expediter needs to work closely with such staff, particularly on high-value and critical items. They can assist him, notifying him immediately when they make changes affecting delivery. Details of significant changes in manufacturing lead times on key items should be circulated promptly to all interested parties. This facilitates the planning of future commitments. Suppliers should be asked if they anticipate variations to current lead times over the coming year.

Too often, user staff state deadline dates on requisitions. They should check that these are valid, otherwise subsequent expediting effort could be misplaced. Staff who plan work, give realistic dates and are flexible should not be unfairly disadvantaged by those who do not.

Liaison with the buyer

Where expediting is divorced from buying, the buyer and expediter must work closely together. The buyer places orders.

The expediter has details of suppliers' past delivery performance, which could influence supplier selection. Sourcing policies are affected by the quality and speed of feedback received from expediters. Buyers can aid expediters by applying additional pressure on defaulting suppliers. Where lucrative future business is to be won, this could stimulate a supplier to resolve a delivery problem.

Where there are cash-flow problems, financial accounts give careful consideration to releasing payments against invoices. Payment might be deferred to a supplier who is running late on deliveries, which impedes the expediter's efforts to progress orders if payment is withheld against outstanding orders. The two functions must therefore work closely together in this sensitive area.

Liaison with stores
Close liaison is required between the expediter and stores staff. When material delivery is due, the expediter should first check with stores for receipt. The material could have been delivered, thus removing the need to contact the supplier. The expediter should notify receipts bay staff of advised or promised deliveries and request that they notify him when the material is received. The expediter needs to be notified of shortages or rejections, as he still has a commitment relating to such consignment(s). Where free-issue materials are to be sent to the supplier, the expediter requires dispatch to be made on the date specified, as delay could result in subsequent expediting problems, as a supplier then has a legitimate excuse if delivery is extended.

Techniques used in delivery management

Materials requirements planning (MRPI)
An expediter working for a manufacturing company may progress bought-out materials to meet internal materials requirements planning (MRPI). An expediter employed by a non-manufacturing organization could deal with major suppliers using this technique. Hence, knowledge of how it operates is of value to him too. MRPI is discussed in Chapter 3.

Line of balance
This technique for assembling, selecting and presenting in

graphic form the essential stages in the production process in relation to a time-scale. It is used in certain specialist industries such as aerospace. Here, too, knowledge of its use and value will assist the expediter. The technique is discussed in Chapter 12.

Delivery management in project work

When an organization plans a project, it may use a network or bar chart for preparatory work to show the timing, activity time-scales and sequencing of all activities. Consider the stages shown below, which could apply to a purchase order placed with a manufacturer:

Stage	Activity
1	Design work
2	Drawing preparation
3	Enquiry issue
4	Quotation/supplier evaluation
5	Negotiation/supplier selection
6	Requisition raised
7	Purchase order placed
8	Manufacturing (by supplier)
9	Transport to stores/site

Assume the materials are required on site by week 50. It is necessary to work back from this date to establish planned start and completion dates for each activity. The supplier might have quoted 20 weeks delivery, but this information would normally be given when he submits his quotation. On major projects where preparatory work is carefully planned, details are required of the manufacturing lead time for key materials. This information should be obtained.

A further service can be provided by the expediter with knowledge of supplier's previous delivery performances. He can comment on the extent of probable delays against times being quoted. More realistic estimates of material supply time-scales can then be included in plans, which should then be capable of being met.

Gantt charts and networks
The use of updated Gantt charts and networks enables expediters involved in project work to see how material priority

sequences are affected. For example, a site activity is delayed and so material required for that activity is not required by the planned date. This delay could affect related items in the plan. If so, they too will not be required by the original planned dates, and progress action on these items can be relaxed and efforts directed more productively elsewhere.

In addition to the above documents being used for site work, they are also used by suppliers for planning manufacture.

Basic steps of expediting

We have discussed two very important expediting objectives, i.e. the need for the expediter to know his suppliers, and the need to be mindful of possible conflict when he seeks (a) to avoid stock-outs and (b) to avoid inflating stock levels. The basic steps to be followed to resolve this conflict are as follows.

Knowledge of commitments

This includes known and anticipated commitments. What purchase orders have been placed and with which suppliers? What is the nature of individual orders and their required delivery dates? Has any work been initiated with a supplier by letter of authorization which needs progressing? A good appreciation of the needs and problems of users will improve the expediting service provided.

Acknowledgements to orders

Receipt of an acknowledgement is the first indication that a supplier has received the order, and important orders need to be treated as pending for regular checking for receipt.

Timing and nature of progress action

When should the next action be made and how, i.e. telephone, telex, letter, urging card or supplier visit? Computer or manual expediting systems may signal actions to take on predetermined dates, e.g. in weeks 2, 4 and 6. This approach avoids missing a progress action through error. However, flexibility is needed. If, when progress action is taken on week 2, serious problems are noted, immediate corrective action could be taken well in advance of week 4. The subsequent computer signal to progress in week 4 gives a formal reminder only.

Determining relative importance of orders

To determine relative importance requires consideration of a number of points, i.e. urgency, complexity, time allowed v. time needed, problems anticipated and consequences of failure to meet delivery dates. The higher the value of an order, the greater the probabilities that the work content (and hence resulting problems) will be higher. Similarly, an order for complex materials, components or equipment may be multi-process and more vulnerable to problems arising during manufacturing. There would be a higher probability of problems arising in the supply chain, too. Other important points are supplier reliability, time allowed for processing work and changing priorities.

Categorizing orders for progress action

New orders being placed can be categorized in four groups for progress action:

- **'A' orders** Assessed probability of late delivery and cost consequences of this are rated 'high'. A planned supplier visit is required at an early date to determine actual progress made during the important early stage of contract, i.e. has production work been programmed and have orders been placed for urgently required materials and long-lead items? Execution of a contract to time is dependent on such action being taken promptly following receipt of an order. Subsequent planned visits would be made as the circumstances demand.
- **'B' orders** These are not as important as 'A' orders but do require regular planned progress actions being taken but exclude, initially, supplier visits. Use would be made of the telephone, telex, or letter. Generally, these orders are not as complex or as critical as 'A' orders and suppliers are more reliable on delivery.
- **'C' orders** These include short lead-time items with low risk of late delivery. Action is to be taken only if materials are not received or advised by due dates. These materials are less critical, so the consequences of delay would not be serious.
- **'D' orders** These will only be progressed when there is a specific request to do so. The orders are of low value, the items

being readily obtainable at short notice from local sources of supply.

Purchase orders can be so categorized at time of placing, but subsequently degrees of importance change for a number of reasons. For example, the reliable supplier of 'B' order material has a serious plant breakdown necessitating urgent discussions at his premises. Obviously, a flexible and balanced approach is required between planned and emergency actions. The expediter is required to be a 'fire fighter' and a 'fire prevention officer'. A customer could cancel or suspend his order, which could result in an 'A' order being cancelled or downgraded in importance.

Level of contact
Some suppliers take a positive approach to progress and have established lines of communication, their progress sections giving customers updated information on progress. However, too many suppliers undertake to inform customers when delays or problems arise that will affect delivery, but do not meet their obligations. One of the expediter's main tasks is to seek meaningful and accurate progress information. It is important that he establishes the right contacts with staff who are not necessarily the most senior officials. When major problems arise that they cannot handle, they will advise him who to contact.

Delivery information
Prompt and accurate information is essential. Information received requires to be interpreted and evaluated. The expediter would consider his previous experience in dealing with the supplier and the market supply situation, which might raise doubts on the validity of delivery promises made.

In probing actual progress made against an order, the expediter could conclude that the supplier is unduly optimistic or pessimistic. The supplier could be confident that he will deliver by a given date but the expediter considers that delivery will be extended, arriving at this conclusion from an assessment of the work outstanding. Meaningful information must be given to inventory control, material control or user departments. For example, the expediter might inform the user that a supplier has promised to deliver in seven days, but he considers the supplier is too optimistic and considers 10 days is more realistic and should be planned for.

Supplier programme slippage
A supplier promises to complete an order in, say, 10 weeks. During a progress check in week 6 the expediter learns that the order is running two weeks late. Can this delay be accommodated in the programme? The required delivery of 10 weeks might not now apply and extended delivery might be acceptable. Where delay is not acceptable, means of overcoming the problem have to be pursued firmly but constructively with the supplier. A number of possible solutions could be considered, which include:

1. Introducing overtime or additional shift working
2. Replanning operations including the transfer of work to other machines or sections
3. Rearranging priorities
4. Sub-letting the whole or a portion of the work or bringing back to the purchaser for completion

The expediter must press his organization's case with negotiating skill, as he is its representative. Sometimes, serious problems arise where he requires the assistance of senior or specialist colleagues. If the options given above are put persuasively and firmly to a supplier, he is likely to reconsider his position and find solutions or part-solutions. A delay might not be avoided but be reduced significantly. However, in pursuing such options, the expediter must not incur additional cost without prior agreement with the buyer.

Multiple orders placed with a supplier
An expediter is often under pressure to progress single orders in isolation. Such pressure should be resisted because of the probable effect on other outstanding commitments placed with a supplier. Priorities need to be under constant review to ensure that materials are delivered in the required sequence.

Multiple-item orders
A multiple-item order sometimes gives one delivery date. If the

date is met, no problem arises. However, if the supplier meets difficulties that delay delivery, the impact might be minimized if materials are processed and delivered in a particular sequence. The expediter should acquaint himself of such requirements and notify the supplier.

Recording progress actions

All progress information should be recorded and made available to all interested parties. User and other staff may require order status data when the expediter is not available. Essential information that should be recorded and available in such circumstances are:

- Information received and the date
- Source of information
- Subsequent action taken
- Next proposed action to take (how and when)

The date of received information is important. A current date is more likely to be valid than one a month old. Such information enables the requestee to decide whether or not to take further action. The source of information, too, could be important. The more senior the status of the person giving the information, the greater validity it is likely to have. Recording subsequent action taken is particularly useful. Precious time may be saved and duplication of effort avoided.

Manufacturing lead times

The manufacturing lead time is the time a supplier requires to complete an order from date of receipt. The sum of the actual individual process times is often much less than the manufacturing lead time. A delivery of 20 weeks quoted for a component could have five processes, each taking less than two days (a maximum total process time of 10 days). With a five-day working week, material would lie idle for 90 per cent of the time. Such a relatively lengthy throughput time often results through inefficient use of resources. Idle time periods are deliberately built into manufacturing lead times to give a reservoir of material at each work station. This ensures better utilization of facilities. A competent expediter is aware of such float or idle time and can assess the supplier's scope for making up for delays occurring in the manufacturing programme. The relationship between manufacturing lead time and total actual process time is important for another reason. A supplier quotes 30 weeks' delivery for work with five days' work content because he has no free capacity until week 29. If the order is progressed before that week, there will be no progress to report. The supplier could say that work is planned to commence in week 29. A problem arises when information is sought in, say, week 28 and the supplier states that, because of delay, work cannot commence until week 30. Many progress checks could have been made prior to week 28 with no indication of pending problems that would delay delivery. The requisitioner or user would have been notified accordingly. Hence, during those 28 weeks there would be no cause for concern and no need to replan work. This is a particular type of delivery problem difficult, if not impossible, to resolve.

The third situation to which the expediter has to give particular attention is when the manufacturing lead time quoted is significantly reduced by delay in releasing the purchase order. This means that greater progress effort is necessary.

Conclusions

Delivery management is a key function, which has been given less consideration in the past than its importance deserves. Efforts made by individual functions to planning, quality, sourcing, price, stores and inventory management are adversely affected if there is no efficient, integrated contribution from delivery management. Expediting, a major part of delivery management, is still viewed as a subordinate activity by some organizations. Fortunately, many organizations recognize that it is more than a mainly clerical job of checking and urging deliveries. Expediters spend a great deal of their time doing work of primary, not secondary, importance. They represent their organizations directly with suppliers and hence need status and support. They do, however, need to operate within the total framework of delivery management, which is a planned approach aimed at minimizing the incidence and severity of delivery problems. The expediter depends very much on the efforts, decisions and actions taken at the earlier stages in the procurement cycle and the cooperation he receives.

Management's recognition of the expediting role and scope is reflected in its philosophy to recruitment, training, status and remuneration. High-calibre staff may need to be recruited depending on the nature and volume of supply commitments. There is serious imbalance where a highly qualified designer or other technical staff set the procurement cycle in motion and are dependent on a very much less qualified person making his contribution later in the cycle.

10

Physical storekeeping management

Introduction

We discuss in Chapter 11 the many reasons why there is the need to interpose stockholding between suppliers and users. Frequently, quantities of an item are bought which cannot be put into immediate use or processing, e.g. bulk buying for discounts, economic manufacturing quantities and economic transport loads. Stores is also the repository for items returned to stock or held in safe custody, e.g. tooling, jigs, patterns and defective or surplus material awaiting return to suppliers or disposal action. While inventory control is not always the responsibility of the stores manager, physical storekeeping is. They share a common responsibility to maintain an adequate balance between supply and demand. One of the particular responsibilities of physical storekeeping is to minimize differences between recorded and actual stock. They must also ensure that materials are available for issue against authorized demand in good condition within the times specified against the required degree of notice. However, issuing procedures must be flexible to cater for genuine emergency situations that arise. Because of the special need for physical storekeeping and inventory control to work closely together, it is the policy in most organizations for the two to report to the stores manager. A point sometimes forgotten by the staff in these two functions is that they are the custodians of materials, with a duty to provide a service to users.

The stores department has increased greatly in importance in recent years, being a major contributor to cost containment. Let us consider the many aspects and activities embraced by physical storekeeping.

The stores function

The total stores function, including physical storekeeping and inventory control, may be illustrated as shown in Fig.10.1.

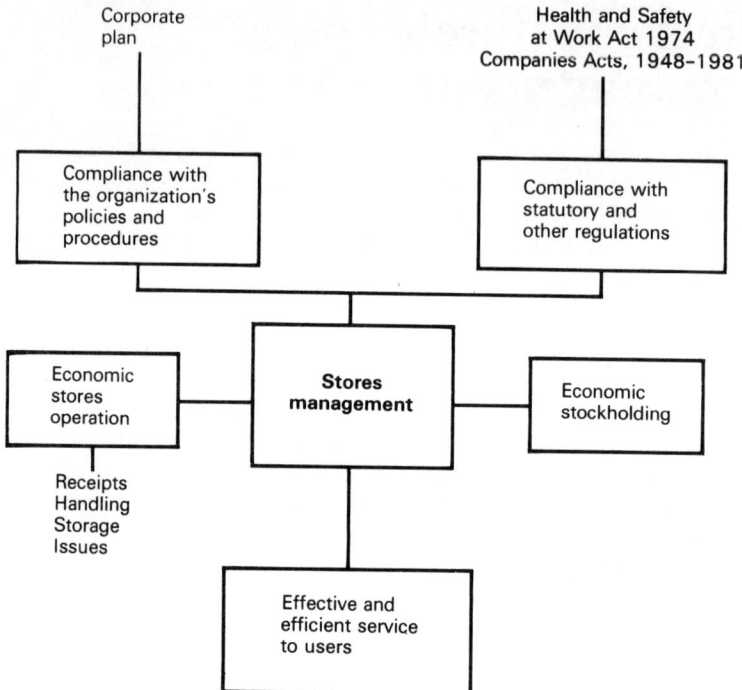

Figure 10.1 The stores function

Types of stores

There are many different types of stores, the main ones in general use being as follows.

General stores

These form the greater majority of stores in the public and private sector, which serve the needs of most users.

Production stores

These stock tools, equipment and consumable materials required to support production in a manufacturing environment. The materials do not become part of the saleable product.

Engineering stores
These stock engineering requirements needed for maintenance and servicing, including consumables. They would also hold in safe custody items of plant and equipment awaiting installation or putting into use.

Finished-goods stores
These are the repositories for completed items pending dispatch to customers. These are also known as warehouses. Their use is discussed in Chapter 13.

Sub-stores
These vary in size and number depending on geographical dispersion of the user units and the incidence of emergency situations that arise. Financial control of inventories cannot be effective without strict control of sub-stores stockholding.

Stationery stores
These stock the organization's range of stationery items.

Special stores
These stock a wide range of materials which by their nature might require segregation or to be located apart from other buildings. Such materials include solvents, petroleum, radioactive materials and, in special cases, explosives. Applicable safety regulations must be strictly observed.

Categories of materials
Materials may be classified in a number of ways relating to their nature or end use. For the purposes of accounting and budgeting, we will consider classification by end use.

Production materials
These are required for processing, i.e. work is carried out to change shape, form or characteristics. The material becomes part of the saleable product. Such material is generally bought-out.

Production components
These are finished parts, sometimes called piece parts, which are not to be processed but are fitted or assembled into the saleable product. These components or parts are bought-out or internally manufactured.

Work in progress
Material in progress lies in production sub-stores or at various work stations on the factory floor. Some material may be routed back to stores for processing externally. Other material will be sent back to stores pending completion of associated materials, whence all will be withdrawn. Both production and engineering requirements are included in this category.

Capital plant and equipment
These items are generally bought-out against capital accounts and held in safe custody in stores until required for use. They are not normally held on inventory charge.

Engineering spares and materials
These include finished components and materials awaiting processing.

Tools, jigs and fixtures
These items are required by both production and engineering departments. They will normally be held in stores in safe custody on behalf of those departments.

General stores
These include the diverse range of materials required in the running of an organization.

Packaging
This is held for packaging saleable products.

Scrap and redundant materials
There is generally a range of scrap and redundant materials awaiting disposal. Stores would normally be responsible for storage pending completion of disposal action.

Contractor materials
These items are received and placed in stores in safe custody pending the arrival on-site of contractors' men.

Material coding

A good coding system must be capable of being understood and applied by all staff required to use it, down to the lowest clerical grades. There should be no possibilities of misinterpretation or duplication. Each item must be specifically identified with its own unique code reference. All codes within the system would comprise the same number of symbols.

Possible future developments should not be overlooked. There could be changes in the nature and magnitude of products or services being provided and coding systems must be designed to cater for this.

Range of coding systems
A very wide range of items held in stock in some large organizations can run to tens of thousands. These are broken down into distinct separate family groupings, with further division into subgroups. Each item will bear its own individual classification, which could include chemical composition, shape, size and dimension. Units of quantity, the inadequacy of which is the source of many problems in stores, and accounting references can also be included.

Types of codes
There are three types in general use, which are alphabetical, alphanumerical and numerical. The latter coding is the most flexible of the three, being ideally suitable to computer application.

CODING CLASSIFICATION
There are two types of classification in use, i.e. by nature of the item and by end use. Let us consider these different approaches.

Nature of the item
The main classifications could distinguish between materials for

processing, tools, cable, chemicals, oils and greases. For example, using the numerical code:

11	Mild steel	16	Chemicals
12	High tensile steel	17	Oils and greases
13	Aluminium	18	Tools, jigs and fixtures
14	Titanium	19	Mechanical spares
15	Timber	20	Electrical spares

The above main classifications can be divided into subcategories. Take code 12 for 'high tensile steel' as an example. The first subdivision could relate to shape:

12/01 Square bar
12/02 Round bar
12/03 Flat bar
12/04 Sheet

Further subdivisions would identify specific qualities, sizes and finish. Taking 'square high tensile steel bar' as an example:

12/01/05/20 HT steel, heat resistant, 20 mm square

End use
A good example of this is used in the car industry, where the various major elements of a car are identified by a two-figure code, e.g.

31	Body	34	Steering
32	Engine	35	Electrics
33	Transmission	36	Internal trim

As in the case of nature of the item, further subdivision is made by allocating additional digits related to the breakdown of components within the group. For example, under 'transmission', the main driveshaft on a rear-axle-driven car might be identified as 33/10.

ADVANTAGES OF A GOOD CODING SYSTEM
A good coding system provides many benefits, which will assist all staff, e.g. materials management, requisitioners, users and accounts. These benefits are as follows.

Identification of item
A good coding system facilitates easier physical identification of items in stock. Lengthy, descriptive titles are avoided as they do not always readily assist in identification, particularly on slower-moving items.

Recording
This is simplified for both mechanical or computerized applications.

Centralized control
This has particular validity in the larger organizations as a good coding system ensures efficient interfacing communication between all manufacturing, storage and user units. It facilitates stockholding comparisons.

Standardization and variety reduction
Such policies would be difficult to pursue without a good coding system that facilitates ready identification of items with possible common application.

Stock records
Stock records, whether manual or computer-based, are the heart of the stores system. Resulting from rapid technological development of computer systems, manual control systems are now being largely superseded. However, whatever system is used, specific inputs of data are required at specific stages in the procurement cycle. The logic has to be right for both systems. Let us consider the manual system. Stock records are used for a number of reasons. Materials must be identifiable, together with their locations. All transactions must be recorded. These include receipts, allocations, issues and transfers. Inventory control is entirely dependent on stock records for initiating stock replenishment. Management and statutory commitments require costing evaluations. Information to be included on stock records is discussed in Chapter 11.

Receipts
Efficient receipt of materials into stores is the foundation on

which all subsequent transactions depend. It is normal practice in most organizations for stores to be notified in advance by purchasing of materials on order. This is done by sending the receipts section a copy order. Action then proceeds as follows.

Raising of goods-received note

Delivered goods are identified and a goods-received note (GRN) is raised. There are exceptions when verbal orders have been placed by phone in emergencies and received goods cannot be identified as no order copy has been supplied. Purchasing should always notify stores of the impending receipt of such items, giving them the allocated purchase order number and item description or references. A specimen format of GRN is shown below:

GOODS RECEIVED NOTE			Serial No.		
Consigner		Advice Note No.	Date of Receipt		
Packages			Purchase Order		
Type		No. Off	No.		
Item Ref. No.	Description	Quantity received undamaged	Standard price	Value	
Receipt		**Inspection**			
Received		Accepted/rejected			
Damage/shortage					
Report No.					
Signed		Signed			
Date		Date			
Stock posted	Signed ....-......	Invoice No.			
	Date				

Acceptance of goods

Acceptance normally includes checking identification with description/references on the order. A quantity check is then done and any discrepancies noted. There would also be a superficial examination for obvious damage or deterioration. Where inwards goods inspection is applicable, i.e. for quality certification or for vendor rating assessment, materials are passed to stores inspection for detailed examination. Where items do not meet specification or are damaged or have deteriorated in transit, the supplier and/or the carrier must be notified promptly (and certainly within the prescribed period). Items would then be returned or collection arranged. Some materials are not readily classified 'acceptable' or 'not acceptable', and these are transferred into quarantine pending examination and a decision being made.

Transfer to storage or to users

Following receipt and subsequent acceptance, goods are normally transferred to designated storage locations. In cases of urgent need, users would be notified and arrangements made for dispatch or collection of the items.

Stock location systems

Materials are stored at fixed or random locations, i.e. an item is always stored at the one location or it is stored at different locations at different times. The choice of method is dependent on consideration of many factors such as nature, size and weight of the item, space utilization, accessibility, handling, volume and speed of turnover of stock. Environmental considerations could determine that certain materials are always stored in locations where special facilities have been provided, e.g. temperature and humidity control. Accessibility and handling may be interdependent. For example, access to storage locations by cranes, forklift trucks or conveyors could be limited by building construction constraints or by the type and proximity of racking and binning. Floor loading figures may not be constant throughout a stores building and this factor could influence the location decision. Let us consider the two methods in turn.

Fixed location

This method has universal application. It has particular merit where there is regular and constant flow of materials to support production or user requirements. Also, demand does not change greatly and rapidly. Minimum time will be required to find the various materials, as stores staff become familiar with their fixed locations. Locations can be set logically by item classification and coding references. There are some disadvantages to the use of this method, e.g. space may not be utilized economically.

The fixed location system is often used for materials required for a specific contract or major works order. This facilitates identification and checking of materials in the one location. Once the contract or works order is completed, any unused materials are checked and returned to stock or disposal action taken. The space freed is made available for other contract materials. As consideration is given to the nature, size, weight and turnover rate of stock, some modification to the system could be necessary to cater for these factors.

Random location
This system is the most economical in the use of space. It speeds up the process of moving items from receipts bay into stock as they can be set down in the first suitable available space. However, a disadvantage is that time could be added at the subsequent issue stage. A typical example of the use of this system is items delivered for the smaller capital projects, which have not been allotted specific storage areas or compounds. Once the items are issued, the space freed becomes available for other project items. Random location storage is particularly applicable in an automated stores. However, in a non-automated stores, storage location decisions are not always made at the appropriate levels of authority. Consideration must be given to what items are likely to be put into stock within the short term, and the choice of location method made within the framework of the stores plan.

It has been said that this method gives more responsibility to storekeepers and makes their jobs more interesting. This has to be balanced against them having to be very much dependent on reference to stock records to locate items. It certainly means that more initiative will be demanded from all stores staff concerned. Individual contributions will have to be increased.

The stores building could be purpose-built or have been

adapted, hence construction and the constraints so imposed can influence selection of the location method. Where there is a fairly constant level of demand for established products, fixed location may be the best option. Where new products are being introduced fairly regularly, fixed locations could prove to be an unsatisfactory method. There is need, however, to differentiate between standard and non-standard materials, as some items have universal application across all product ranges while others are required specifically for one product only. Fixed location is more likely to be more appropriate for standard than for non-standard materials.

Flow of materials

Efficiency of the stores operation is very much dependent on the planned input and output flow of materials. Flow can be considered in terms of volume, direction and speed in that sequence. Volume is related to the levels of stocks held in stores and demand. Direction of flow is also dependent on stores layout, administration and control considerations. Ideally, materials should flow in one direction without reversals or inter-crossing, but this ideal is not always achievable. The most economic total stores operation is achieved through a compromise between space utilization, deployment of handling equipment and direction of flow. Changing patterns of product demand, too, is a significant influencing factor. The final aspect, speed of flow, is proportional to call-off rates, i.e. determined by user departments and stores operating efficiency levels, i.e. availability and capability of staff and handling equipment to locate and retrieve materials and move them to the point of issue.

Interference to flow in the form of bottlenecks can seriously affect the service to users and be costly and time-consuming. Material picking work needs careful planning to minimize such interference. A high proportion of storekeepers' time will be spent picking and marshalling items for issue.

Shelving, bins and racking

Greater efforts are being directed to maximize the use of floor space and building height in existing buildings. The philosophy is 'think cubic'. In the planning of new stores buildings, the fullest consideration should be given to the wide selection of shelving and racking systems. A number of innovative, specialist manufacturers are competing to supply high-density, low-cost storage facilities.

Shelving and bins
Shelving is designed to store all types of goods, excluding particularly lengthy or bulky items which are best suited to storage or racks. There are a number of different types of high-flexibility shelving systems. The two in general use facilitate the extension of the unit sections or modules, in length and height, by means of (1) bolting or (2) clipping. Hence, standard shelving units are readily adaptable for all stores layouts (see Fig.10.2). Where headroom allows, high-rise shelving can be considered. Some types are convertible and their installation could be the first stage to fully automatic storage later should the need arise. Multi-tier shelving with above-ground platforms is an alternative option of a cost-efficient installation, and gives high-density, hand-picked storage without the use of mechanical equipment, except for the possible use of conveyors. In addition to the wide range of fixed shelving, many types of mobile shelving are in general use. While there are obvious height constraints to the use of such shelving, large savings are made in floor space, as the number of gangways is reduced to one, which is not fixed.

A very wide range of bins, vertical storage carousels, cabinets and containers are manufactured. Collectively, they satisfy all binning requirements for the smaller items. Their designs cater for space utilization, loading capacities, access and picking times, division or extension, transportability and, where applicable, security.

Racking
Racking is a storage facility that differs from shelving or binning as it is normally used for storing lengthy, large or bulky items such as the following.

1. **Bars, sections and tubes**   These racks are of three types. Pigeon-hole racks are used for light bars, sections and tubing, which are stored at right-angles to the aisles. The two main disadvantages are that mechanical handling cannot be used where aisles are insufficiently wide to give end clearance when

Figure 10.2   Impex shelving system (courtesy of Dexion Ltd)

putting items into or retrieving from storage. Antler racks, which have horns or lugs, are used for the heavier bars, sections and tubing. To facilitate mechanical handling by overhead cranes, stacker cranes and side-loaders, these items are generally stored horizontally, lengthwise to the aisles. The third type of rack is the vertical rack, which minimizes the use of floor area and maximizes the use of height. The disadvantages are the need for headroom clearance to facilitate storage and retrieval, difficulty of securing to lift and possible buckling of light items under their own weight. Racks can be fixed or free-standing depending on current and anticipated use.

2. **Plates and sheets**   Heavier plate and sheet may be accommodated in vertical racks constructed of cross-members and supporting uprights. Such racks facilitate stock rotation where materials are subject to and affected by weather, as rainwater will drain quickly. Plate cramps would be used for lifting. A more economical way to store large quantities of such items is to store on the ground using spacer bars when lifting. The disadvantage of ground storage is the difficulty of operating a first-in, first-out procedure, which could be necessary because of anticipated deterioration, e.g. corrosion. Lighter and smaller plates and sheets would be stored on pallets or in horizontal racks.

3. **Cable**   Most heavy cable is stored on wooden drums. The drums are stored on racks, which are constructed with single horizontal tubes to support them and to facilitate loading and retrieval.

4. **Drums**   Racks are used to store drums holding various types of liquids, e.g. oil, and powders. These racks are normally of strong construction to support heavy loading. The drums may be placed on or retrieved from the racks by crane, pulley block or forklift truck.

Material handling equipment

In recent years, stores have been subjected to technological development on a large scale. This is particularly true of mechanical and electrical equipment. The degree of sophistication of such equipment previously seen in manufacturing departments has now been extended to stores applications. There has been a revolution in the mechanization of the stores operation, resulting from the very wide range of highly specialized equipment available on the market. The wide variety of materials to be transported or moved ranges from large heavy items to lighter fragile ones. Goods have to be lifted and lowered, sometimes moved from one floor to another. Economic operation of stores means optimizing the use of floor space. Constraints so imposed in operating areas have meant that equipment such as high-reach forklift trucks have to work in narrow aisles with widths sometimes limited to 1½ metres or less. Materials may have to be lifted to considerable heights, sometimes up to 30 metres. Some equipment has to negotiate tight, constricting corners.

Benefits sought
Materials handling equipment is introduced into stores to achieve one or more objectives. These are (1) an improved service to users, (2) reduction in costs and (3) improved control. Benefits gained result from increased handling capacity, speed of movement and accessibility. Certain types of injuries to staff are reduced, particularly those relating to lifting strains and cut hands. Because of the use of more scientifically designed handling equipment, damage to materials in stores is also reduced. Obviously, increased vigilance is required from all staff within stores to prevent accidents as the benefits of mechanization are pursued.

Expenditure
With the manufacture of increasingly specialized mechanical handling equipment, the costs of these items have soared. The benefits sought from their use must be measured in operating economics and in safety terms. Full consideration must be given to the suitability of equipment for the particular working environment within the foreseeable future. New equipment should first be viewed under similar working conditions to ensure that it will meet full requirements, with particular emphasis on safety. Life-cycle costing must be evaluated, taking full account of capital expenditure invested, operating and maintenance costs, workload capability and anticipated life. Return on capital employed would be compared on the various options being considered. Equipment standardization may be under consideration, but this must not be pursued at the expense of limiting essential flexibility.

Safety considerations
We have commented on the increasing numbers of specialized

mechanical handling equipment now in use in stores. Coupled with this is the increasing attention directed to space utilization and volume and speed of material input and output flow. These developments demand that special emphasis be given to accident prevention. Equipment must be properly maintained and operated strictly in accordance with manufacturers' instructions. Operatives must be properly trained and tested at prescribed intervals and their performance should be under periodic review to ensure that satisfactory standards are maintained. With the increasing volume and speed of operations, greater vigilance is required from all stores personnel. A good housekeeping policy is essential. Gangways must be kept clear of hazards. Warning systems should be employed, particularly when equipment is operating around blind corners. This provides additional safeguards to on-board television cameras and monitors, which enable drivers to view what is happening on the other side of the mast or around the corner. Statutory regulations relating to lifting gear, which include periodic inspection and testing, must be strictly observed.

Communication with drivers

In the smaller and medium-sized stores, supervisors are in regular communication with drivers. However, in some of the largest stores and warehouse operations, supervisors and inventory controllers require direct communication with drivers who operate for long periods away from the vicinity of the office. This is achieved by the use of radio and/or on-board computer. In the latter case, the truck operates from an induction wire guide system to which the computer lines are incorporated. Stock control can be more tightly controlled by status updating of receipts and issues as they occur, noting stock-outs and damage. The driver uses the keyboard to indicate each action taken. The extent of such status updating is, however, dependent on time constraints imposed on the busy driver.

TYPES OF EQUIPMENT

There is an increasing sophistication and specialization of the various types of powered equipment now being operated within stores. Material handling publications and sales literature regularly introduce new developments in this ever-widening field.

Powered trucks

These are generally powered by diesel engine or electric battery. Powered trucks are driven in the sitting or standing positions or controlled by walking operators. In some stores, trucks (pulling trailers) operate on fixed circuits and take their power from live rails below ground level. They are often fitted with warning alarms as an accident prevention measure. While powered trucks have largely replaced hand-operated trucks in major stores, hand trucks continue in regular use in the older, more congested stores buildings.

Forklift trucks

These are powered by diesel and petrol engines or electric battery. There has been a revolution in the development of these machines, with an increasing number of variations from the original basic designs in regular use a few decades ago. Over a period of about 40 years, these developments have included high-reach, side-loading and turret trucks. The original forklift trucks carried overhanging loads outside their wheelbases. Hence, they were heavily counter-balanced and had wide turning circles. Their height reach was also limited because of instability under load. The design of high-reach trucks that carry their loads within their wheelbase was a major step forward in the service that could be provided. Improved steering design, too, now enables trucks to turn in very constricted spaces. The more recently developed turret trucks operate within narrow aisles and can turn through 90 degrees to enter or retrieve goods from the racks. Examples of forklift trucks are shown in Fig.10.3.

Many attachments are available for use with 'forklift' trucks, including fork extensions, crane beams and hooks, drum grips (for handling drums) and booms for inserting into steel rings and wire coils, side-shifts, load and carton clamps, rotating fork units and paper roll clamps, load stabilizers and carriage backrest extensions.

Cranes

Many types of cranes are used in stores building and stockyards. These include diesel rubber-tyred mobile cranes, which operate within and outside the stores building. They are more versatile than electric overhead travelling (EOT) cranes, which operate

Figure 10.3 Forklift trucks
(a)   Foer 15.1. Counter-balanced capacity: 1600–400 Kg, depending on model

(b)   Foer 15.1. Capacity: 1600–4000 Kg, depending on model

(c)   Seven 1.5 LPG SC 158. Capacity: 1500 Kg

on overhead gantry girder rails (where headroom under roof structures allow). EOT cranes, too, can be used for inside and outside storage. Another type of track crane is the goliath or portal crane, which runs on tracks at ground level. A variation to this, which allows more floor space to be used for storage, is the semi-portal crane. This has one track set at ground level with the other set at a higher level on a girder normally attached to the stores or stockyard building structure. The use of these track cranes, which operate within stores buildings, is reducing as the 'think cubic' philosophy develops (i.e. increased heights of racking), which imposes severe constraints on crane movement.

Conveyors

There are two main types of conveyors, gravity and power-operated. The gravity conveyors generally operate over fixed paths where there is sufficient height of the loading over the delivery point and the weight of the goods is sufficient to create movement. These conveyors are of the roller, wheel or chute type depending on the nature of the material to be carried. For example, the wheel models are suitable for light packages. Power-operated conveyors are of roller, belt or slatted wood design and can be fixed or portable. Conveyors can be supplied to handle unit loads on pallets. Tracks supplied in various widths and lengths can be built up from standard sections. Curved sections are also available, varying from 30 to 90 degrees. Selection of a conveyor must take into account the nature of the materials to be carried, their volume and weight and required speed of operation, which may be fixed or variable and one-way or reversible. A range of vehicle loading conveyors or elevators, weatherproofed for external use, are also in general use.

The stores layout finally determines which conveyor system is most suitable for a particular application. As in the case of forklift trucks and cranes, safety considerations are of paramount importance, requiring full compliance with applicable regulations and operating instructions.

Types of storage and adequacy

Storage may be classified as covered, i.e. stores buildings, and open, i.e. stockyards.

STORES BUILDINGS

The size and type of stores buildings depend on a number of factors, which include siting, size and nature of the organization's operations, whether they are to be purpose-built or converted, and future plans.

Purpose-built v. converted installation

The purpose-built stores is designed normally to suit operational requirements and financial constraints. There are obvious advantages of using this type of building. An efficient layout can be planned which takes full account of materials to be handled and stored. Space utilization is carefully considered against material handling requirements and constraints. Building structure and floor design can incorporate special features for guide tracks and power and/or control lines to handling equipment. The main initial disadvantages are the relatively heavy expenditure and the time taken from the design stage to becoming operational. In recent years, building costs have increased at rates higher than general inflation.

Another important disadvantage is the difficulty in forecasting building requirements beyond, say, 10 years. Buildings are designed to be operational for periods of at least 25 years (in many cases 40 years or more) and this is reflected in the high installation expenditure. For comparison, it will be noted that mobile equipment operating in a stores environment, such as forklift trucks, will probably have an operational life of under 10 years.

The use of converted buildings reduces costs and time to put into use. Planning effort is concentrated in seeking to make the best use of available space and constraints that are imposed such as site location, headroom and structural features.

Single- v. multi-storey

Single-storey buildings are the more widely used of the two types. They have many advantages over multi-storey. All activities take place at one level, facilitating better logistical flow and control. High-reach trucks can be used to optimum advantage as there are no ceiling constraints. Structural costs are reduced and scope for storage is increased because floor loading problems can be minimized.

The main advantage of the multi-storey buildings is its more economic use of land. This is particularly important in or near cities, where the price of land is high. Construction costs are higher because of the need for deeper foundations and stronger walls required to support ceilings and roofs. Maintenance costs, too, are higher, as working heights are greater for roof repairs and cleaning of window lights and rainwater goods.

STOCKYARDS

It is extremely costly and unnecesssary to put all materials into a covered stores building. Stores buildings can be very expensive and hence they are designed to take only those materials which must be stored internally. There are many heavy, large and, indeed, smaller items that do not deteriorate under weathering conditions which can be stored in the open subject to security considerations.

Materials stored in the open include two categories. The first category does not normally require protection against the weather, e.g. iron castings, structural steelwork and rubber- and plastic-coated cables. Some of these items have a shorter turn-round period than the others. A second and larger category of materials does require protection by wrapping, painting, covering in plastic sheeting or cocooning by spraying of a protective film. The most economic methods should be used appropriate to needs. Cost of application can be high and time-consuming.

Stockyards are generally sited close to main stores buildings for security and administrative purposes. Lighting is required for security and to facilitate authorized operation and access during the hours of darkness. The ground surface could be tarmac, concrete or screed with chippings, depending on the nature of the materials stored and the types and weighting of cranes in use. Appropriate racking, stillages and hard-standings would be provided as required.

Centralization v. decentralization

Centralization v. decentralization of stores may be considered in two situations: (1) the organization operating on one site and (2) the organization operating on two or more sites. Centralization of stores is primarily adopted because of the benefits to be derived from the economies of scale and centralized control.

There are a number of aspects to be considered and these include the following.

Nature of the goods
The location of the centralized store relative to the operating locations of users is of primary importance. Frequent lengthy and time-consuming journeys made by users travelling to stores to collect materials must be avoided or minimized so that their time is used more productively.

Receipts control
The benefit gained by grouping staff at one location is centralized control over all inward goods receipts. This must be considered against lengthier communication lines and double handling of some items.

Issue control
Improved control must be gauged against lengthier lines of communications and adequacy and promptness of response in emergencies.

Transport
The economies of scale include within the calculations the cost of storage, handling, transporting and security. Operating a centralized stores can result in frequent lengthy journeys being made, incurring costs that could outweigh the savings required from centralization.

Security
This aspect is relevant to both storage and transport. Centralizing stores provides greater scope to improve security within the stores and to minimize loss through theft or damage. Balanced against this is the potential additional security risk when valuable and attractive materials are transported on frequent and lengthy journeys.

Stocktaking and inventory control
Control is best achieved when all materials and records are held at one location.

Level of service provided
This is a function of material availability and prompt issue to and receipt by users. Heavy loss can be incurred if production delays result through shortfalls in the delivery service. The distance factor, which relates to both transport and communications, can be of vital importance. The promptness and adequacy of response in an emergency situation may be the deciding factor in the choice between centralized or decentralized stores.

Standardization and variety reduction
Such assignments are tackled more effectively under centralized control, when all materials and records are held at one location.

Vulnerability
The decision to centralize stores and 'put all one's eggs in one basket' sometimes proves to be a poor one. Examples are often quoted where catastrophes have occurred at centralized stores and depots, resulting in heavy loss of stock. A recent case related to all spares required to service a major national operation, which were housed at one location and were destroyed by fire, with disastrous results to the operation. Whatever the degree of stringency applied to safety precautions, accidents do occur. The advantages sought through economy of scale and centralized control can be lost as the result of one catastrophe.

Vulnerability to loss is related to two factors: (1) degree of probability of a loss-making situation arising and (2) the probable degree of loss likely to be incurred. A careful evaluation is required to seek realistic calculations from which a considered decision may be made. The experience of other organizations should be sought. Local fire officers and security officers are available to give advice and recommendations.

Compromise on centralization v. decentralization
Many organizations adopt a flexible approach to the subject of centralization. They operate a system that is largely one of centralization with limited local decentralization, which gives scope for users to obtain materials from sub-stores in emergencies.

This is particularly relevant where walking distances to and from a centralized stores within a large site are great. Non-productive time is thus significantly reduced.

Automated storage

Automated storage is relevant to the storage of materials required for processing or use within an organization and also for finished goods awaiting distribution to customers. While automated storage applies, therefore, to input and output materials, it has had wider applications to finished goods, and we therefore include this subject in Chapter 13.

Security

There are three main areas of concern, which are physical, administrative and personnel.

Need for secure stores

Efforts made by inventory control and physical storekeeping staff to provide an efficient, economical and effective service to users is nullified unless such efforts are supported by adequate security. Without such security, items may not be available for issue against demand. Secondly, cost of replacement and rectification could be high. Let us consider the main aims of security of stores, which are:

1. Avoidance of loss, particularly through theft
2. Avoidance of damage
3. Avoidance of deterioration

The main points to be considered in ensuring an adequate secure stores are now discussed.

Location

Where a stores building is located in a high-risk security area, special precautions have to be taken. Close liaison is required with local police, fire and security specialists.

Building construction and access

Generally, most break-ins into stores are made via doors or windows. Thieves generally do their work in the minimum of time with minimum noise. Doors and windows with their locks and fittings must therefore be strong and secure to deter or delay entry.

Incoming goods procedures
This is a key area where strict control procedures are required, particularly when collusion between stores staff and transport drivers is suspected. This can be a particular area for concern.

INTERNAL STORES SECURITY
This aspect covers both physical procedures and systems/ documentation. Access to stores must be strictly controlled. Very high-value attractive items should be stored within secure internal compounds, cabinets or safes, depending on their nature. The number of key-holders must be strictly limited.

Storage conditions
Different types of items require different storage conditions. For example, instruments should be stored in dry conditions to avoid ingress of moisture. This may be achieved by the use of sachets of silica gel crystals. Timber needs to be stored and supported in such a way to allow the free flow of air to prevent warping and cracking. Temperature control may be required.

Security checks
Administrative security is an important element within total security. This includes random checking of stocks. Frequent but random spot-checking also assists in minimizing discrepancies and giving earlier warnings to facilitate investigation. Weaknesses in systems are then identified and security procedures strengthened.

Security of attractive items
The incidence of theft will be highest for high-value items and lower-value items in general domestic use. Copper valves, fittings and pipes may be of a type not readily usable in the home, but could command good prices in the market. Items such as gloves, light bulbs, torch batteries and the wide range of bolts, screws, nuts and washers have universal use. These are attractive items. Where items are issued from stores on a one-for-one

basis (i.e. a new item supplied against the return of a faulty or worn one), it may be necessary to destroy or effectively dispose of the returned item. Failure to do this could result in the old item being again handed in to stores in exchange for a new one, with the cycle being repeated. Where a usage rate is, exceptionally high, special measures may be required, as there could be collusion between stores and user staff.

A good way to deal with low-value but attractive items is to identify them, record details of usage and take preventive measures to avoid theft. Theft can be prevented in a number of ways, e.g. increasing security or reducing the attractiveness of an item. The standard bayonet-type electric light bulb is an attractive item, being used in the home. It could be economical to discontinue it's use and replace with a costlier non-standard bulb and new socket. Theft of light bulbs would then be significantly reduced or eliminated completely.

Special security methods
Advice should be sought from security specialists such as fire officers, insurance investigators and local police crime officers. They advise on structural and other necessary changes required in stores, particularly to doors and windows. They advise also on the type of alarms to install and their siting, fire-fighting equipment, lighting, closed-circuit television and patrol requirements.

Managerial responsibilities
Effective security is not achieved unless the stores manager effectively plans, organizes, delegates authority, motivates staff and introduces effective means of controlling and measuring. Regular audits are required to ensure full compliance with security policies and procedures. Good communication with all interfacing departments is essential, as they too must support such policies and procedures. Key points for consideration and implementation are:

- Issue of stores security policies and procedures
- Selection of staff
- Delegation of work
- Training of staff
- Use of appropriate methods and procedures
- Application of effective controls

Health and Safety at Work Act, 1974

Health and safety is of importance to staff in all the functions embraced by materials management. It is particularly so to the stores function as stores is generally the largest employer of staff within materials management, with responsibility for handling, moving and storing a wide range of materials using a variety of mechanical handling equipment. Full compliance with the requirements of the Health and Safety at Work Act and other regulations is essential to prevent accidents occurring that cause injury or loss of life to stores or other personnel. Failure to comply is a criminal offence, with penalties related to the degree of personal responsibility of the persons concerned. The fundamentally new approach of the 1974 Act is that responsibility is directed from corporate bodies, e.g. companies, to named individuals. These include defaulting members of management and staff. Accident prevention is a primary responsibility of all managers and their staffs. The particular relevance to stores is two-fold, as accidents can result in:

- Possible depletion of manpower resources and hence interference with the stores services being provided to users.
- Possible damage to items in stores as a secondary effect.

Causes of accidents
The five most common causes of accidents in stores are:

- Projecting materials, particularly into aisles and walkways, from bins, racks, stacks or moving loads.
- Slippery floors usually resulting from spillage of liquids such as water, oils and greases. These should be cleaned promptly and procedures implemented to minimize recurrence.
- Falling materials usually resulting from inadequate placing of items into bins or racks, unsafe stacking on insecure lifts by forklifts, cranes or other lifting equipment.
- Collision with mechanical handling equipment. This requires extreme vigilance particularly in the narrow confines and congestion within the older stores.
- Falls by persons, e.g. from ladders.

Issues

We have stressed that stores exists to provide a service to users.

This service should be both effective and efficient. Materials should be issued against reasonable and authorized demand. Some stores managers have taken the view that materials held in stock are their property, a right to be jealously guarded. Where this belief still exists, it should be promptly dispelled. The stores manager and his staff are the custodians of materials. Their responsibility is to ensure its ready availability for issue to legitimate users giving appropriate notice.

Authorized signatories

This is a well established procedure for ensuring that responsibility for stocked items is transferred to legitimate users. The practice in many organizations is to produce a list of authorized signatories. Such a list will be updated. Problems arise when particular individuals are not available to sign and procedures must cater for such emergencies. Normally, the issue note would be passed to a senior or another nominated person for signature.

Identification and retrieval of materials

To ensure that materials in stock are available for issue to time requires a number of objectives being met. Firstly, correct identification is essential. Secondly, location should be as recorded. Many users experience lengthy delays while stores staff locate required items. Retrieval is the next consideration. An item might be located quickly. However, it may not be readily retrievable because of the way it has been stored. It could lie at the bottom of a stack of material or special lifting equipment may be required. 'Thinking cubic' is a most important philosophy for stores staff. However, such a philosophy can be taken too far, with resulting disadvantages. The correct balance must be sought between space utilization and quality of service.

A final appropriate point is the manner in which material is protected to prevent damage in stock. A particular example concerns the breakdown of the production line in a major company. Stores received an urgent request to issue a gear wheel. Following a lengthy delay in locating the spare part, an even lengthier delay ensued because it was over-protected. It took several hours to chip off the very hard protective coating applied prior to putting into stock. The right balance must be sought between the degree of protection and retrieval time.

Material must leave stores for use in good condition, which means the manner of its handling must be satisfactory. The right types of handling and transporting equipment are required, which includes, in special cases, supports and securing devices. Handling procedures must be adequate to facilitate the smooth transfer from the stock location to the user, avoiding damage in transit.

Economic issue quantities
Users must obviously bear the primary responsibility for determining issue quantities, except in special cases where units of issue have been designated by stores, e.g. items in boxes of 20. However, the stores manager and his staff can often significantly reduce the incidence of abnormal issue rates. Consider the example where particular sized bolts and nuts are to be used on a major assembly contract on-site over a period of several months. Assume the usage rate is 1000 nuts and bolts a week. Would it be reasonable for the user department to withdraw six month's requirements at one time? If they did, there would be strong probabilities that high losses would occur, with a subsequent request for replacements. Control needs to be exercised in determining what are economic issue rates. This takes into account marshalling and handling costs, paperwork, transport costs, site or sub-store costs and security.

Transport
Stores may provide transport for internal and external distribution of materials to sub-stores, depots or users. External transport considerations are dealt with in Chapter 13. Internal transport arrangements generally follow the form of a milk-round where deliveries are scheduled to the various departments on specified days and times during the week. Appropriate authorized documentation is submitted giving the required notice to enable stores issue staff to marshal requirements and load vehicles.

Surplus, scrap and redundant stock
We discuss the disposal of surplus, scrap and redundant materials in Chapter 14. Responsibility for disposals does not generally lie with stores. However, whichever department has responsibility, stores has a major part to play, as it will be

responsible for holding and safeguarding much of the material awaiting disposal. This material has to be adequately labelled or marked and segregated from usable stock. Where special disposal procedures apply, these must be adhered to, including necessary highlighting of hazardous materials and instructions on their handling.

Relationships with other functions

The purchasing and stores functions provide the essential links between suppliers and users. Stores has a dynamic role to play. It needs constantly to be in close communication with purchasing and users to ensure that it anticipates problems rather than just reacting to them. There are many points for consideration which come within the responsibility of physical storekeeping such as storage conditions, accessibility, shelf life, item deterioration and protection. Where special loads are scheduled for delivery, there might be need to consult with users on craneage, handling and storage requirements. Stores may hold tools and equipment in safe custody on behalf of users.

Stores efficiency

Stores efficiency can be measured in a number of ways in conjunction with inventory control (and purchasing) such as:

- Percentage of issue requisitions honoured
- Level of production delays resulting from non-availability of material

However, the efficiency of physical storekeeping can be measured in isolation from other functions. Let us consider one important aspect.

Inward goods

The smooth handling of inward goods is a key area. Vehicle arrivals need to be planned to avoid excessive delays resulting from queuing. Suppliers must be notified of the times during which stores are open to receive goods. Where queuing is a problem, the time of acceptance of the last daily delivery should be specified. Suppliers must be notified of holiday and other periods of closure to avoid making abortive journeys. Consider the following situation relating to queuing. The manager of a large stores receives numerous complaints from key suppliers. He decides to investigate vehicle unloading delays. Data obtained show that an average of four vehicles an hour arrive at stores. Vehicles are unloaded on average at six per hour. By using the Poisson theorem the following statistics are established.

Let the arrival $= A_r$ and the unloading rate $= U_r$. Then

$$\text{Utilization of the receipts bay} = \frac{A_r}{U_r} = \frac{4}{6} \text{ per hour}$$

$$= 67 \text{ per cent}$$

This means that when a vehicle arrives the probability of having to queue is 67 per cent.

$$\text{Average number in queue} = \frac{A_r}{U_r - A_r} = \frac{4}{6 - 4} = 2$$

$$\text{Average time in queue} = \frac{A_r}{U_r(U_r - A_r)} = \frac{4}{6(6 - 4)} = \frac{4}{12} \text{ h}$$

$$= 20 \text{ min}$$

The loss resulting from queuing is estimated to be £2.50 per minute. Management considers a recommendation that the rate of unloading vehicles could be increased to eight per hour by deploying more storekeepers in the receipts bay. It is estimated that additional cost incurred would be £120 per hour. Would this money be well spent? Applying the Poisson theorem (where now $A_r = 4$ and $U_r = 8$)

$$\text{New average time in queue} = \frac{A_r}{U_r(U_r - A_r)} = \frac{4}{8(8 - 4)}$$

$$= \frac{4}{32} \text{h} = 7\frac{1}{2} \text{ min}$$

The reduction in the average queuing time is thus $(20 - 7\frac{1}{2})$ minutes $= 12\frac{1}{2}$ minutes. Average number of vehicles arriving to unload is four per hour, so the total queuing time saved is $4 \times 12\frac{1}{2} = 50$ minutes. At a cost of £2.50 per minute this gives a saving of $50 \times £2.50 = £125$ per hour. The administrative cost outlay to employ additional staff is £120 per hour. On the basis of staff working a 35-hour week, this additional staff deployment would yield a weekly savings of $£(125 - 120) \times 35 = £175$.

This estimated savings might not warrant employing additional staff. Arrival and unloading rates need to be carefully checked over a realistic time-scale, which caters for seasonal and other influencing factors. The estimated loss incurred through vehicle queuing would also require verification over a similar period. Supplier goodwill is an aspect that cannot be readily measured quantitatively but is nevertheless a very important one. Security is another point to consider. The less time suppliers' vehicles are on an organization's premises, the fewer opportunities there are for drivers to leave their vehicle and commit malpractices.

Conclusions

Materials management cannot be soundly based unless it embraces an effective, efficient stores operation. It has generally been the case in the past not to recruit highly qualified staff to work in stores. However, physical storekeeping assumes increasingly greater importance as efforts are directed towards an integrated professional approach to materials management. Advances gained in inventory management must be matched by advances in contribution and status of physical storekeeping as a more scientific approach is directed to this function. Hence, greater thought is required to recruitment of stores personnel. The function, generally, needs to be better planned within an overall materials management staff training and development career structure.

11

Inventory management

Introduction

Cost of inventories can be one of the largest figures in the balance sheet. The words 'inventory' and 'inventories' used throughout this chapter refer to stockholding, i.e. goods held in stock. Organizations are also concerned with buildings, plant and equipment inventories. These comprise lists by reference codes and descriptions of all buildings, items of plant and equipment of significant value owned by them as fixed assets and included in the balance sheet.

Why do we need to hold materials in stock? The simple answer is that it is generally not possible to operate just-in-time or other forms of stockless buying to eliminate inventories. Goods cannot always be delivered direct from supplier to user. Hence, there is the need to interpose a regulated reservoir of stock between the two. Consider Fig.11.1.

The supply of a very wide range of goods follows this pattern, for a number of reasons. Let us consider the main ones.

Supply and demand

It is impossible to match deliveries with usage rates, because each may fluctuate greatly and at short notice.

Requisition v. order quantities

It is not always possible to order requisitioned quantities because of order quantity constraints imposed by suppliers. Such constraints include economic manufacturing quantities, minimum order quantities and minimum order values.

In the case of economic manufacturing quantities, a buyer could require, say, 100 items but the manufacturer has to set up production to produce an economic minimum batch quantity of, say, 1000. For standard items the buyer might find other buyers who collectively would take up the full production and could act

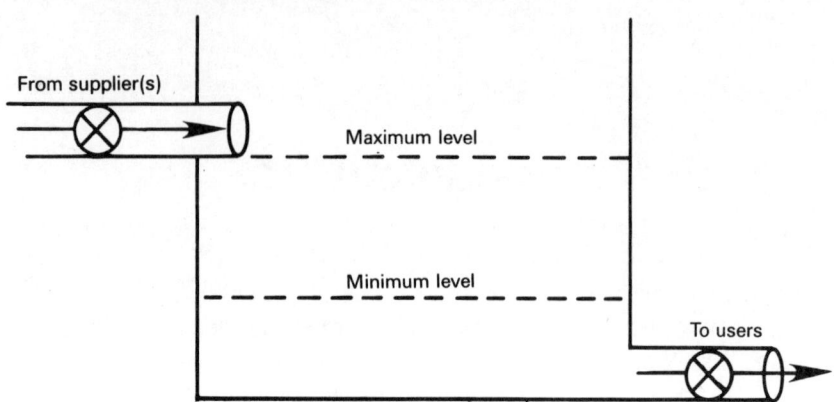

Figure 11.1 Regulated stock reservoir

on their behalf as lead buyer. Minimum order quantities are also included under economic manufacturing quantities but they relate mainly to boxed or packaged quantities. For example, where 20 small, low-value items are required, the supplier might not break down a boxed quantity of 50. The buyer has to take the full quantity or seek supply elsewhere, where similar constraints may also apply. In the case of minimum order value, five items costing £3 each, i.e. a total order cost of £15, could be required but the supplier will not accept such a low-value order. He considers it uneconomic to process an order under, say, £25 and so sets a minimum order value for that amount.

Economic purchasing
This includes economic order quantities (EOQs) and obtaining discounts for higher quantities related to price breaks. It is also sometimes advantageous to advance delivery dates to avoid price increases pending.

Economic internal production
This is dependent on available economic batch quantities of materials for processing which cater for rejects and spoilage. Work on materials in production could be suspended necessitating bringing forward other work in the programme to optimize the use of machines and labour. Alternative standby materials are, therefore, held in stock for use in such situations.

Work in progress
This can be considered in relation to all processes where support material has to be available in case of material delays, modifications, rejection or spoilage.

Over-manufacture
A higher than target yield could be achieved during batch production through a low rejection rate. Hence, the surplus material is put into stock to meet anticipated future demand.

All-time requirement
A supplier gives notice that he is ceasing manufacture of particular materials or components. He might, however, as a special concession, undertake to make one last batch quantity to meet a buyer's forecasted future requirements. Careful assessment would thus be needed to minimize serious under- or over-estimating of probable demand.

Purchaser supply (free-issue) material
It might be more economic to buy and stock certain materials to provide as 'free-issue materials' for subcontracted work. This applies when the purchaser can buy these materials at prices that the supplier cannot match. Hence, it is advantageous to buy quantities and hold in stock for this purpose.

Finished stock
As in the case of matching supply with user demand, it is not always possible to meet customer demand with completed items supplied direct from the production line. Where packaging was required, this might need to be undertaken in the finished-goods warehouse.

Economic transport quantities
The quantity specified sometimes forms a very small portion of an economic transport load. Hence, a larger quantity has to be ordered to make the consignment a viable one.

Strategic buying
A forecast shortage of key material required for production

might necessitate management instructing purchasing to buy a stipulated large quantity. This would be put into stock as an investment to ensure availability over a specified production period, e.g. 3, 6 or 12 months cover as appropriate.

Cost and financial aspects of inventory levels

Inventory levels and values have most important cost and financial implications for an organization. The cost and financial accounts departments are obviously closely concerned but so, too, are users, customers and tax inspectors. Let use consider the various aspects that affect or are affected by stockholding. This is shown diagrammatically in Fig.11.2.

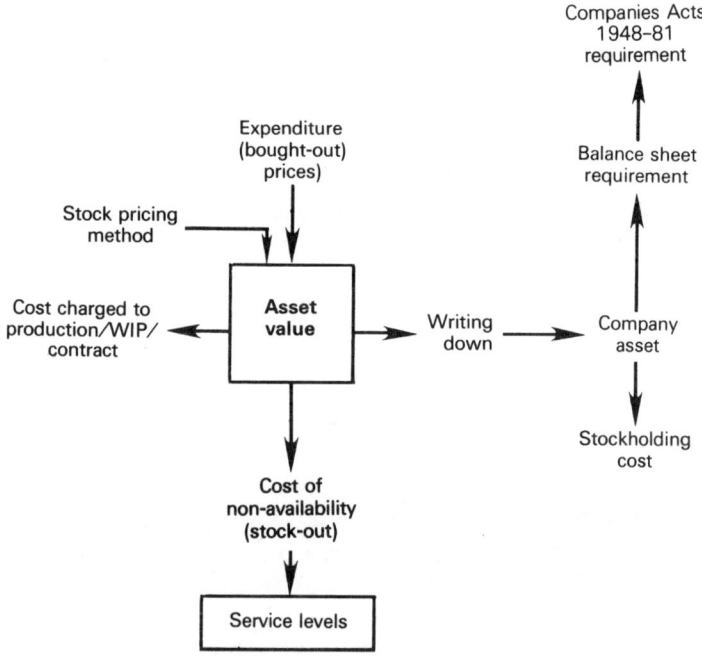

Figure 11.2   Cost and financial implications of inventories·

It will be noted from this figure that there are five separate cost/financial elements, which are:

1. Expenditure
2. Asset value

3. Stockholding cost
4. Non-availability cost
5. Charged-out cost

Expenditure
This is very much within the sphere of responsibility of purchasing, who have the main impact in this area. Expenditure is a function of unit price (related to buying skills, sourcing and timing of supplies and quantities bought). Phasing of payments is also related, as items may be delivered and put into stock but their cost is reflected in the balance sheet as a 'debit' until payment is made.

Asset value
When materials are received, put into stock and paid for, they become a current asset in the balance sheet. Frequently, stock valuation may be the highest single figure on that document. Stock incorrectly valued, being under- or over-stated falsely, deflates or inflates profit.

Materials can deteriorate in stock or become obsolescent. Hence their inventory values would be written down each year in accordance with an agreed policy. This policy would apply too where excessive surpluses of stock existed, e.g. stockholding of a particular material represents five years stock related to anticipated usage. In such circumstances disposal action would be taken to reduce the stock and to write down its value.

Stockholding cost
It normally embraces four elements, which are:

- Loss of investment opportunity. This is the interest that could be earned if the capital tied up in stock was invested. For example, if stock levels were reduced by £50 000 and this sum was then invested at 15 per cent interest for a period of one year, this would yield £7500.
- Stores operating costs. This includes rent, rates, insurance, depreciation, staff salaries and wages.
- Loss, deterioration and damage. Loss includes theft, obsolescence and misplacement.
- General administrative costs. These include general office and related non-direct stores costs.

Cost of non-availability

This varies significantly depending on circumstances existing at the time. When stock-outs occur, users and customers sometimes have alternative options which they can take. While criticality varies, levels of service must be determined below which stock levels must not fall. Service levels are determined in a number of ways:

- Customer service levels, e.g. 98 per cent — this means that 98 out of every 100 demands from external customers must be met.
- Plant operation service levels, e.g. 97 per cent — plant is required to operate 97 per cent of total available hours. Stock control has to support that requirement.
- User service level, e.g. 96 per cent — 96 out of every 100 requisitions submitted by production, engineers and other users must be met.

Service levels v. cost of inventory is not a linear equation but follows the hyperbolic form. This means that as service levels to manufacturing or processing are increased, the cost of supporting stockholding increases at a higher, increasing rate. The long- and short-term requirements of the accountant, user and customer need to be carefully evaluated to achieve the right balance between service and inventory levels. The curve is illustrated in Fig.11.3.

Non-availability of stock can result in a number of serious consequences within an organization such as:

- Cost of production delays. This includes three separate elements. Non-availability of material required for production may result in idle machines and manpower. Resources might have to be utilized less efficiently to meet commitments. In the case of an engineering spare not being available, this too could produce a similar result. Cost of recovery could involve special deliveries or overtime working.
- Delay to the provision of a service. This might be critical as in the case of urgently required medicines for patients (NHS) or spares for a city's public transport, e.g. bus or underground service.
- Loss of investment opportunity. In the case of material

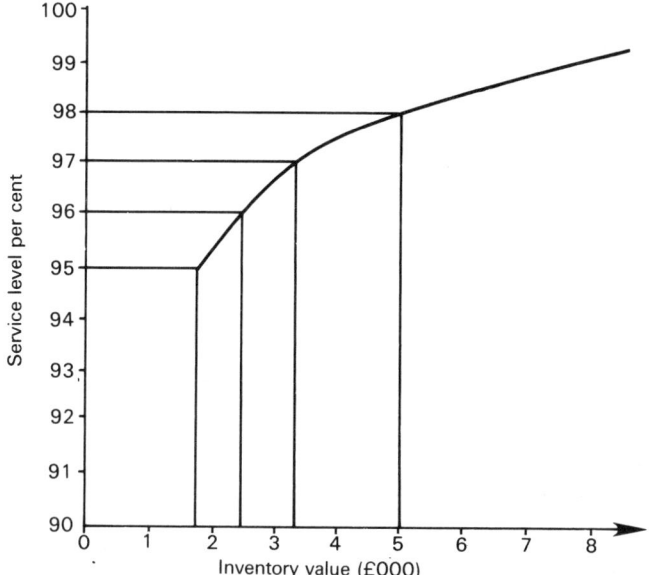

Figure 11.3 Service v. inventory levels

required for the installation of new plant and equipment its non-availability could delay commissioning. Earnings on capital employed is then deferred (i.e. loss of investment opportunities).

• Loss of customer satisfaction. In this case delay in supplying goods to a customer or delaying completion of his capital project would be to his dissatisfaction. This could adversely affect relations and, in the extreme situation, result in loss of future business.

Charged-out cost
The charges made to users for items they withdraw from stock varies with the prices paid by purchasing and the stock pricing methods used. Work being processed for a customer's order may thus show differing unit material costs for different batches. The influence of stock pricing policies on the charged-out costs of materials is considered in the subsection below.

Methods of pricing stock
It is purchasing's responsibility to buy materials, components,

tools and other items to put into stock. Unit prices first have to be determined. Do they include or exclude such elements of cost as cash discounts (payment settlement terms), carriage inwards, packing charges and insurance? There are a number of different stock pricing methods in use. Each has advantages and disadvantages. Some are more appropriate to a particular organization's operating needs than others.

Cost price
This is the actual purchase or bought-in price. It is the only one of the five methods that does not need stock adjustment accounting. Different consignments of the item may be held in stock at different prices. Items could be priced on the basis of FIFO = first in, first out or LIFO = last in, first out.

The main disadvantage to the use of cost price is the difficulty in comparing job costs. One job will be charged disadvantageously, at a higher material cost than another. Secondly, many calculations are required where market prices change rapidly. In times of falling prices, stocks would be overvalued.

Average price
This system has much to commend it. Each item bears an equitable share of total cost. Fresh calculations must, however, be made after each receipt into stock.

Standard price
Because of problems encountered in the use of the cost price and average price methods, standard or factory value pricing was introduced. All items are charged into stock at standard prices. This simplifies stock recording. Subsequently, items are charged out to production, contracts, work in progress and budgets at standard prices. This avoids unfair weighting to some cost centres or products. This method cannot operate successfully without realistic forecasting of the standard prices over the budget period. This would normally be one year.

Market price
This is sometimes known as replacement price (the current market price), i.e. the price to be paid to replace an item issued from stock.

Selling price
This is a distribution oriented method of pricing. It is aimed at assessing the performance of sales depots or finished stock warehouses.

Setting stock levels
Stock control should be a dynamic function, with the stock controller reacting to all signals both internal and external, that suggest revision of stock replenishment procedures relating to (1) quantities to procure or (2) timing of purchases or internal manufacture. He should anticipate probable changes in material usage and replenishment rates. The process of looking at stock items in this way is called reviewing. There are two types of review, reorder level and cyclical.

Reorder level
This approach aims to control stocks between agreed upper maximum and lower minimum levels. To cater for fluctuations in usage and replenishment rates, the minimum figure is set above zero to provide a buffer or insurance stock. The time to reorder is when there is just sufficient stock of an item to satisfy the forecast maximum demand during the replenishment period or lead time. This pattern is shown in Fig.11.4.

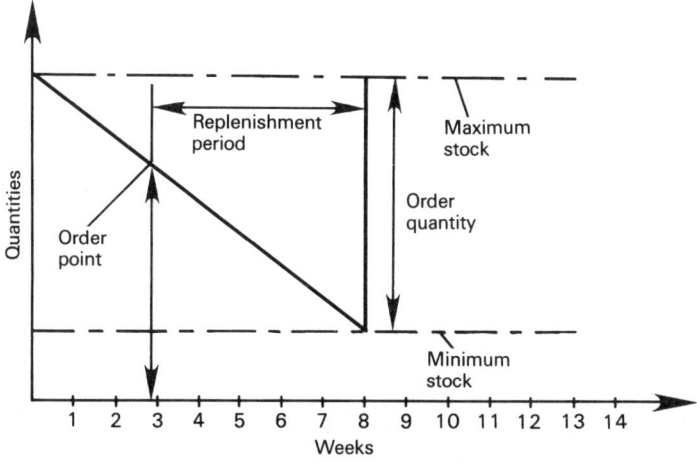

Figure 11.4   Stock reorder cycle

The figure illustrates the situation in simple terms. Stock-out could, however, arise if the usage rate or replenishment period exceeded the maximum values forecast. Conversely, excessive stockholding results if demand is reduced and deliveries are made earlier than forecast. There are permutations to usage and delivery rates, some resulting in a balancing out, which do not result in stock-outs or excessive stocks, e.g. a high usage rate compensated by a shorter lead time. The pattern of excessive stock and stock-outs is shown in Fig.11.5.

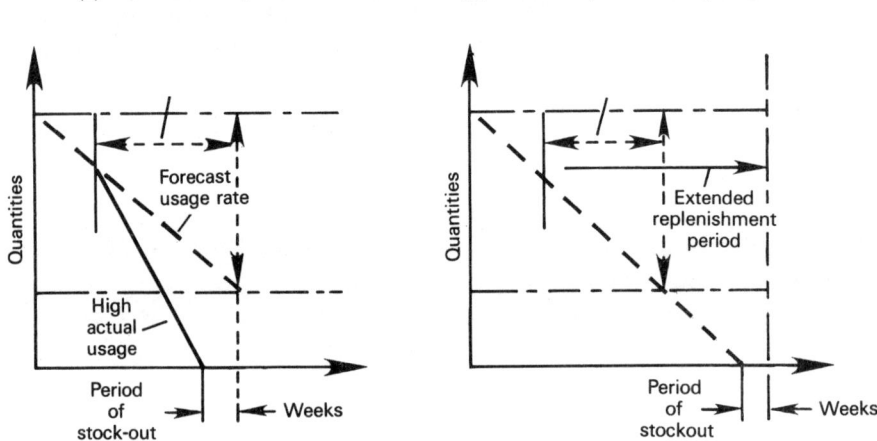

Figure 11.5 Effect of variations in usage and replenishment rates

The stock controller determines order level and order quantities on the best possible forecast of demand and replenishment rates. The fundamental problem is one of accurately forecasting the subsequent cycle. The order quantity determined for delivery on completion of the first cycle has to cater for actual usage and replenishment rates in the subsequent cycle. Failure to set the right order quantity could result in stock-out or excessive build-up of stock during this second cycle (see Fig.11.6).

Cyclical review
In this approach, the whole range of items is reviewed systematically on periodic cycles. An ABC classification approach is desirable. The range of stocks can be classified by usage value

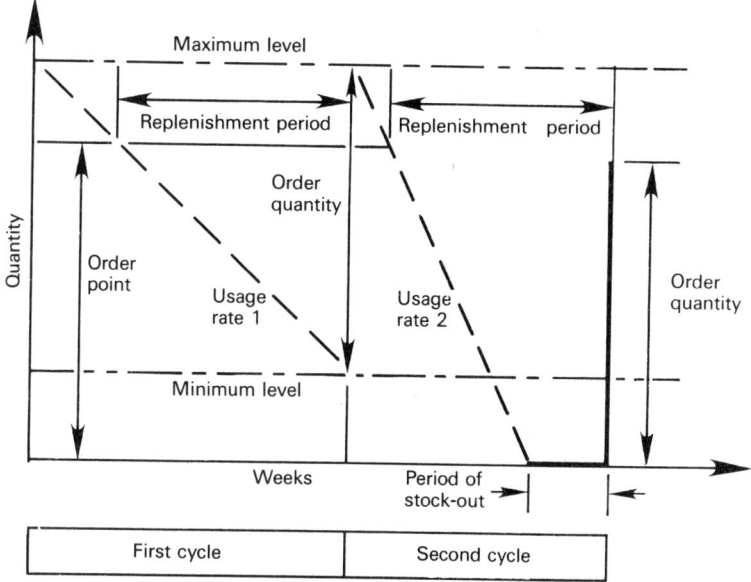

Figure 11.6   Forecasting for the second cycle

in accordance with the following well known rule, which states that:

> In any given group a small number of items will account for the largest proportion of the usage value.

To undertake this exercise it is necessary to determine the usage values of all stocks in descending order of value, i.e. unit values × annual usage. ABC analysis could then be made. A pattern might emerge, for example, where stockholding could be divided into three groups of items:

- 'A' items: 10 per cent of the range accounting for 60 to 70 per cent usage value.
- 'B' items: next 20 per cent of the range accounting for a further 20 per cent of usage value.
- 'C' items: remaining 70 per cent of the range accounting for 10 to 20 per cent of usage value.

Review periods could be applied accordingly. For example, 'A' items reviewed weekly, 'B' items reviewed monthly and 'C' items three-monthly. This is shown in Fig.11.7.

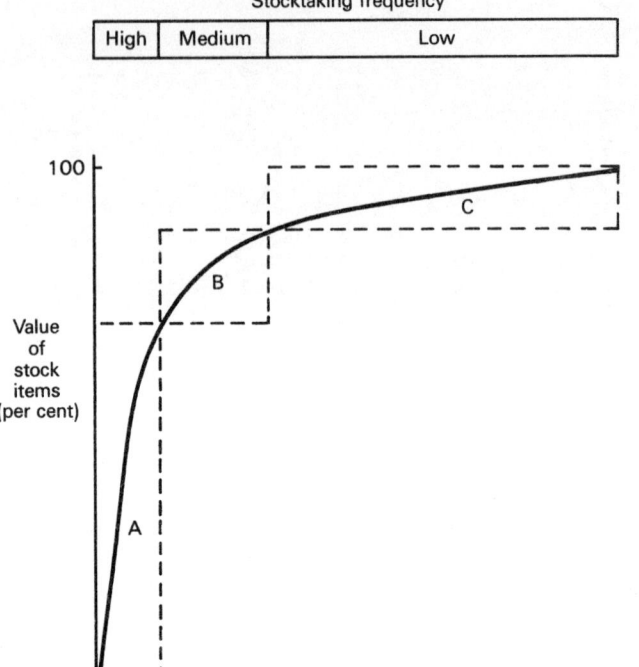

Figure 11.7   Stock review periods related to ABC analysis

The curve of the line will vary significantly between organizations, depending on the differentials in cost and usage rates between items.

ECONOMIC ORDER QUANTITIES
The economic order quantity (EOQ) principle is applicable to low-value/high-usage items. The approach seeks to minimize the total costs of two elements, i.e. stockholding and order-placing costs. The interaction of the two is shown in Fig.11.8.

Order-placing cost = Cost of placing order × Number of orders placed (for annual require-ment)

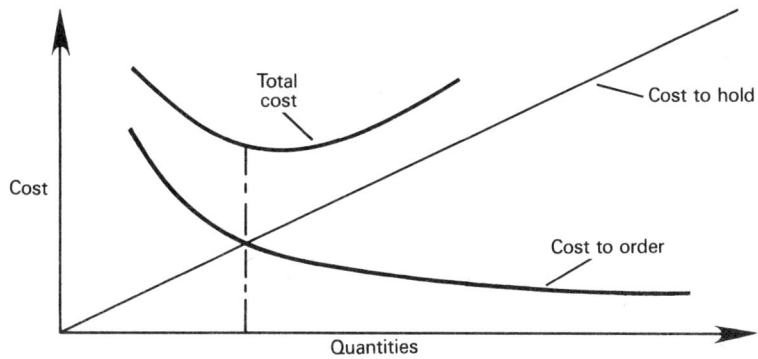

Figure 11.8 Stockholding v. order-placing costs

Stockholding cost =   Unit price of item × Average
quantity in stock × Cost of holding
stock (as percentage of average
stock value)

From these two equations is derived the EOQ formula, which is
as follows:

$$EOQ = \sqrt{\frac{200AP}{IU}}$$

where P = cost of placing an order, U = unit price of the item, A
= annual usage and I = cost of storage expressed as a percentage
of the value of the average stock.

Consider the following example. A company uses 1000
'Widgets' each year at a cost of £4 each. The cost of placing an
order is £24 and the cost of holding stock is 30 per cent.
Then:

$$EOQ = \sqrt{\frac{200 \times 1000 \times 24}{30 \times 4}} = \sqrt{\frac{200 \times 1000 \times 24}{30 \times 4}}$$

$$= \sqrt{40\,000} = 200$$

Constraints to use of EOQs

The concept of the EOQ is a good one, but there are a number of constraints limiting its use. Usage and replenishment rates must not fluctuate too greatly. Aspects dealt with previously in this chapter also restrict its application. These include economic manufacturing and minimum order quantities, minimum order values and economic transport loads. Other points include shelf life.

The EOQ equation is dependent on an accurate evaluation of the order-placing cost. Some organizations quote standard figures. However, costs incurred can vary significantly from one order to another. On some orders administrative work is minimal. This applies when competitive quotations have recently been obtained and a repeat order is to be placed with the previous supplier. In other situations, sourcing, negotiation and supplier selection precedures may be lengthy, incurring very much greater cost. Evaluating order-placing costs realistically could be a difficult and an uneconomic task.

Stockholding cost, the other element of the EOQ equation, is also often simply stated but difficult to evaluate. For example, a figure of 30 per cent may be quoted. This includes all elements such as loss of investment opportunity, rents, rates, etc. The figure quoted for loss of investment opportunity, e.g. 15 per cent, could vary significantly from one year to the next. It could also vary greatly during one year.

Inflation is another factor that must not be overlooked when setting a percentage for cost of stockholding. For example, by EOQ calculation four orders are placed for a particular item at regular intervals through the year. The item price increases 12 per cent over the year, which means that the average increase over the year is 6 per cent. This factor should be taken into consideration in determining the loss of investment opportunity element of the stockholding percentage. In this case it would be, more realistically, $15 - 6 = 9$ per cent.

Annual contract for call-off

It will be appreciated that a frequently used alternative to the EOQ approach is the placing of one order for the required annual quantity of an item for call-off as required. The advantages are that one set of purchase order documentation is raised and stock levels are greatly reduced. However, a number of batch quantities would be received and handled together with related invoices requiring processing and a number of payments being made. Instead of one delivery date there would be more with possible increased progress action being required. Also using this approach generally results in the buyer being committed to a fixed price for the contract period, e.g. one year, which may not be favourable as advantage cannot be taken to seek competitive quotations.

STOCKTAKING
However efficiently stock is controlled, discrepancies will occur between actual and recorded levels. These must be investigated to determine how they have arisen so that corrective action can be taken to prevent recurrence. Stock must be valued correctly. Recorded quantities must be correct, shortfalls being identified promptly and stock replenished to support operational requirements. There are two approaches to stocktaking.

Periodic stocktaking
Stocktaking establishes stock valuation for the balance sheet. It is undertaken at prescribed intervals during the year (possibly quarterly) or at the financial year end. Production may then cease, with no receipts and issues being made. A large number of clerical or audit staff might be required to work during a highly concentrated period. Usually stores close for normal business (often but not always over a non-working weekend). Overtime working rates would add to stocktaking expenses.

Continuous stocktaking
Continuous stocktaking enables groups of items to be checked regularly during the year. This means that within a 12 months' period all items can be counted and checked. It would not be necessary to suspend normal stores business during this check, so there would be no interference with the operations of the enterprise.

The ABC analysis application is suited to continuous stocktaking. As the Companies Acts, 1948–81, requires an accurate stock evaluation, the higher-value 'A' items should be checked near to the financial year end date to reduce the degree of error that may accrue due to discrepancies between actual and recorded stock quantitites. To meet the needs of legislation and management, stocktaking must be carefully planned and efficiently executed. A high degree of care and attention to detail is demanded. Control of the operation is normally assigned to a senior member of the materials management or supplies management team. An important objective is to prevent malpractice or fraud. An outline plan of stores with rack, bin or compound locations provides the basis from which stock areas can be allocated to pairs of checkers. There may be a requirement for moving or lifting equipment with additional lighting also being necessary. The accident prevention provisions of the Health and Safety at Work Act, 1974, must be not be overlooked.

It will be important to distinguish items held on stock, i.e. on inventory value, from capital plant and equipment held in safe custody and already charged out on receipt direct to capital expenditure schemes. Also lying in stores there may be written-off materials awaiting disposal action and materials that are the property of user departments or on loan from other organizations. Purchaser supply material already charged out ready for dispatch on a subcontract to a supplier should also be noted.

Forecasting

Good forecasting is the firm foundation on which a successful stock control system can operate. Both usage and replenishment rates with their probable fluctuations need to be forecast. That forecast must be monitored and corrective adjustments made promptly as adverse trends develop. Calculating how much to order and the timing of release of orders can then follow.

Forecasted usage rates may relate to previous demand patterns closely or to a limited degree only. However, future rates could be independent of previous usage patterns. Indeed, in the case of the launching of a new product or the installation of new capital plant and equipment, there will have been no previous usage of materials or spares. In looking at probable future demand patterns, it will be noted whether or not items are recurring or non-recurring. For example, usage rates of particular engineering spares during the first year's operation may be significantly different from the manufacturer's forecast and may be very different from usage in the subsequent year.

Past usage rates often fluctuate period by period but without developing an upward or a downward trend, the moving average remaining fairly constant. Trends could, however, show increases or decreases following a straight-line moving average. Where the increase or decrease was not constant but was being applied at, say, 5, 10 or 20 per cent each period, this would be a proportional trend of hyperbolic form. Usage rates may follow a seasonal pattern with much higher demand occurring at particular times of the year. Good examples of this pattern are summer and winter clothing, where demand may fluctuate violently. This will be true, too, for some non-standard engineering spares which cannot be lifed. A part issued from stores and fitted to capital plant could give satisfactory service for several months or fail during its first day of operation.

Taking manufacturing industry product life cycles as an example, usage rates for materials and components required will vary during the cycle. Consider Fig.11.9.

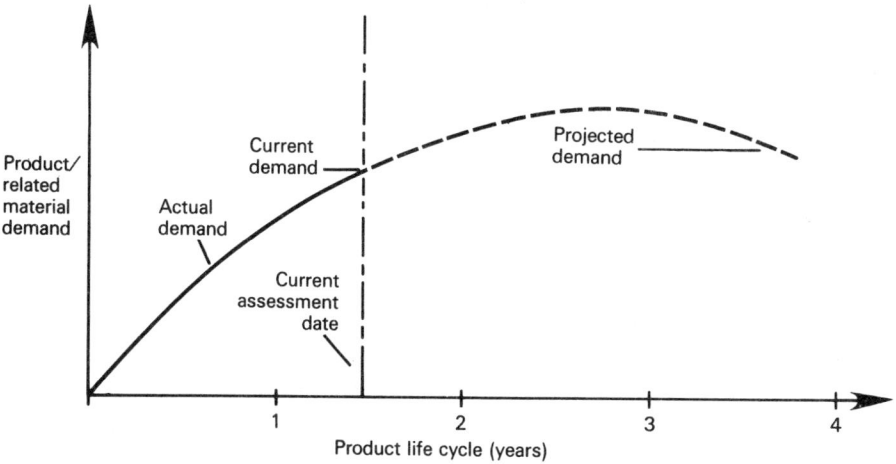

Figure 11.9 Material usage relationship with product life cycle

In this example it will be noted that the usage trend curve varies throughout the product life cycle. While the normal demand curve follows this distribution, the total cycle time may extend or contract from that predicted. Actual demand could also fluctuate greatly above and below the normal demand trend curve for a number of reasons, including climatic changes or customer fickleness. The effect of competition from other products could also influence demand.

Where forecasting is related to previous usage/demand, stock controllers have the choice of three methods to use:

1. Moving average
2. Weighted moving average
3. Exponential smoothing

Consider the usage pattern of an item over the past 12 months as shown below and in Fig.11.10.

Period	Forecast	Actual
1	18	20
2	20	25
3	26	30
4	28	25
5	26	28
6	28	30
7	33	35
8	36	40
9	42	40
10	40	45
11	42	45
12	45	50

Moving average
Consider the moving average over the last six periods. This would be

$$\text{Moving average} = \frac{35 + 40 + 40 + 45 + 45 + 50}{6} = 42.5$$

It will be noted that this is a low figure, having been exceeded by each of the last three period figures. Hence, it is not a good forecast figure for period 13.

Weighted moving average
If more weight is given to the more recent usage figures taken over the last six periods, the forecast will be more realistic. Maximum weight would be given to the last period (period 12)

with decreasing weight over the previous five periods. The weighting scale can be varied. In the following example, the weighting runs from 6 to 1 as shown:

12	50 × 6 = 300
11	45 × 5 = 225
10	45 × 4 = 180
9	40 × 3 = 120
8	40 × 2 = 80
7	35 × 1 = 35
	21 940

Therefore

$$\text{Weighted moving average} = \frac{940}{21} = 44.8$$

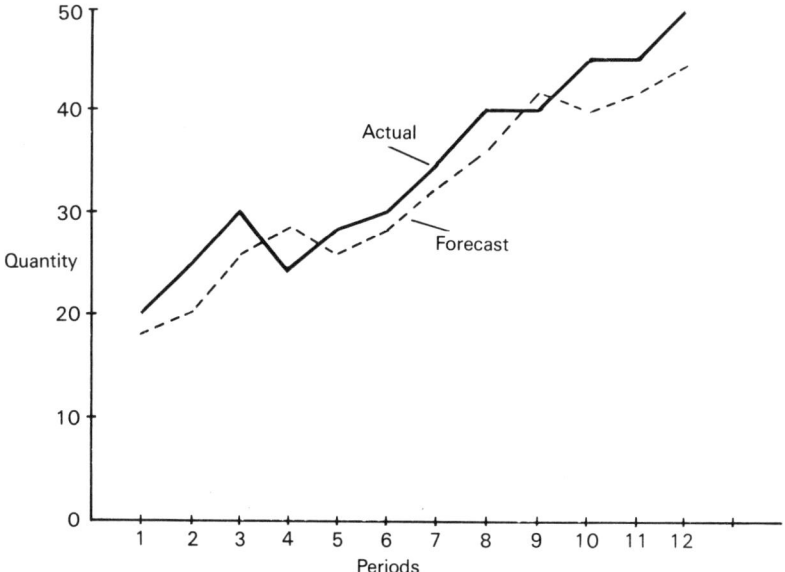

Figure 11.10   Actual v. forecast usage rates

This is a more realistic figure, but is still marginally below the usage rates of periods 10 and 11 and significantly below period 12 usage. It would not, therefore, be a good basis from which to forecast usage in period 13, without modification.

Exponential smoothing

This is a particular kind of weighted moving average which considers actual v. forecast usage for each period. More weight is given to the more recent figures than the older ones. For example, looking at the above weighted moving average figure of 44.8 at period 12, how may we best forecast for period 13? It would be noted that, in period 11, a probable usage of 42 was forecast for period 12. This is an under-estimate of 3, the actual usage being 45. There is need to seek to differentiate between a real trend and a random fluctuation. This can be tackled by settling on a compromise between forecast and actual figures.

The basic equation of exponential smoothing is based on the form:

$$\text{New forecast} = \alpha \times \text{Latest actual figure} + (1 - \alpha) \times \text{Old forecast}$$

where α (the Greek letter alpha) is the smoothing constant. It represents a value between 0 and 1 (with figures of 0.1 to 0.3 normally being used). We will use $\alpha = 0.3$ in the equation. Thus

$$\text{Forecast for period } 13 = 0.3 \times 50 + (1 - 0.3) \times 45$$
$$= 15 + 31.5 = 46.5$$

which looks to be a more realistic forecast than obtained using the other methods.

Forecasts are rarely 100 per cent accurate and are generally likely to be under- or over-estimated most of the time, the degree of error varying from low to high. This could apply equally to usage and replenishment rates. Successful forecasting also requires recorded v. actual stock figures to be reconciled.

Replenishment rates

Two situations need consideration; firstly, the forecasted rates for the current cycle of ordering. The supplier of a particular item might quote a delivery period of, say, 10 weeks. How successful in maintaining promises has he been in the past? The extent to which he has exceeded quoted deliveries can be readily established. Hence, a quoted figure of 10 weeks could be more realistically assessed. Order points and order quantities might require being related to, say, 11 or 12 weeks if these times are more likely to be achieved. The order processing period will be included as part of the total replenishment period. The time from release of requisitioning instructions from stock control to receipt of materials into stores may thus be:

- Assessed/standard order processing period
- Quoted/confirmed manufacturer's lead time
- Extended delivery adjustment factor (where applicable)

Intelligent use of supply market signals also assists stock control. For example, consider the purchase of differing shapes and sizes of steel castings, where the current delivery periods for the range vary from 12 to 30 weeks depending on size and complexity. Extended delivery of one or two items could indicate probable corresponding movements across the whole or part of the range and, hence, such probabilities require investigation.

Good inventory control is dependent on purchasing's advice on probable significant changes in delivery periods. Will currently quoted delivery periods change during the coming months and by how much? To provide this information, purchasing must keep in touch with major suppliers. A particular material may be in short supply, resulting from reduced output. Alternatively, output might be constant or increase, but customer demand could increase at a higher rate, leading to scarcity. Purchasing must look for indications of reduced output or increased demand for key materials. In the case of common usage materials, e.g. copper v. aluminium, increased demand for one could quickly stimulate increased demand for the other. Close liaison with stock control will ensure that corrective action is taken to increase quantity requirements or to advance deliveries.

Standardization and variety reduction

Standardization and variety reduction assist towards more efficient stock control. They reduce stockholding and facilitate more economic buying through aggregation of quantities. Consider the following situation, where there are two companies 'A' and 'B', associated members of a group. They manufacture between them four products. each product comprises a number of parts. For this example we focus attention on five constituent parts 'a', 'b', 'c', 'd' and 'e', used across the range of products as shown in Fig.11.11.

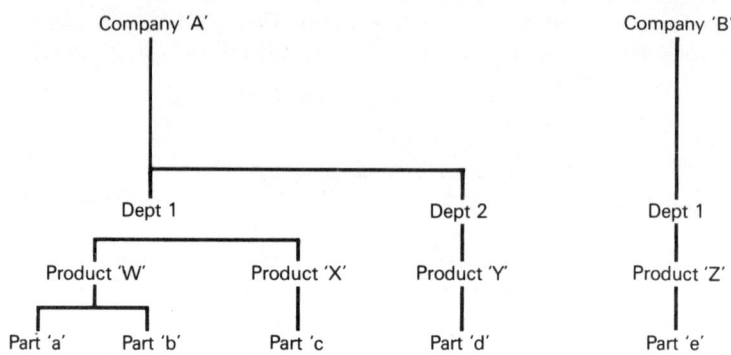

Figure 11.11

Each department in each company has specified its own requirements, and all five similar parts are held in stock. It is first necessary to determine if a standard specification could be produced which meets the needs of each department for these five parts. If this can be achieved, all parts could be designated, say, part 'a'. Only one part has then to be bought and stocked, with savings benefits to purchasing and inventory control. In emergencies, a part could be transferred from one company to the other. If this degree of standardization cannot be achieved, the requirements of the four products might be met by reducing to, say, two or three parts.

What is achievable for products applies equally to engineering spares. There are many similar possibilities in manufacturing and non-manufacturing organizations where general and consumable items could be investigated for commonality as above. A balanced approach is essential, otherwise the operation would be loss-making. Standardization can be taken too far, seriously restricting purchasing's scope to source. For example, a decision is taken to standardize on one type of electric motor in three sizes to be supplied by one selected manufacturer. This reduces spares holdings and gains significant discounts by buying larger quantities of the reduced range. However, the supplier could later consider that he has a captive market and increase prices excessively. He could experience manufacturing problems which affect quality or delivery. Ultimately, he may go into liquidation and leave the market. All these situations would have serious consequences for the standardization programme.

Another important aspect for serious consideration is timing. Setting a standard too early might result in missed opportunities later, including reduced scope to take advantage of technological developments.

A good example of variety reduction is oils and lubricants. A survey carried out in a major company disclosed the use of a very large number of different grades. Manufacturers of plant and equipment had specified that their own oils or greases must be used or material guarantees would be nullified. However, once guarantee periods expired, no such constraint could apply. Specialists undertaking the survey reduced the range by approximately 60 per cent, yielding enormous savings to purchasing and inventory control.

Variety reduction yields buying benefits, e.g. discounts for larger quantities, but such benefits can be lost through uneconomic usage. For example, a particular brand of paint is bought for maintenance in three sizes (1, 2 and 5 litre tins). The price of the 5 litre tin is extremely attractive, as it costs only three times the price of the 1 litre size. It is therefore decided to stock this one size of tin. However, tradesmen regularly requisition from stores the 5 litre tins, frequently using as little as 2 litres for immediate requirements. The tins are put on one side and when reopened some weeks or months later the contents have solidified and are unusable. Obviously, this is not an economic approach to variety reduction.

Computer application to stock control

Most organizations operate some form of computerized stock control but may be considering further development.

Benefits sought from computer application are generally three-fold. Firstly, to assist towards the reduction in inventory levels. Secondly, to provide a more efficient service to users. Thirdly, to reduce administrative costs. These benefits are derived from computer technology, which provides:

- Speedier storage and retrieval of data
- Ability to handle urgent complex forecasting

- Speedier arithmetical calculations relating to inventory levels
- Prompt updating facility for all users
- Quicker and better decision making from a wider range of options

Computers reduce the volume of documentation and tedious clerical work, freeing staff for more productive and creative work.

AREAS OF APPLICATION
There are a number of areas of application, important ones being as follows:

- Forecasting
- Stock status reports
- Stock replenishment signalling
- Obsolescence and slow-moving stock identification
- Standardization and variety reduction investigation
- Reorder point and quantity calculations
- ABC classification

Important aspects for consideration are now discussed.

Suitability of proposed system
The foremost consideration is that it is designed to meet the needs of all users. Another possible requirement is a viable and economic capability for future development. One major temptation to be resisted is being over-ambitious, i.e. avoid 'using a sledge-hammer to crack a nut'. This has much relevance to computer application.

Selling of proposals to staff
It is vital to win the support of all staff involved in the new proposals, as there will be some natural reluctance to change. Legitimate concern of staff must be anticipated and handled sensibly, with prejudice and inertia being overcome.

Smooth transfer of application
This applies to a change from manual to computer application or further computer development. A realistic time-scale must be

set with a clear cut-off point. The viewpoints of all involved should be considered. Temptation to retain major elements of the superseded system as a back-up must be resisted. Failure to do this will result in a costly and inefficient hybrid system being operated. Visual display unit (VDU) monitors need to be located to achieve optimum results. Security of the system includes input and output control authority, confidentiality and avoidance of loss of data. There may be need for systems compatibility to embrace customers and key suppliers. The services of a fully trained and competent systems specialist could be required with particular specialism in materials management.

Stockless buying

Stockless buying methods have been used for many years and include (1) the supplier holding the stock and releasing against call-off and (2) imprest stock, where supplies are delivered to the purchaser and stocked on his premises but payment is only made against withdrawals from stock. Inventory values are reduced in both cases. In the first case storage space is also freed, but there is dependence on transport in an emergency situation.

Buyers should be mindful that savings achieved using stockless buying can be offset by the paying of higher prices than might otherwise have been achieved. For the buyer to achieve savings sought from stockless buying, the supplier has to stock additional materials or accept deferment of payment, both at some cost to him. In recent years a more dynamic approach has been taken on the subject of stockless buying, called just-in-time buying.

'Just-in-time' (JIT) buying

The need to exercise strict control over inventory levels is a fundamental requirement of materials management. Increasing efforts have been directed to greater planning and control of stocks. A dynamic approach introduced in recent years that demands total commitment from management and staff is just-in-time buying. This is a zero stock policy that is very much a philosophy in its country of origin, Japan. It has been suggested that the stimulus for conceiving and developing JIT buying grew from the acute shortage of space in Japan. It is highly probable, however, that Japanese businessmen took a more radical view of inventory levels than their Western competitors. They were prepared to apply a high degree of risk management and operate without the security of buffer stocks. Too often, many organizations in the West have pursued the reverse policy, that of JIC (just-in-case) buying and built up stocks excessively to reduce high-cost stock-outs. JIT buying may not always prove to be the panacea its promoters believe. Materials management is concerned with minimizing the true total cost at the point of use. Eliminating stockholdings (a major element of cost) must therefore be an attractive objective. However, reduction in inventory costs must not be offset by incurring greater cost elsewhere through implementing JIT.

Claims resulting from the successful implementation of JIT are many. Because of the strict, planned, logical and integrated approach involving all functions and suppliers, savings claimed are not restricted to inventories and stores space. Figures quoted at a JIT conference held in 1987 are as follows:

- 25–60 per cent reduction in cost of quality
- 35–75 per cent reduction in raw material inventory
- 40 per cent improvement in total output
- 40–80 per cent reduction in total space requirements
- up to 25 per cent reduction in direct and indirect labour costs
- 90 per cent reduction in processing lead times
- up to 100 per cent reduction in finished-goods inventories

FOUNDATION FOR JIT
The introduction and application of JIT must be based on sound foundations. A number of conditions thus need to be met. Let us consider these.

Forecasting and planning
Maximum time and attention must be directed to good forecasting and planning. JIT margins are, of necessity, extremely tight ones and hence results achieved will depend on the quality of this input.

Zero defects

Material or component batches must conform totally to specification. This requires that stringent quality assurance appraisals are undertaken prior to placing contracts. Subsequently, effective monitoring of supplier capacity and performance is required.

Compliance with specification and quality requirements is essential. JIT cannot succeed unless it is based on achieved zero defects. There has been much development of quality circles in Japan where full worker participation has been encouraged. There is an awareness that everyone has a responsibility for quality. Companies in the West must encourage a similar approach.

Meeting delivery dates

Specified material or component batch quantities must be delivered by due dates. This places a special responsibility on the supplier, who may need to hold buffer stocks to cater for shortfalls in his production. It may also be necessary for him to operate flexible working, e.g. overtime, weekend or extended shift working, to meet the daily or weekly commitment. Strict control must be exercised over transport to ensure that completed items are not delayed in transit.

It has been estimated that there are approximately a quarter of a million manufacturing corporations in Japan, two-thirds of which employ fewer than 30 people. Work flow is thus capable of being regulated to closely held limits related to small capacities. Since the advent of the 'second industrial revolution' in the West, there has been a significant increase in the development of small businesses. This trend, if continued, can materially assist the application of JIT in the future.

Batch quantities

Small batch quantities must be manufactured at economic cost. This can be achieved by (1) the utilization of smaller, more flexible machines and (2) significant reduction in operation set-up times by the use of specialized adaptable equipment and specialized labour (incurring higher cost). These are two areas of specialism where the Japanese have been particularly successful. UK buyers must ensure that their suppliers of key components and materials are similarly equipped to produce small batch quantities economically.

Plant and equipment must be subject to a high standard of planned maintenance to minimize breakdowns.

Administrative requirements

Delay problems will still occur even when the foregoing requirements are met. Production delays result if items are not adequately identifiable or related material assurance or performance certification is not provided. Consigning details must also be clear and adequate to ensure that deliveries are made to the right destinations. The implementation of a zero defects policy applies equally to documentation and identification as it does to material. Documentation requires effective monitoring and auditing.

Schedule flexibility

JIT does not operate successfully where individual usage rates fluctuate greatly. A reasonably uniform flow is required. Schedules must be planned, giving agreed degrees of notice of forecasted changes in demand. Such notice will be dependent on the nature and quantities of requirements.

JIT selectivity

Assembly, particularly flow line, may generally be better suited to JIT application than manufacturing. As we discussed above under 'Batch quantities', a number of small suppliers using batch production would be required to provide the JIT support. An analysis of requirements would also be required to determine which items are best suited for JIT application. The demand pattern, value, volume, criticality and supplier capability and reliability are key points for consideration.

The supply chain

The performance of key suppliers is very much related to the performance of their suppliers. Full attention must be directed to ensure that key sub-suppliers are embraced within the total integrated JIT effort.

Scheduled deliveries

Frequently, there is not one terminal delivery date but a series of scheduled dates. Such schedules could be flexible, the supplier being notified of minimum and maximum quantities required each week, month or period. The expediter could give advanced warning of significant changes in required take-off. This would follow receipt of instructions from production and planning control. There is a need, therefore, to maintain close and effective communication between the two functions.

Obsolescent and slow-moving stocks

From time to time demand for items in stock ceases or reduces. The task of inventory control, working closely with design, users and purchasing, is to anticipate such changes in usage rates at the earliest possible stage.

Obsolescence

Materials and components become obsolescent for a number of reasons. Manufacture of a particular product may discontinue and, hence, demand for items held in stock for the product ceases. This applies also where the product is subject to changes in specification and existing items are superseded by new ones. Plant and equipment may be taken out of commission and, similarly, demand for supporting maintenance spares would cease. Modifications to plant and equipment would also result in demand ending for items held in stock.

Production planning must notify inventory control of the date on which product manufacture is to end. Stock control levels set for related items should then be regularly reassessed as efforts are directed to run down stocks. The ideal situation at which to aim is to hold just sufficient stock to support production on the last day of manufacture. This approach is required, too, for plant and equipment spares. However, this situation is a more complex one. Some spares are held in stock as an insurance in case of a breakdown, the timing of which cannot be predicted. Such spares are not lifed spares and hence their usage rates cannot be determined. Plant and equipment might not break down during the whole period of its operations. Hence, spares held as an insurance against possible breakdown could remain in stock after these units are taken out of commission.

It may be possible to use, or modify for use, particular obsolete materials for economical application elsewhere. Discussions would be required with designers and users.

Slow-moving stocks

Most stock items turn over at least once per year, i.e. the average number of the item in stock is, say, 100 and the annual usage rate is 100. Many items will turn over more frequently than this, possibly up to 10 times per year or more. The higher the turnover figure, the lower will be the inventory value.

The term 'slow-moving' applies to stock items where the turnover rate is significantly lower than is acceptable. A turnover rate of twice per year may be acceptable to some organizations while others aim for a much higher rate of six times per year or more. This would be dependent on the nature of the operation.

As in the case of obsolescent stock, alternative uses should be considered. Failing this, action would be taken to dispose of stock surplus to requirements.

Conclusions

Inventory control is required to be a very finely tuned operation. It has to keep the balance within close margins. Capital tied up in stock must be held to specified budget levels. Stock-outs must be minimized to provide specified levels of service to production or other users, e.g. 97 per cent or 98 per cent. With its closely associated functional partner, physical storekeeping, it provides the essential interface between users and purchasing. As pressure grows to reduce inventories further (and this is evident in the importance of JIT), inventory control will continue to be a key constituent within materials management. Forecasting techniques, particularly, must be developed so that this function can meet its ever-increasing commitments.

12

Production control management

Introduction
Production planning is responsible for determining and offering good, realistic dates to meet user and customer requirements. This is the first stage of the process of production planning and control. Its task is to plan the right product at the right time at an acceptable cost to meet customer or user needs. Subsequently, efforts must be directed to ensuring that these requirements are met. Production control takes responsibility for this second stage, to translate expectations into reality. A good plan must be backed by effective monitoring and control.

Objectives
Production control's function is to progress work to meet the materials plan. This requires systematic measuring to detect variations between 'actual' v. 'planned' progress. Such measurement enables divergences to be identified promptly, allowing maximum possible time to take corrective action.

Production flow analysis
Production or material planning should have, initially, considered three important requirements relating to production flow. These are minimizing the cost of handling and movement, seeking the shortest throughput times and making the most efficient use of all facilities. Failure to meet these objectives can result in heavy cost. Actual production flow must, therefore, be under frequent review and analysed to highlight bottlenecks and other areas of weakness that require correction.

Shop loading
The main objectives of shop loading are to ensure that production programmes are met and to achieve this economically. Let us consider the various aspects.

Meeting production programmes
Production control has to deal with planned and unplanned commitments. Production planning would have initially determined the sequence in which planned work is to be scheduled to commence to meet required completion dates. Production control then ensures that they have all relevant order details and documentation, and draws out all required materials and directs them to specified work centres.

Optimizing the use of plant and equipment
Many different types of problems occur in the production department, which demand prompt and effective corrective action. A machine may break down, necessitating work being directed to another one if the fault cannot be remedied quickly. An effective scheme of planned maintenance minimizes the incidence of breakdowns, but these cannot be prevented completely. Flexibility of operators is important so that they can be moved to operate other machines if the need arises. An operator may be absent or taken ill and his work assigned to another.

Skill is required to integrate emergency commitments (unplanned demands) into the production programme to minimize interruptions to programme and optimize the use of plant and equipment. Work process times and sequences are key elements for consideration in achieving these objectives. Their significance is discussed under Johnson's rule below.

JOHNSON'S RULE
Consider the following example, where a series of 10 jobs, each requiring two processes, are to be sequenced through two work centres, a planing machine 'A' followed by a boring machine 'B'. Completion of all 10 jobs is required by the same date, i.e. there is no particular order of priority. Machining work is routed first to machine 'A' in each case. The main objective is to maximize the utilization of both machines. This is achieved by applying 'Johnson's rule'. The stages for applying this rule are shown below in the table.

Job no.	1	2	3	4	5	6	7	8	9	10
Time (h) on 'A'	10	8	11	6	9	5	4	8	3	5
Time (h) on 'B'	3	6	5	2	8	7	6	10	9	8

The rules to be followed are:

1. Select the lowest available processing time. If this time relates to the first machining operation, this job should be loaded first; if to the second, load the job last in the available places in the loading sequences.
2. The loaded job should now be deleted from the list for subsequent action. The remaining jobs are then examined.
3. Select the lowest available processing time and go to 1 and repeat.

If two jobs have the same processing time:

- On the **first** machine: sequence so that the job with the longer time on the second operation is done before the job with the shorter time.
- On the **second** machine: sequence so that the job with the shorter time on the first operation is done before the job with the longer time.

Hence, following Johnson's rule the loading sequence would be revised as follows:

Job no.	9	7	10	6	8	5	2	3	1	4
Time (h) on 'A'	3	4	5	5	8	9	8	11	10	6
Time (h) on 'B'	9	6	8	7	10	8	6	5	3	2

The two job loading sequences can now be plotted, the original numerical one and the one using Johnson's rule.

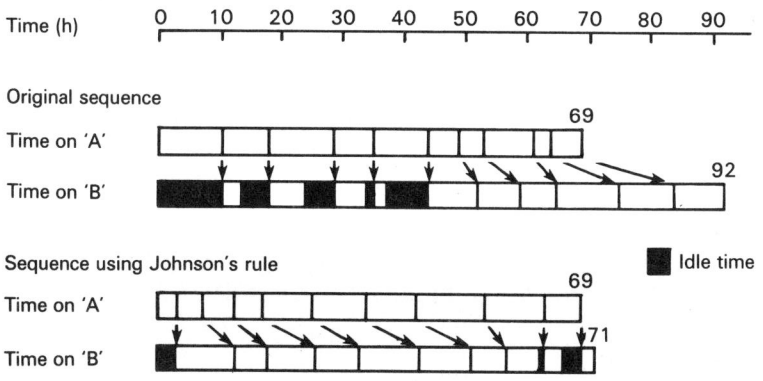

Machine utilization for the two loading sequences can now be compared:

	Original loading	Revised loading
Total time	92 hours	71 hours
Utilization of 'A'	100%	= 100%
Utilization of 'B'	64/92 = 70%	64/71 = 90%

The significant improvement in the utilization of machine 'B' will be noted. By revising the loading sequence, the delay in commencing work on machine 'B' is reduced from 10 to 3 hours. Subsequently, the idle time between processes on machine 'B' is reduced from 18 to 4 hours.

Documentation

This is a vital element for both production planning and production control. With increasing application of the computer to production control, the use of some of these documents will diminish. However, the details included and sequence logic will continue to be retained. The main documents normally applicable are:

- Drawings, specifications, part lists
- Routing and operation sheets
- Tooling details
- Standard times, grades of labour, machine capacities
- Sales programme order or order book
- Production programme
- Shop and machine loading schedules
- Production instructions
- Materials requirements schedules or purchase requisitions
- Materials availability reports
- Completion of production reports

Work in progress

We discussed in Chapter 11 the need to minimize inventory levels. Materials in stores may be held on inventory charge or in safe custody, e.g. items have been charged out direct to capital projects. Items held on inventory will ultimately be issued, as follows:

- To production for processing, fitting or assembly
- To users for use or consumption
- To suppliers as free issue

In the case of items in the first category, these will normally be taken off inventory charge and charged against a works order 'work-in-progress' account. The cumulative value of all materials in the processing/assembly/fitting cycle can be high. It is an area demanding strict financial control. The longer the time material issued from stock remains in the work-in-progress account, the more likely it is to attract additional charges. The inventory controller's responsibilities normally cease when materials are issued. Production control take over the responsibility to work to the production plan and achieve target throughput times. They must ensure that all charges allocated to particular work-in-progress accounts are legitimate ones.

Reservoirs at each work station
The value of work in progress is reflected by the material build-up or queuing at each work station. Production control must investigate promptly the reasons for excess. An increasing queue size at one work station denotes that capacities are not balanced or that delays will occur at subsequent stations through a shortage of material. One skill demanded of production control is an ability to anticipate problems arising which will adversely affect materials levels at each work station. In the ideal production environment, material should arrive at each work station on a 'just-in-time' basis. However, there are many production environments where this ideal situation is not achievable.

Economic batch loading
Production/material planning will have initially considered what quantities of completed items are required by what dates and for which customers. Some customers require their orders to be delivered in scheduled batch quantities over stipulated periods. The conflicting requirements of a number of customers can also necessitate batch production.

The determination of economic batch quantities is dependent on whether materials are being produced for direct supply to one or more customers. In many situations, batch quantities are required to replenish stocks from which customers draw. Other key elements to be considered are bought-in prices, which may relate to quantities purchased, inventory costs, production plant utilization and, finally, setting-up costs. Batch production will apply where group technology is operated.

Input/output control

Production input/output control often needs to be finely tuned. There may be a need for very sophisticated feedback systems that signal, promptly and accurately, current or anticipated significant fluctuations in the material input flow or in demand (the output flow). Consider the example where a factory producing product 'A' dispatches completed items to a finished-goods warehouse. Subsequently, goods are dispatched to a number of regionally based distributors. Finally, goods are sent to individual customers. Customer demand can vary greatly up or down with no common pattern between the regions.

Production planning and control must respond promptly to changing patterns of demand. This is not always achievable if reliance is placed on feedback from the finished-goods warehouse. There are three factors to be considered relating to changes in demand, which are:

- Amplitude of demand
- Time lag
- Harmonic factor

Consider Fig.12.1.

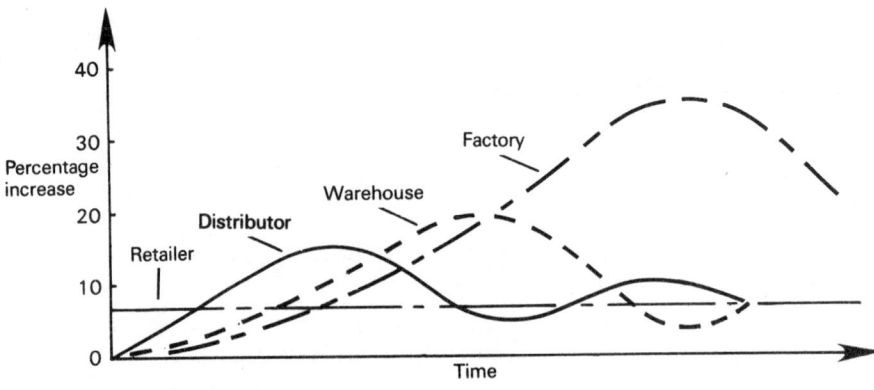

Figure 12.1 Instability of demand response

Note the increasing intensity and instability within the system. There is an obvious need to interpose a decision-making 'black box' between all pairs within the system (Fig.12.2). Demand response can then be monitored promptly and simultaneously. Ideally, prompt knowledge of customers' intentions would materially assist the factory's production planning and control. A good example is the use of guarantee cards. Not all customers complete and post guarantee cards to the manufacturers. Assume, however, that in the case of a particular type of men's shaver, 70 per cent of customers normally post their cards, of which 500 are received. If this figure increased to 600 in a particular week, what might this variation suggest? Demand might have increased by 20 per cent but may not be attributable to seasonal fluctuations. There could be a

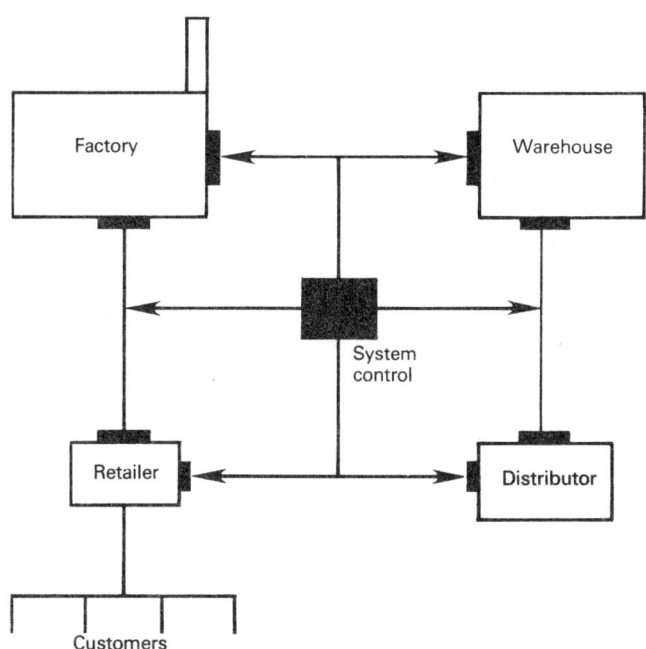

Figure 12.2   Demand feedback control

legitimate unanticipated increase in demand or a higher-than-normal percentage of customers completing and returning the guarantee cards. Demand might have increased following an advertising campaign in the press or on TV. Market research staff need to inform production planning and control promptly of their assessment of the situation. Is there a legitimate increase in demand and, if so, how much is it and over what period of time is it likely to be sustained?

Changes in customer demand can also be gauged promptly in other ways. Consider the sale of goods in supermarkets. Here a computer link between sales check-outs in the stores and head office enables the actual daily sales of each of the very wide range of products to be compared with anticipated sales and seasonal trends. Particular attention would be given to the high-volume, high-value 'A' items. A prompt evaluation of 'Why?', 'How much?' and 'For how long?' will need to be undertaken and the individual factories notified promptly of changing schedules.

Line of balance

Line of balance is a technique particularly suitable for control of production of fluctuating or repetitive batches. Specifically, it enables the quantities of items to be determined which must be completed by intermediate dates to ensure that progress is 'on-line' to meet the final completion or delivery schedule date. Line of balance is a multi-stage process, which commences with the batch schedule. It compares actual v. planned progress against delivery schedules. A line-of-balance chart can be constructed from which forward projections can be readily determined for each stage or activity at particular review periods. Hence, for example, any shortfalls in completed quantities required in, say, four, six or eight weeks' time can be predicted, enabling remedial action to be taken or reprogramming done, whichever is applicable. Consider the following schedule for a 'Widget' component, which is to be made in batches over a nine-week period. The required weekly batch and cumulative quantities are shown in the table below. Actual v. planned comparisons can be made at regular review periods. For this example the position is shown as at week 3.

Week no.	Completion of items		Cumulative completion	
	Required	Actual	Required	Actual
1	20	15	20	15
2	20	15	40	30
3	20	30	60	60
4	25		85	
5	25		110	
6	25		135	
7	30		165	
8	30		195	
9	30		225	

This schedule can be constructed graphically as shown in Fig.12.3.

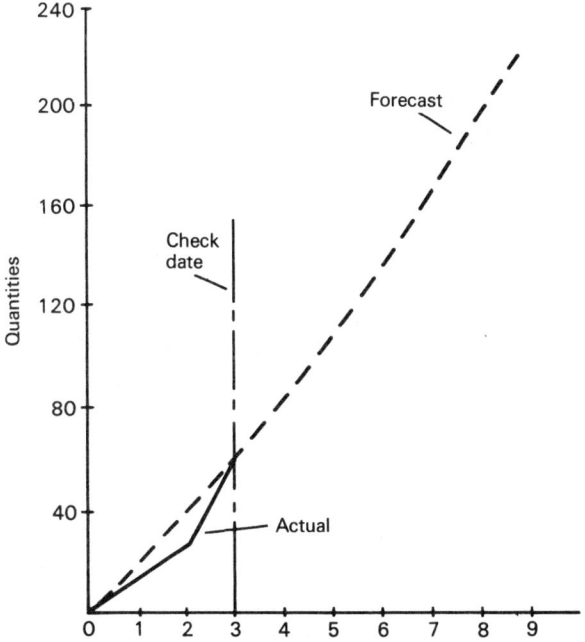

Figure 12.3 Cumulative completions

The 'Widget' component may embrace few or many operations, each one with possible widely differing process lead times. For this example, let us consider that the component comprises two sub-assemblies with purchased and made-in parts (with their respective lead times) as shown in the operation programme (developed as an arrow diagram) in Fig.12.4. It will be noted that the programme is in weeks, with items 1 and 2 having the longest lead time of five weeks.

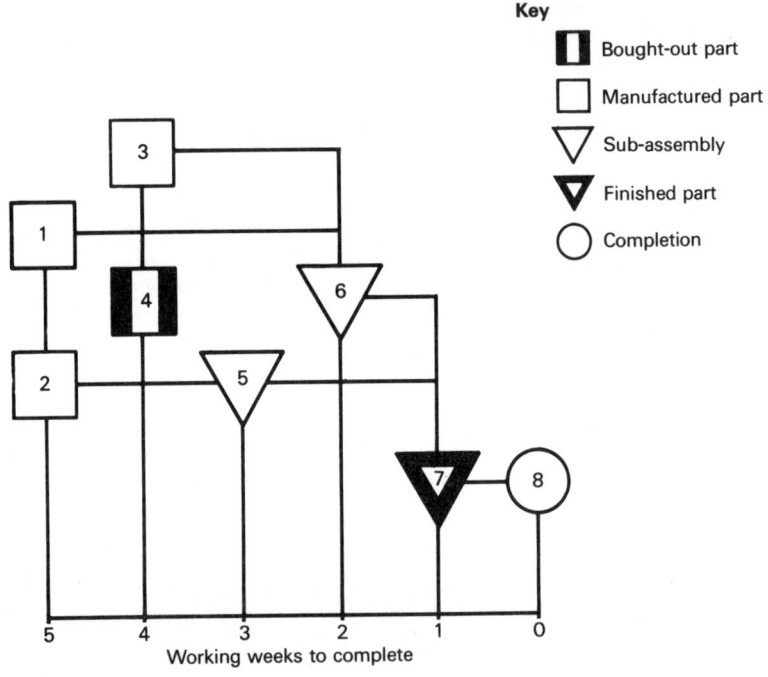

Figure 12.4   Operation programme

The final process is to construct the line-of-balance diagram by integrating the operation programme (Fig.12.4) with the cumulative completion (Fig.12.3). This is a multi-stage process as follows:

1. Construct Fig.12.3.

2. Construct to the right of 1 the vertical lines of the 'operation number' vertical bar chart.
3. Using week 3 as the datum point, construct a vertical co-ordinate from week 3 to intersect the 'cumulative number of units' curve. Work forward to the right and construct vertical coordinates for each operation in turn to cross the curve. Take operation 1 first, which has a lead time of five weeks. Hence for this operation the vertical coordinate would be drawn at week 8 (3 + 5).
4. At the point of intersection, construct a horizontal coordinate to extend to the right and draw the top from the top of the vertical bar for operation 1.
5. Proceed to construct the vertical and horizontal coordinates for operations 2 to 8, similarly. It will be noted that in the case of operation 8, it is only necessary to draw a horizontal line striking across to the right from the intersection at week 3 on the curve. The line so constructed shows the actual progress of operation number quantities required (60) to be completed at week 3 to meet forecasted 'Widget' quantity requirements, which is 60.

To determine if there are shortfalls in quantities for each of the other operations we need to construct the line of balance on the histogram to check against actual inventory and work-in-progress quantities.

Taking operation 5 as an example, this has a lead time of three weeks and it will be noted that by drawing a vertical coordinate upwards to intersect the quantity curve this gives a forecasted requirement of 138. It will be noted from Fig.12.5 that the inventory check showed a total of 128 available, a shortfall of 10. Action would be required immediately to speed up the process to overcome this.

Line of balance thus starts from a given actual cumulative datum point (in this example, week 3), with an item quantity of 60, and then is constructed using the cumulative curve. A number of assumptions are made:

1. Lead times will not change from the figures given in the operation programme.
2. Actual cumulative totals beyond week 3 will be as scheduled.

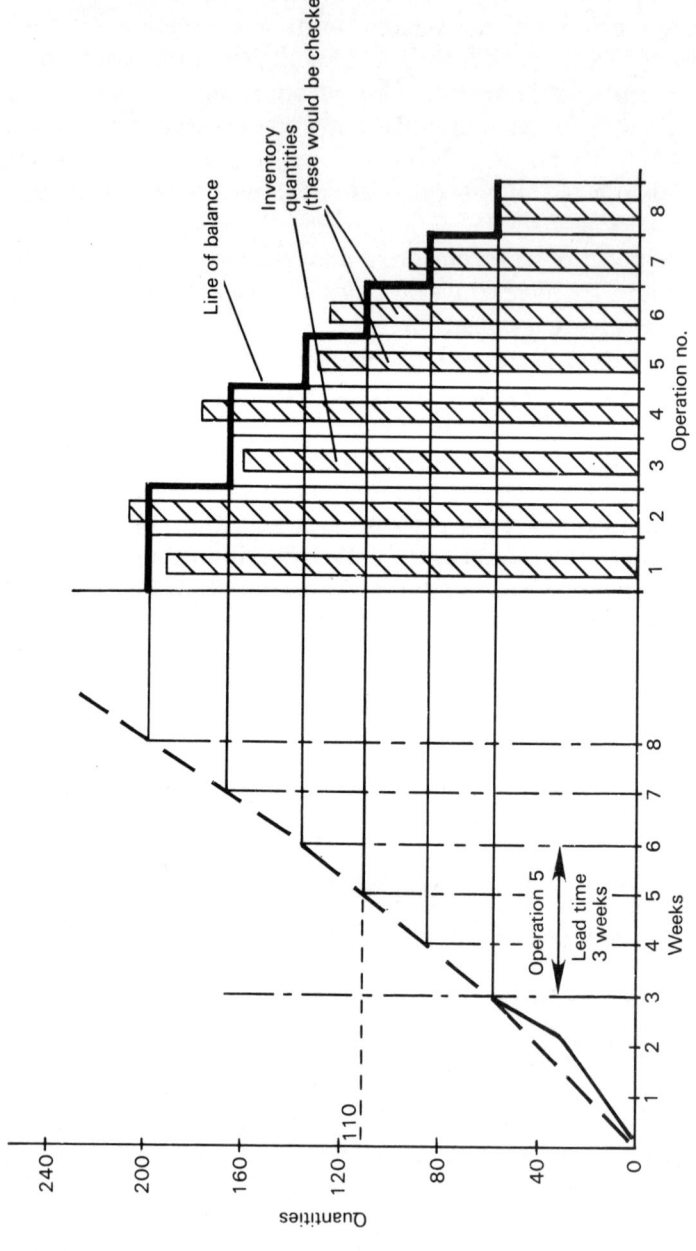

Figure 12.5 Line of balance

Sub-contract control and release
Production control may be involved in sub-contracting, the need arising for a number of reasons.

Work speciality
This type of work will normally have been identified as being suitable for sub-letting, as it is not within the organization's field of specialism. Alternatively, the work could not be processed economically within the company, and, hence, the intention to sub-let would be noted and catered for by production planning. Close liaison will be required between production control, production planning and purchasing to ensure release of materials with full instructions and documentation by specified dates.

Capacity problems
Shortages of capacity may create short-, medium- or longer-term problems. In the short term, work might have to be sub-let as a matter of extreme urgency as a result of, say, a machine breakdown. In the longer term, a decision might have been made to take a machine out of service for a period for overhaul. This, too, would result in a temporary shortage of capacity.

Customer specified
Material planning should be notified at an early date of the intention to sub-let. Production control will be involved, particularly if they are engaged in preparatory operations. They need to maintain close contact with purchasing to check arrangements made with the supplier nominated to carry out the work entailed. Specifications and drawings may be required for dispatch to the subcontractor. Tooling, jigs and fixtures could also be required.

Quality control/inspection requirements
We discussed quality control relating to bought-out materials in Chapter 6. Production control has to work closely with quality control on stage inspections during the various processes on the shop floor.

Contractual
Points for consideration include indemnities, ownership,

confidentiality, use, scrap and spoilage, which we have discussed in Chapter 8.

Work study

Work study is a technique particularly important to production control because of the nature and the magnitude of the interface between men and machines, hence, its inclusion in this chapter. Work study has been defined as 'The systematic examination of activities in order to improve the use of human and other material resources'. Work study has universal application in supply, service and transport industries in both the public and private sectors. It is not now restricted to overalled operatives working in manufacturing industry, as it was in the first half of this century. Work study has combined with 'organization and method' (O&M) within productivity management and hence now has a much wider sphere of influence and application.

Work study comprises two quite separate studies. The first is method study (determining the best way of doing a task) and the second is work measurement (determining how long the task should take).

METHOD STUDY
Determining the best way of doing a task depends on whether or not the task is to be done for the first time. When it is, consideration would be given to similar applications to use as a basis for pursuing the study. For an existing task the study requires to be a systematic and critical examination of the present method in order to make improvements.

Systematic analysis
The analysis of an existing task must follow a logical systematic procedure commencing with the selection of the task. Many tasks require analysis, hence the need to be selective in choosing the one giving most scope for achieving significant improvement. All data relating to the task and how it is carried out are recorded. This is followed by critical examination of the data. From this analysis the new method is developed. It is important that all implications of the change in method are considered, as the full benefits anticipated from change are not always fully realized. There can be loss as well as profit. The new method is

recorded in the way used for the initial study. All persons concerned in operating the new method need to be trained and to acquire appropriate skills. The new method is then installed as standard practice and its use monitored to check possible deviations and reasons why.

There is much scope for the application of method study within the functions embraced by materials management, particularly in production planning and control. The main objectives sought from the use of this technique are (1) to increase productivity and (2) to improve working conditions. The attaining of these objectives is demonstrated by reduced costs or better value for costs incurred. Such a study should be carried out at the material planning stage. For an existing job or process, the details of each element or stage are recorded in the sequence in which it is done, the time duration for each element also being recorded. The study includes productive and non-productive time elements for both men and machines. The method study process can be developed in a number of ways depending on the nature of requirements.

Activity symbols used
Standard activity symbols have been adopted for universal application which cater for the various stages of work under method study, and are:

Operation   This denotes that material or documentation is being worked on in some way

Inspection   This denotes examination, checking or verification in some way. It may relate to quantity or quality

Transport   This denotes movement without actually being part of an operation or inspection

Delay   This denotes a temporary storage awaiting an operation, inspection or transport

Storage   This denotes storage, which has been planned or required

Material flow chart

This can be developed using activity symbols to depict the flow of, say, iron castings, which are to be issued from stores to be machined and assembled with other items. In the example given below, the flow chart shows all activities with their standard symbols, up to and including the machining of the casting.

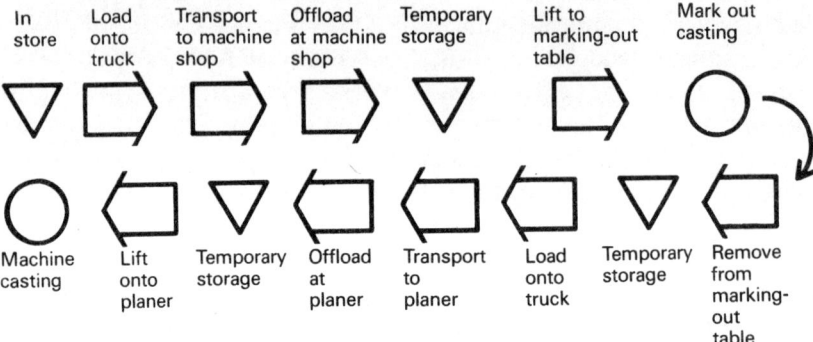

In store | Load onto truck | Transport to machine shop | Offload at machine shop | Temporary storage | Lift to marking-out table | Mark out casting

Machine casting | Lift onto planer | Temporary storage | Offload at planer | Transport to planer | Load onto truck | Temporary storage | Remove from marking-out table

Outline process sequence chart

This chart is used to show the productive activities of operations and inspections. Its use may be demonstrated in the following example:

Issues   Marking out   Machining   Inspection   Finished goods

Multiple activity chart

This charting method may be used to show the simultaneous activities of two or more persons or a combination of the activities of a person (or persons) and a machine. The productive and non-productive periods, i.e. working and idle time, can be given for each. The chart may be prepared in the form of a process chart or a bar chart. Consider the following process chart machining example with six activities:

	Stage 1	Stage 2	Stage 3	Stage 4	Stage 5	Stage 6
Operator	Load and set up	(idle)	Re-set	(idle)	Inspect	Remove
Machine	(idle)	Rough machine	(idle)	Finish machine	(idle)	(idle)
Time (min)	10	40	5	60	10	10

The total process time is 135 minutes, during which the operator is not actually working (i.e. he is idle) for 100 minutes or 74 per cent of the time. Attention would be directed to giving the operator other work so he may be gainfully employed during these idle periods. Where the situation permitted, work might be found on another machine.

WORK MEASUREMENT
Subsequently, measurement of 'actual' v. 'planned' performance can be carried out once the methods have been determined and standardized. There are three basic approaches to work measurement, which are dependent on the nature of the organization and the types of work done.

Time study
This method involves the direct measurement of selected work using the stop-watch. The various stages in the measurement process are:

- Division of the job into separate logical elements.
- Timing of each element. This requires an adequate number of readings being made to give an acceptable degree of accuracy.
- Rating of the level of effort for each time taken.
- Calculation of the basic time for the operation.
- Adjusting the basic time with the inclusion of allowances to cater for unavoidable delays, personal needs and fatigue.

Activity sampling
This method involves observing work being carried out to estimate times. It will be used in the following situations:

- Determination of allowances to include in standard times.
- Analysing of the distribution of work activities within a group.
- Estimating of machine utilization.
- Determining indirect labour time standards.

Synthetic or analytical method
This is a method of indirect work measurement in which synthetic times for basic motions or elements are built up to give methods time measurement (MTM) and predetermined notion time standards (PMTS). Times are predetermined for such

hand activities as reaching, moving, grasping, turning, positioning, applying pressure and releasing. Additionally, the method caters for eye travel and focus. Other movements of the body may be applicable, such as in a lifting movement or where legs and feet are involved. This method is particularly applicable to high-volume repetitive bench assembly work.

In all of the above approaches to work measurement, standard times have to be determined. This is done by adding time allowances appropriate to the individual situation. Where working conditions are severe, a higher allowance would be given. The fatigue factor would also be considered, as would the layout and tooling used. Standard times are thus calculated from the data provided by the methods employed in work measurement plus the provision of allowances.

Conclusions

Production control is the direct link between production supervision and production planning. It thus has the frequently difficult task of reconciling conflicting requirements between these two greatly differing functions. We have discussed a number of differing approaches to managing materials and it will be noted that operations management provides the best scope for resolving such conflict, as each of the three functions report to one manager or director.

Production control operates at the final material input stage to manufacturing, and, hence, the success of its contribution depends very much on the effectiveness of the preceding functions in the supply chain. Hence, measurement of its achievements must take into account the quality of such contributions.

While we have dealt with production control separately from production planning, the two functions are often closely integrated, with duties overlapping, particularly in the smaller organizations.

13

Distribution management

Introduction
Distribution has been defined as 'The performance of all business activities involved in moving goods from the point of processing or manufacture to the point of sale to the customer'. In practice, the distribution function generally tends to be considered as covering the stages from receipt of request for goods to be dispatched to the finished-goods warehouse to actual receipt by the customer.

While principles of distribution are valid for all types of organizations in the public and private sectors, e.g. manufacturing, service, supply, or transport, application will vary considerably depending on the nature and volume of products. Another important factor is the customer market, which may be local, regional, nation-wide, EC or world-wide. Hence, the choice of mode of transport and time factor also varies.

Objectives
The primary objective of distribution management can be expressed in simple terms. It is to provide an efficient and effective service to the customer market at target economic cost. This is measured by the quality of service being provided against cost incurred.

Functional activities
Many warehouse activities are similar to those discussed in Chapter 10. These include receipts and putting into stock of goods. Other activities that have special relevance to finished-goods warehouses include the following.

Picking planning
Finished-goods warehouse or central depots provide a regular service to customers. A pattern will emerge of the type and

anticipated quantities of items required. Retrieval (picking) of materials from widely dispersed locations within the warehouse has to be planned to optimize the use of all resources at minimum cost. Sequence of picking requires careful planning as a flow line operation, which considers the nature, size and weight of goods, rack or bin locations and heights, and volume and frequency of demand. Item value or attractiveness also influences choice of location for reasons of special security. The methods of handling and transferring goods to the dispatch bay is dependent on the nature, size and weight of goods. Stacking is another important aspect. Item 'A' can be stacked on item 'B' but not the reverse. Item 'C' might need to be completely separated from item 'D' to avoid possible contamination.

Transfer to dispatch bay
Smooth and speedy transfer of picked items is impeded by bottle-necks in the flow line to the dispatch bay. We discuss later in the chapter the time criticality period from receipt of customer requirements through the various stages of identifying, locating, picking, packing and loading items onto vehicles for dispatch by road to customers.

Forecasting requirements
We discussed in Chapter 10 the need for regulated reservoirs of materials to cater for fluctuations in supply and demand. Similarly, there is need for regulated levels of finished-goods stocks to be interposed between production and the company's customers. Fluctuations in supply to and demand from the customer market result for various reasons. Heavy seasonal demand necessitates regular batch production throughout several months of the year. In the case of some items, it is more economical to set up machines to operate for a short period only to produce estimated annual requirements. Completed items are then dispatched to the warehouse. When interruption to production is anticipated, stockpiling may be necessary to ensure a smooth flow of goods to customers. This requires the use of good forecasting techniques, which take into account all probable influencing factors. Customer demand could vary for many reasons, quite apart from seasonal effects. A trade recession might be developing which reduces demand. One particular

manufacturer may be increasing his share of the market. Adverse publicity of the product might temporarily affect demand.

Marketing and sales are the functions concerned with forecasting future demand, but, generally, non-manufacturing organizations involved in distribution do not have these functions. However, whatever the nature of the enterprise, trends in volumes dispatched can be analysed. Depots or customers would be asked to give forecasts of their requirements over the coming 12 months. These would be updated at specified intervals. Specialized forecasting techniques would be used so that considered judgement can be made on probable future levels of commitments. Such techniques include exponential smoothing, which we discussed in Chapter 11.

Finished-goods warehouse

As the name implies, a warehouse is a stores for finished goods awaiting distribution to customers. Warehouses are located at factories, at a central distribution point, or at a number of geographical locations depending on distribution requirements. Some goods have limited life, as in the case of fresh foodstuffs, where the rule 'first-in, first-out' is a good one and is generally followed. However, for the great majority of finished goods, life constraints apply to a much less critical degree and storage space limitations could make it difficult to apply the rule because of retrieval problems, e.g. double handling.

Automated storage

The decision to consider installing automated storage will stem from an organization's wish to meet specific objectives, the three main ones being:

1. Reduction in the cost of storage
2. Improvement in the level of service to users or customers
3. Improvement in control of all aspects of warehouse activities.

Factors for consideration

The decision whether or not to automate a warehouse can be a lengthy process in which very careful consideration is required. Important factors are as follows.

- Cost of installing suitable equipment. This is high and could include for significant alterations to an existing, not readily adaptable, building.
- Available funds and alternative investment opportunities.
- Forecast of probable long-term requirements included in the corporate plan, particularly possible changing patterns in the nature and volume of future material flow. This is a major requirement. Automation is costly, and hence evaluations must project forward possibly 10 years or more.
- Dependability and vulnerability of the proposed automated system. In the event of a power cut or other cause of stoppage, what effective alternative means of material location, access and retrieval is available for the period of emergency? Project costing might need to cater for the inclusion of a standby generator which could 'trip-in' in the event of power failure.
- Evaluation of probable savings. There are many contributions to savings, which include reduction in stock levels, improvement in the service to users and redeployment of staff. Additional savings are also achieved through faster turn-round times of vehicles.
- Selection of equipment. A number of major manufacturers have installed a wide range of automated warehouse equipment within the UK in recent years. Warehouse managers and project development staff should visit other organizations who have similar operations. This enables all involved to study the operations of the different types of equipment, applications and working environments. In discussion with other warehouse managers and staff, points could arise which suggest that one installation is more suitable than another subject to possible modifications, e.g. eight-high stacking instead of ten-high because of roof height constraints.

One example of an automated storage system is shown in Fig.13.1.

Distribution planning
Distribution planning is influenced by a number of key factors. Ultimately, this planning has to relate to main warehouse or central depot locations. These might have been determined

Figure 13.1 Automated warehouse: system for 'The Bathroom Warehouse' (courtesy of Mannesmann Demag Ltd)

some time ago by the geographical dispersion of the customers they served, i.e. sub-depots, local distributors, wholesalers and individual customers. Consider Fig.13.2. This shows distribution from one central point.

Regional depots may be widely dispersed geographically. They could differ greatly in size, i.e. by their individual volumes of service to customers. With the passage of time, demand remains static, grows or contracts in the different regions, possibly with no common trends. Centres of gravity of customer markets may shift, with one particular regional depot assuming

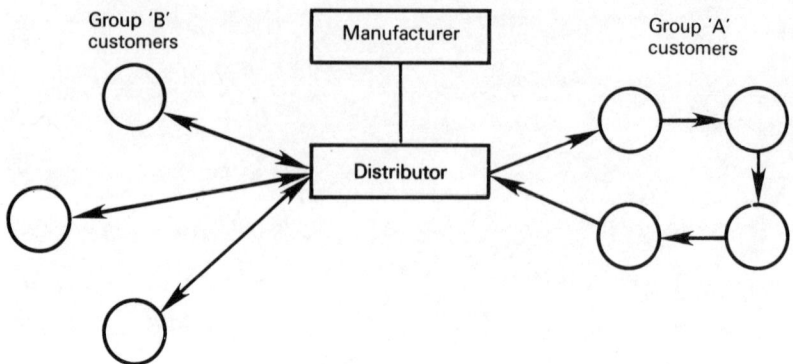

Figure 13.2   Distribution pattern — single manufacturer

greater importance than another as it handles an increasingly larger volume of products. It could be necessary to re-site a depot to give prompter response to customer markets. Another important point is that local site constraints might result in a depot being moved to another suitable site in the region where planned expansion can proceed. Reducing customer demand in one region could result in its depot having to close, with remaining commitments being transferred to the nearest one.

Another scenario relates to the situation where an organization has a number of manufacturing units dispersed over a large geographical area, for example, as applies in the United States or in Europe. In such a situation, a particular product would be produced and available in differing quantities at a number of widely dispersed locations. Customers with their varying demands for the product are similarly widely dispersed. The organization is thus concerned in developing a distribution system that will achieve customer satisfaction at total minimum cost.

Consider Fig.13.3, which shows an example of distribution from two manufacturing centres in Europe.

Assume that in this example the product supply quantities and individual demand quantities are as shown in the tabulation below, which is known as a distribution matrix.

The quantities to be supplied by Birmingham and Zurich to the five individual customers located in Europe would be developed as a linear equation, which included all elements of cost and time factors.

To From	Paris	Dusseldorf	Hamburg	Milan	Toulouse	Available for supply
Birmingham						50 000
Zurich						70 000
Required	30 000	25 000	40 000	20 000	5 000	120 000

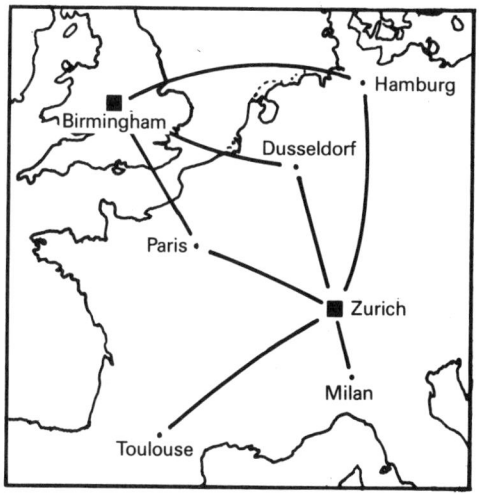

Figure 13.3   Distribution pattern — multiple manufacturing centres

Industrial, commercial and economic situations are in a state of continuous change, however gradual, so distribution planning must be under regular review. Such planning is greatly assisted by the use of linear programming, which enables limited resources to be allocated to competing demands in the most effective way possible. Linear programming is a highly specialized subject, which is not within the scope of this book. There are a number of books on linear programming available on the market for interested readers.

Customer liaison
In many manufacturing organizations, sales liaison with main warehouse must be close. Sales staff make regular visits to

customers. Promises given of firm delivery dates for orders need to be supported by warehouse stocks and distribution capabilities. Obviously, it is unwise for false promises to be made, as this affects companies' reputations. Hence, sales staff must keep updated on warehouse stock availability. They could be the initial focal point of customer complaints and be called upon to arrange return and replacement of substandard goods. In addition to receiving complaints from customers, they might receive constructive suggestions on ways of improving a product, its packaging or method or timing of transport. Such information should be passed promptly to the warehouse and other involved department(s) for consideration and action.

Transport planning

Transport may account for a significant percentage of an organization's total operating costs. It has been estimated that transport costs can represent 25 per cent or more of the total cost of many products. Hence, transport is a key area within distribution management, demanding the fullest consideration particularly on the following main aspects.

Determination of requirements

The types and number of vehicles need to be determined to support operational requirements. Consideration would be given to forecasted longer-term distribution patterns.

Ownership v. leasing v. hiring

Increasing consideration is being given to the economic cost of operation rather than the prestige of ownership. Government policies have prompted the growth of leasing. The advantages and disadvantages of ownership, leasing or hiring of vehicles is discussed later in this chapter.

Road Transport Acts

Transport of goods by road is subject to a number of Acts of Parliament. Construction and use of vehicles and trailers must conform to regulations laid down. Size, length, axle loading and emission of fumes to atmosphere are some of the aspects covered. Vehicles must be examined within one year of purchase to ensure that they conform to required standards. A vehicle test certificate and a plating certificate will be issued if the vehicle meets requirements. The latter certificate verifies fitment of a plate that details the weights at which the vehicle may be operated.

All drivers of heavy goods vehicles must be licensed and adequately insured against third party risks with an authorized insurer.

International movement of road transport, wide, long and dangerous loads are also covered by individual Acts. Transport managers must keep abreast of current and impending regulations. Acts relating to road transport are amended from time to time. Croner's Publications publish a manual *Croner's Road Transport Operations* issued in loose-leaf binder form. Subscribers receive monthly updates on all relevant amendments to regulations.

VEHICLE OPERATING OPTIONS

An organization has the choice of options for moving materials from central depot or finished-goods warehouse to distribution points. These are self-owned fleet, leased fleet and the use of hauliers.

Self-owned fleet

The main advantage of owning vehicles and employing drivers is that this gives complete control over both. An additional advantage, if required, is the opportunity to advertise the company and its products. There are disadvantages, as problems will be experienced if there are peaks and troughs in distribution commitments. Facilities will be required for servicing and routine maintenance, demands on which could fluctuate greatly. Hence, additional and probable high expenditure would be incurred. Vehicles may operate well below capacity or lengthy periods, with little or no scope for building up loads or part-loads for return journeys. Once unloading is complete, empty vehicles must be dispatched promptly back to the warehouse or central depot. Time devoted to determining product manufacturing costs must be extended to include also the determination of realistic transport costs.

Another important aspect relating to self-owned vehicles is vehicle replacement policy, which should be catered for within the corporate plan. Consideration is required of a number of points. Vehicle development is one. Are significant changes predicted in future distribution patterns to the customer market? This might affect the nature, volume and weight of vehicle loads. Vehicle legislation is also a key point. What could be the effects of new legislation under discussion in the EC on UK vehicle users? Vehicle axle loading has been a particular major issue in recent years. Drivers' working hours too, may again come under review.

A company, making the decision to project a better image in the customer market, might need to re-examine its policy in the design of its vehicles. Should the old fleet be run down quickly and be replaced with a more economic and eye-catching model?

Leased fleet

One alternative option to the self-owned fleet is leasing vehicles on contract. Here, too, control may be exercised over drivers and vehicles, and advertising might be negotiated as part of the contract. Costs can be accurately determined as there are no hidden elements. Garage or maintenance or servicing costs are not incurred. Economic contracts require vehicles and drivers to be fully employed. As with self-owned fleets, it is not always possible to arrange economic loads for return journeys.

Leasing differs from hiring as leasing generally involves one user or customer only for a period of possibly three to five years or the economic life of the vehicle. The owner aims to recover all expenditure incurred in buying vehicles and operating costs plus required profit from leasing arrangements. Frequently, a financial house acts as an intermediary between lessor and lessee. In hiring, the owner hires out vehicles on a daily, weekly or monthly basis to several users. He aims to recover his expenditure and make his profit from a number of individual contracts of differing durations made with various hirers.

Key financial considerations relating to the self-owned fleet v. lease decision will be very much dependent on a number of internal and external factors. Chancellors of the Exchequer exercise some influence. They can stimulate investment in vehicle production, make tax adjustments and give other allowances in their budget proposals. Points for consideration in choosing between self-owned and leased fleet options include:

- Availability of funds
- Alternative investment opportunities, i.e. rate of return on capital
- Cash flow
- Interest rates
- Tax concessions
- Effect of inflation

By leasing, a vehicle can be used at today's prices but payments are made out of tomorrow's income, freeing working capital for more productive use. Rentals are fixed at the outset and do not fluctuate. Hence, leasing also aids budgeting and cash flow.

Other important considerations include the need for flexibility in the type of vehicles required. With a leasing contract, an organization could be committed to operating a particular type and size of vehicle for a period of three to five years. A contract release clause might be negotiable allowing termination of the lease at an earlier date for a stated payment. Anticipated technological developments in vehicle design is another important factor that might make leasing the favoured option.

A leasing contract includes such aspects as:

- Period of lease (primary and secondary) and cessation
- Use, replacement, maintenance and insurance of vehicles
- Lessor's and lessee's respective rights
- Time of payments
- Applicable law

Use of hauliers

This is the final option that a company can consider. This option might be favoured because a company does not become committed to a long-term contract of a year or more with fixed haulage rates. Hence, there is full scope to seek competitive tenders and negotiate the lowest rates for very short periods, which can include negotiating rates for each delivery.

Generally, the most suitable vehicle can be provided for each load. The company will not be directly concerned with vehicle capacity utilization on return journeys. Contract rates will, however, reflect this important economic fact. A major problem for the company is that it cannot exercise control over vehicles or drivers. Advertising will not be possible as a particular vehicle may work for the company one day and be assigned to another company the next day. Where peak commitments coincide with the needs of others, difficulty may be experienced in obtaining vehicles when required.

Distribution contract

We have discussed above the three transport options that can be considered where distribution management operates within materials management. A number of large companies who previously owned or leased their transport fleets have now contracted out their distribution requirements, in some cases including warehousing. This new approach to distribution has resulted from the companies concerned deciding that it would be more profitable to concentrate their specialisms on manufacture and marketing and to leave the problems of distribution to established experts in that field. This is a logical development of specialization. Companies who contract out distribution requirements have evaluated the cost of losing direct control against the increased professional specialist capability gained. Initially, emphasis is mainly directed to reducing distribution costs for the same level of service. As more distribution experts come into the market and competition grows, the emphasis becomes more evenly divided between reducing distribution costs and satisfying increased customer demand to reduce local stockholdings. This development is taking place in parallel with the increasing application of JIT, which is designed to eliminate inventories. Fundamentally, this form of partnership between a manufacturer and a distributor is not different from other forms of partnerships where there are clearly defined divisions of responsibilities. Aerospace provides two examples. The European Airbus is one, where a number of companies each produce major parts of the aircraft. The second relates to most jet airliners, where the airframe is made by one company and the engines by another.

Contract distribution is, however, outside material management's area of operations, as control of distribution passes outside the company to a third party interposed between company and customers.

Packaging and pallets

Packaging is being used increasingly for manufactured items not only to protect them but also to provide a more suitable shape for handling and transporting. Packaging also facilitates the advertising of the contained item.

Unit loads may be made up from cardboard cartons, work boxes, sacks, stillages or pallets depending on requirements of handling, transporting and storing. Pallets are designed in many forms from the basic platform to box structures and provide two-way or four-way entry by truck forks.

Packaging is a specialized area where advantages sought are balanced against cost and weight. Security, too, is of increasing importance, so that the method of packaging is often designed to prevent easy access for theft.

Packaging is also considered within the supply chain where the customer requires items to be packaged in a particular way to meet the requirements of his customer.

Use of containers

Products for distribution are not always loaded directly into the transporting vehicles. It is often more economical to pack containers for loading onto vehicles for dispatch. This reduces the time vehicles are out of service as loading and unloading times can be greatly reduced. The use of containers provides a number of other advantages. The unit load will be larger, being consolidated from what was previously a number of smaller packages. Security will be improved.

Types of containers

Containers may be classified as thin-skinned, insulated or refrigerated. Other classifications include general cargo, top-loading, half-height and open-sided. They are designed to be suitable for transport by road, sea or air.

Lengthy, overseas and disrupted journeys

A number of major problems may arise in the use of containers. Where they are exposed to weather conditions, they should be inspected to ensure that they are in a satisfactory condition. This includes both visual internal and external examination. Structure and attachments require checking for damage or deterioration, particularly through ingress of water. This requires the examiner to check the inside of the container for signs of dampness. During periods of dry weather it is advisable to close the container doors and check internally for chinks of daylight. Where light shines through, water may also enter.

Materials must be adequately secured against movement by the use of floor stops and internal lug attachment fittings with appropriate strapping or rope. Firm packing would be inserted between items to prevent chafing. This is particularly important where the journey will not be a smooth one and includes frequent handling. The dispatcher may be responsible for the total journey or the risk may pass at an intermediate stage with split insurance. This applies, for example, where goods are consigned overseas on a FOB (free-on board) basis, i.e. at a specified port or airport in the UK. In special circumstances it might be necessary to prove adequacy of loading before dispatch by photographing each stage of the loading. This step might need to be taken following cases where customers had previously wrongly complained of loading inadequacies. In special circumstances, also, the customer's representative could witness loading. This avoids subsequent claims being made against the dispatcher.

Mechanical handling aids
We have discussed a wide range of mechanical aids in Chapter 10. Many of them are equally applicable in finished-goods warehouses.

Documentation
Each consignment, i.e. each vehicle load, should be given a unique sequential consignment number. This identifies the dispatching section or loading area and destination. All details of the load would be recorded on the loading sheet, together with vehicle reference number and dispatch date. The type of stores and total load might also be included. This enables queries or investigations to be handled expeditiously if the need arises. The number of copies will vary with an individual organization's requirements. The warehouse (the dispatcher) would retain a

copy. The driver may be required to take two or three copies for the authorized recipient. Any queries or discrepancies would be detailed on the appropriate copy and returned promptly to the warehouse for investigation. A final copy would be sent to accounts.

Export requirements
This is a highly specialized area where requirements are dependent on nature of goods, method of transport and country of destination. The Treaty of Rome to which Great Britain is a signatory includes within its many requirements a common transport policy. This seeks, as one objective, the free circulation of transport services within the EC.

Manpower measurement
Required manpower levels are dependent on a number of factors, which will relate initially to the levels of service to customers that must be met, e.g. 95, 96 or 98 per cent. These will include the following.

Vehicle or container loads
From assessments of customers' requirements, unit and size of vehicles and containers, average unit loads and average number of loads per week can then be calculated.

Dispatch cycle
Consider a central depot that supplies six regional depots. Each week, central depot receives computer print-outs from each regional depot specifying their stock replenishment requirements. The overall inventory policy is to hold minimum stocks in the regions. Hence, the ordering/delivery time-scale must be short. For example, on day −1 computerized order requirements are received at central depot from a regional depot. On day 1 the details are passed to the packers for action. All withdrawals of items from stock, necessary palletizing or packing, and preparation of documentation would be planned for execution and completion on this day. The vehicle or container would be loaded on day 2 ready for dispatch early in the morning on day 3. These stages are shown in Fig.13.4.

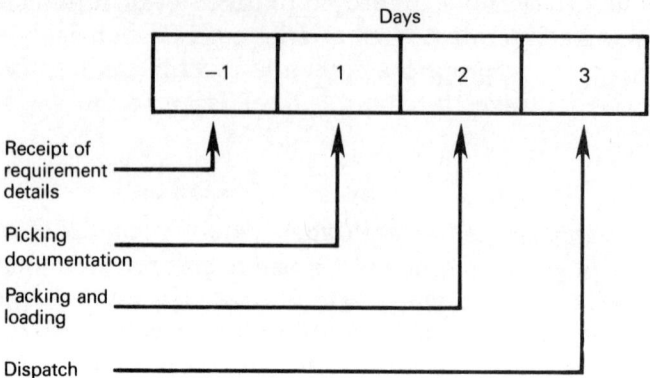

Figure 13.4 Dispatch cycle

Time performance standards
These will vary from one organization to another. Peaks and troughs may be experienced in the workloads of dispatch staff responsible for carrying out a wide range of duties. Their major duties would be directly concerned with the dispatch activities scheduled to be performed on days 1 and 2. These duties could be classified as 'time-critical'. Other duties such as repacking items for return into stock and raising of related documentation would be classified as 'non-time-critical'. Management's aim is to ensure that required effort is concentrated on the former category work. Once commitments have been met, attention could turn to handling the less important secondary work. Obviously, full control is required over this secondary work, otherwise major problems could develop, seriously jeopardizing efforts that should be devoted to 'time-critical' items. The central depot's objective is to provide the specified level of service to each regional depot, and time is a vital element of this service. Flexibility of manpower is thus essential, so that resources are deployed to optimum advantage under changing workload conditions.

Warehouse security
We have discussed in Chapter 10 many aspects of security relating to materials in stores on the material input side of an organization's operations. Security in finished-goods warehouses

is similarly important. Indeed, in many respects it might be considered to be more important, because all goods have been fully processed and, in some cases, will be in an operating condition. Hence, they will generally be of higher value. Also, as they are to be dispatched for actual use rather than processing, they will be more attractive and hence become a higher security risk. The risk factor can be considered to have two elements. The first is value and attractiveness. The second is probable ease of removal. Size and weight are the two important aspects relating to this. Another point is that removal might be a two-stage process. Goods have first to be removed from the warehouse, unless they have been intercepted at some other point in the material transfer process. They then have to be removed from the organization's premises. This is normally accomplished by being secreted on one's person, hidden in some form of bag or haversack, stowed in the boot of a car, stowed in a heavier vehicle such as van or lorry, or stowed within a container load for interception and retrieval later.

It will be noted that in the first three cases it is possible for one individual to remove goods unaided. In the other cases some assistance may be required, e.g. collusion between warehouse and dispatch staff. Transport drivers and staff at receiving depots could also be involved. The incidence of theft will be minimized if management select and appoint competent and trustworthy staff, give reasonable remuneration and apply effective controls. Such controls would include spot checks at each stage in warehouse handling and dispatch cycles, particularly on high-risk items.

Conclusions

Planned coordinated effort deployed at the material input and processing stages must be matched by effort sustained during the final warehousing and distribution stages. The full rewards of good materials management will be earned only when customers are provided with a satisfactory service. Warehousing and distribution teams must achieve this at economic cost. Finished-goods warehouse must, therefore, have equal consideration with other functions when resources are being allocated.

14

Disposal management

Introduction
Disposals management facilitates the conversion into cash of unwanted plant, equipment, components or material. In manufacturing or processing organizations, efficient disposal is of particular importance. However, great scope exists, too, for cash conversion of unwanted material in service, supply and transport industries. However, efforts must not solely be concentrated to providing an efficient disposals system. Attention must be directed also to determining the reasons why items become available for disposal. Periodic statements are issued on the value of sales of disposed items with comparisons made between one month's figures and another's. Concern is expressed if there is a significant reduction in the current month's figures compared with the previous one or a year-to-date figure. Such concern would be justified if this reduction in sales reflected lower selling prices. However, improved efficiency in the way materials are specified, bought, stored, processed and used will result in less scrap being produced, with corresponding lower cash conversion figures. Companies are not in business to produce scrap. The reasons why items become available for disposal must be investigated using a selective approach that compares use with disposal values but does not ignore administrative costs. Corrective measures can then be introduced to minimize future levels of unwanted items, particularly 'A' category ones. There may be shortcomings in the procurement cycle or during subsequent processing or usage, and corrective action is aimed at preventing recurrence. Items become available for disposal for a number of reasons:

1. Poor design/inadequate specification
2. Acceptance of faulty material
3. Change in production programme (reduced demand)
4. Excessive build-up of supplies (over-ordering)

5. Obsolescence/rationalization
6. Deterioration/damage in-company

Many departments can contribute to an investigation, including design, which, although outside materials management's sphere of responsibility, has a major role to play at the start of the procurement cycle.

Range of materials for disposal

The variety and range of materials for disposal are virtually endless and depend on the nature and magnitude of operations in the manufacturing, supply, service or transport industries (public or private sectors). They include metals (ferrous, non-ferrous and precious), timber, plastics, rubber, general stores, chemicals (liquids and powders), waste oils and greases.

In addition to such surplus or scrap material, production plant and equipment, office equipment and vehicles also become available for disposal.

Disposal objectives

The main objectives are as follows:

1. **Conversion into cash**   Seeking the best prices for items for disposal. These would be related to the cost of preparation and handling or disposal. Where market prices for the material for sale are subject to significant fluctuation, e.g. copper scrap, timing of the sale is important.
2. **Disruption to internal operations**   Unwanted items cannot be allowed to build up indefinitely. They need moving, monthly, weekly, daily or more frequently, to avoid stopping production or other work.
3. **Space utilization**   Space limitations could be a crucial factor in initiating disposal action.
4. **Accident prevention**   Good housekeeping is desirable as an aid to preventing accidents. Hence, the need to remove unwanted materials.
5. **Theft avoidance**   It is the moral duty of any employer to remove temptation to steal. Prompt removal from the premises of unwanted materials for sale is thus a desirable objective.

6. **Administration cost**   Efficient disposal of unwanted materials frees staff to devote time more economically to identifying, locating, handling and retrieving wanted materials.
7. **Strategic**   In disposing of unwanted items, there must be no disadvantage to the organization. For example, what would be the effect on its market position or on the sales of new products if redundant products or their key components were released to potential competitors and customers? Strict control procedures are essential to prevent loss arising in this way.

Stages in the disposal process

There are seven possible stages requiring consideration to determine the method of disposal. Many items are not classified as scrap but have a use value. Disposal operations should follow a methodical sequence, which will be dependent on a realistic time-scale. Consider the following check-list:

1. **Alternative internal use**   Can an item for disposal be used elsewhere within the organization? It could have significant use value, and this possibility must not be overlooked.
2. **Use by associated company**   Can the item be used by an associated company? This may require checking before offering for sale elsewhere.
3. **Use of spare parts for internal use**   If the item is a piece of plant or equipment, is it economically viable to dismantle to recover parts as spares for future use?
4. **Offer for sale as usable**   Once it is established that an item is not required for internal use or by associated companies, details can be circulated to other organizations. An item in usable condition attracts a higher price than one sold for scrap.
5. **Offer for sale as scrap**   If an item cannot be sold as usable, details should be circulated to scrap merchants or other possible interested parties.
6. **Offer for free disposal**   If there is a negative response at stage 5, there being no reasonable prospects of selling, can the item be collected and disposed of free of charge? This possibility should be pursued.
7. **Pay for disposal**   Finally, as the last resort, when all other checks have proved to be fruitless, it might be necessary to

pay for disposal. This would require the services of an appropriate 'refuse' collector to remove the unwanted item(s). The lowest possible price should be negotiated for such a service.

Optimizing the value of sales

An item designated as disposable can attract significant added cost before leaving an organization's premises. It is important to have a continuous process for disposing of unwanted material. However, a balance sometimes has to be struck between obtaining the highest possible prices and making up parcels of material to attract the interest of merchants. Consider the following aspects.

Segregation

A merchant wishes to buy scrap of a consistent high quality to an established specification. Hence, scrap might have to be segregated at the point of generation. An example is phosphor-bronze castings. A foundry originally supplying high-quality castings would generally pay the highest possible prices for scrap produced from its products.

Cutting or baling of material

Consider the following example. A merchant supplies scrap steel bars to a local steelworks who require short bars for loading directly into a furnace. Hence, material so supplied is attractive to both the steelworks and the merchant. The latter could collect and deliver direct to his customer. The disposer, however, requires manpower (which incurs additional cost) to carry out this cutting process. Similarly, compressing and baling certain types of scrap provides a more attractive parcel and encourages a merchant's speedier response to collect and remove from the disposer's premises, but also incurs additional cost.

Stripping of cable

Prior dismantling or stripping of material may facilitate examination and so be advantageous to do. Electric cable is a good example. It is sometimes cost-effective to strip electric cable, particularly heavy copper core cable, in readiness for sale. This would depend on the type of cable and manpower availability. Fig.14.1 shows various stages of added costs that could be incurred in preparing materials for sale.

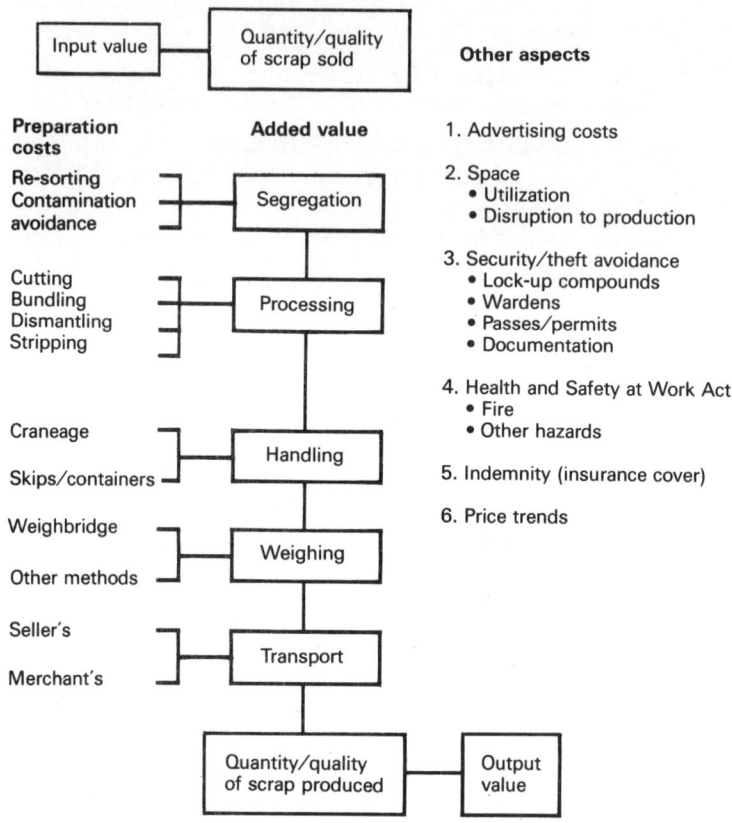

Figure 14.1   Disposal costs — optimizing the value of sales

It will be noted from the right-hand side of the figure that consideration could be required on a number of aspects that incur cost. Advertising is a good example. For example, consider the case of a manufacturing company which has a contract to produce 200 plain shafts. Through a manufacturing error the shafts are made too small and are unacceptable to the customer. Assume the loss incurred is £1000. It is not beyond reasonable possibilities that there is a customer located somewhere in the world to whom these incorrectly made shafts would be suitable and perhaps urgently required. However, it would probably cost over £1000 in advertising and take a great deal of time to locate such a potential customer. Disposals generally have to be managed within very restricted advertising budgets to be cost-effective.

The disposer has to evaluate the economics of who segregates and processes. What cost will be incurred at each stage shown in Fig.14.1? At what stage will the difference between price obtained and cost incurred be a maximum? This evaluation must consider facilities, specialism and manpower availability. The longer-term view must be taken. Skips and pans are a good example. Should the disposer or the scrap merchant provide them?

Disposal of capital plant

We have discussed the procedure for offering items for sale. Some items are specials, others are standard. A lathe that becomes redundant, specially designed and manufactured to meet the needs of a particular company, is most unlikely to be readily usable elsewhere within a group without modification. A standard item might be suitable for internal use within a group. There are a number of points to consider when dealing with the sale of second-hand plant.

Authorization for sale

Individual company policies may vary. Generally, a Board of directors or similar body will have initially approved the purchase of an item of plant or equipment if its purchase price was above a stated figure. If such an item has not reached the end of its planned life, i.e. it is not fully depreciated, this body would normally be required to authorize disposal. This point must be checked when applicable, and where such authorization applies it must be given in writing.

Residual v. market value

Plant might have been purchased for, say, £100 000 with an estimated 10 years' productive life. Production commitments might change after a period of, say, four years, so the plant is taken out of the line. It could be stored for an extended period of, say, two years, when the decision is made to take disposal action.

If the plant has been depreciated on a straight-line basis, its book value could be £40 000. However, its market value could be much higher because of recent high inflation. Demand for new plant of this type could be high, with very extended deliveries resulting. The price commanded by a second-hand item can thus sometimes be higher than the stated price of a new one. Consider Fig.14.2, which illustrates price implications.

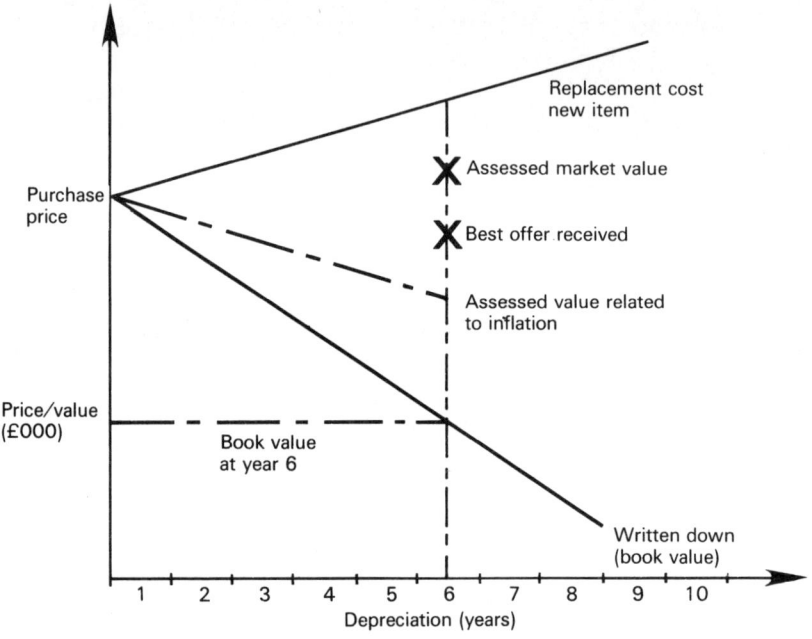

Figure 14.2   Disposal of capital plant — valuation

Value might be related to type, condition, age and current demand from the home or overseas customer market. An emergent nation embarking on a programme of industrialization could require such type of plant. Extended delivery of a new item would influence the market price of the item for disposal. In the above example, the disposer would aim to obtain a higher price than the best offer received. His minimum target figure is the assessed market value. Attaining this objective will be dependent on how realistically it was assessed. The value of any supporting spares held requires assessing and including in the total package price sought. Dealing separately with spares generally results in obtaining lower prices, particularly for plant not to standard specification.

Guarantees are not normally given when offering such plant for sale because the plant has been used and it is not usually possible to demonstrate its capabilities. As in the example above, a machine might be taken out of the production line and stored for an extended period. Years may elapse before a disposals decision is taken. In such circumstances the disconnected machine must be examined where it stands and valued by potential buyers on that basis at their risk. All available data and documentation relating to the plant should be made available for examination by potential customers and for supply with the plant when it is sold.

Disposal of hazardous materials

The Health and Safety at Work Act, 1974, specifies the obligations of the seller to the buyer for the sale of goods, which includes plant, equipment, components, and materials of all kinds, e.g. metals, plastics, rubbers, timber and unused chemicals and catalysts. Used chemicals, spent catalysts and residues are dealt with under the Disposal of Poisonous Waste Act.

The person responsible for disposing of hazardous materials must comply with such requirements. There are a number of points to consider.

1. Material is to be adequately identified with appropriate labelling and documentation.
2. Material is to be made available in such condition and at a suitable location to facilitate safe collection and transport.
3. Adequate instructions are to be given as to safe method of transport and subsequent handling, use and disposal.
4. Where the item for sale is a tank, drum or container, it is to be free from hazardous contamination.

Conditions of disposal

Generally, purchasing is responsible for dealing with merchants or other interested companies on disposals. The buyer is thus required to wear a seller's hat when undertaking this task. In his buying role he seeks the keenest prices for goods purchased. He is now required to obtain the highest prices for disposed items. Previously he negotiated purchasing conditions. Now he has to negotiate seller's conditions. This is a reversal of his normal buying role. Hence, adequate conditions of sale are required. Specimen general conditions of disposal giving an outline of main clauses are included in Appendix 4.

Responsibility for disposals

Responsibility for disposals varies from one organization to another. There are generally four options to consider.

Sales responsibility

Sales could be considered to have a good case to handle disposals because its staff are skilled in selling. This is an area in which they are the experts. Selling is the reason for their existence and disposals is primarily a selling activity. However, most sales staff would much prefer to sell the glamorous new product to selling redundant material. Perhaps the best case against sales being responsible for disposals is that it does not come within materials management's sphere of activities.

Stores responsibility

A good case can be made for stores. The stores manager can claim that his department is best equipped for this task, as it controls most of the materials awaiting disposal within stores or adjacent stockyard areas. It also supplies labour for handling and segregating materials for collection, and is generally responsible for the security of materials awaiting disposal.

Purchasing responsibility

The best case can be made for purchasing to be responsible for disposals. Purchasing staff are trained to handle contract procedures. They are very much involved in price and price negotiation. Initially, they bought materials now awaiting disposal, and hence know the market sources of that material to which in some cases it may be resold, e.g. return of turnings and offcuts to the original suppliers. For some items such as office equipment, e.g. typewriters, suppliers of new equipment offer trade-in allowances on return of the old items.

Perhaps the only question-mark against the case for purchasing is one of psychology. A good buyer does not necessarily make a good seller if he has spent many years 'on the other side of the counter'.

Separate disposal department responsibility
In some large manufacturing organizations, e.g. the volume car industry, recycling of particular materials is done on a large scale. In such circumstances, responsibility for disposal of such materials might need to be assigned to a separate specialist department.

Provision of skips and pans
Where these are required for the disposal of heavy or bulk material, consideration must be given to who will provide, the merchant or the disposing organization. Provision of skips or pans can be a costly investment, particularly if a large number of large-sized items are needed. Many materials deposited into skips and pans for disposal will be sold by weight. Hence, the need to ensure, when applicable, that tare weights are marked. This is done by stamping the details, securing a reference plate or by forming the letters and numbers by welding rod, the latter method giving a more positive secure result.

Skips or pans would be located at appropriate filling points adjacent to production or other scrap-generating departments. Collection of scrap often operates on a 'one-for-one' system, i.e. an empty container is left when a full one is removed.

The weight of the container contents can readily be determined, as road vehicles are required to carry tare weight details. Vehicles would pass over a weighbridge to determine the weight of material for disposal leaving the organization's premises.

Suspension
A 'suspension' clause should be included in contracts relating to disposals. Two relevant aspects are (1) the avoidance of labour disputes and (2) malpractice or suspected malpractice while the merchant's employees are on the company's premises.

Cancellation, arbitration and legal construction
Standard clauses would be included to cater for situations that might arise.

Conclusions

Disposals is a function or activity that is frequently treated as relatively unimportant. It could be the last entry under 'responsibilities' in a buyer's job description and thus is often a poorly organized activity. Savings potential in terms of the total benefits to be derived can be substantial. Cash conversion, i.e.prices obtained, is readily measurable but the other aspects discussed are also important, e.g. preventing particular key items getting into the hands of potential competitors or customers and freeing valuable space.

Financial evaluation of balance sheets

Consider the following financial data taken from ABC Limited.

Balance sheet data

ABC Limited

Financial Data

	£
Shareholder's interest	500 000
Long-term credit	100 000
Current liabilities	400 000
(short-term credit)	
Fixed assets	300 000
Long-term investments	50 000
Current assets	600 000
(short-term assets)	
Profit before tax	100 000
Sales	1 100 000

Note: The short-term assets of £600 000 included in the above data comprise:

Short-term deposits	30 000
Cash	50 000
Raw materials	200 000
Finished goods	180 000
Debtors	140 000

Financial ratios

For simplification, we give target ratios for ABC Limited against which we may measure balance sheet data.

Let us consider some of the revealing ratios, commencing with solvency ratios. These are as follows:

1. **Current ratio**   The target figure is 2:1. The ratio is

$$\frac{\text{Current assets}}{\text{Current liabilities}}$$

From ABC's figures we have

$$\frac{600\,000}{400\,000} = 1.5:1$$

This is not a good figure compared with the 2:1 target ratio. It denotes that £1 worth of current liabilities is covered by £1.5 worth of current assets.

2. **Liquidity ratio**   The target figure is 1:1. The ratio is

$$\frac{\text{Liquid assets}}{\text{Current liabilities}}$$

Liquid assets = short-term assets − stock

ABC's figures give

$$\frac{£600\,000 - £380\,000}{£400\,000} = 0.55:1$$

This figure does not give much confidence. Each £1 worth of current liabilities is covered by 55p of cash or near-cash items, i.e. only 55 per cent of current assets are readily convertible into cash if such action became necessary. This ratio, known also as an acid or quick ratio, is more useful than the current ratio.

3. **Vulnerability**   This relates to the order and extent current assets would be realized if required to cover the demands of current liabilities. In this example, ABC Limited have current liabilities totalling £400 000 and hence would need to realize current assets as follows:

- All the company's cash   £50 000

- All the company's debtors   £140 000
- All the company's short-term deposits   £30 000
- Sell all the finished goods   £180 000

Total   £400 000

It will be appreciated that this is a very vulnerable position for ABC Limited to be in, as it would face a very difficult task, particularly in the short term.

The second set of ratios are operating ratios, which are as follows.

1. **Stock turnover**   Target figure is three times per year. This ratio is

$$\frac{\text{Stocks} \times 52 \text{ weeks}}{\text{Sales}}$$

ABC's annual sales were £1100 000 and stocks of raw materials and finished goods were £200 000 + £180 000 = £380 000. This gives a stock turnover figure of

$$\frac{380\,000 \times 52\text{(weeks)}}{1100\,000} = 35 \text{ weeks}$$

This gives a low stock turnover of 1.5 times a year compared with the target figure of 3 times per year. Inventory levels are too high, too much capital being tied up in stock.

2. **Profit as a percentage of sales**   The target figure is 15 per cent. This ratio is

$$\frac{\text{Profit} \times 100\%}{\text{Sales}}$$

The relevant figures are Sales = £1100 000 and Profit = £100 000, which gives

$$\frac{100\,000 \times 100\%}{1100\,000} = 9\%$$

Profit is well below the target.

3. **Return on capital employed**   Target figure is 20 per cent. The relevant figures are Profit = £100 000 and Capital

employed (fixed assets) = £300 000. This gives a ratio of

$$\frac{100\,000 \times 100\%}{300\,000} = 33\%$$

Return on capital is good, being well above target.

Appendix 2

Consumer Protection Act, 1987 (Part 1)

An EC directive is implemented in UK law by Part 1 of the Consumer Protection Act, 1987, which came into force on 1 March 1988. Goods supplied after that date are subject to the provisions of the Act. These provisions are additional to liabilities that already exist under English law.

Implications of the Act
The main difference between liability under the Act and under existing common law is that, if the injured party can show that:

- There is a defect in the product
- The defect caused 'damages' as defined in the Act

then liability will be imposed irrespective of whether the defect was due to negligence unless the producer can show

- 'Availability of a defence' permitted under the Act

Definition of 'goods'
These include raw materials and components intended for both private or commercial use (excluding agricultural goods and buildings).

The producer
Part 1 defines the 'producer' as the manufacturer of the raw material, component part or finished article. It also includes any person who applies an industrial process. This definition is significant, as it provides that the following persons are jointly and severally liable for a defect:

- The producer, as defined above
- Any person who puts his name, trademark or other distinguishing mark on the product, such as brand or logo (i.e. holding himself to be the producer)
- Any person who imports a product into the EC

Action can be instituted against one or more of the above persons.

Retailers
These are not covered by Part 1 of the Act. They are not liable for defective products unless they fail to disclose to the injured party on request within a reasonable period the name of the supplier of the defective goods.

Defect
There is a defect in a product if:

> the safety of the product is not such as persons generally are entitled to expect. Safety shall include risks of damage to property as well as loss of life or personal injury.

Determining level of safety
This considers the manner of marketing of product, purpose for which product has been marketed, overall packaging and presentation of product together with any instructions or warnings on handling and use. A new, safer product does not necessarily mean the superseded one was unsafe (but the word 'safer' may imply there was need to make the product safer because of a defect).

Literature
All catalogues, operating instructions, leaflets and packaging that give technical or other information and/or suggest possible use(s) for the product must not give misleading impressions as to usage or operation and must be consistent. A defect could result through improper operating or maintenance instructions rather than any defect in the product. Producers should give clear warnings of the dangers of such misuse.

Damages
This includes loss of life, personal injury and loss to property or

land. For property damage to be recoverable the claim must be for £275 or more and the goods must have been intended for private use, occupation or consumption by the claimant.

Loss or damage to the product
Such loss or damage through product defect is not recoverable under the Act. A claim founded in contract or negligence would be pursued as a completely separate action.

Period of liability
The writ must be issued to pursue a claim within the limitation period, which is three years from the date the loss or damage occurred. This date is deemed to be the earliest date at which knowledge of the material facts of the loss or damage were known to the claimant. However, the Act does set a maximum time limit of 10 years from the relevant time, i.e. time of supply. After 10 years the liability of the producer is extinguished. This is covered by the Prescription of Obligations and Limitations of Actions clause within Part 1 of the Act.

The significant point is that the product manufacturer may still be liable within the 10 year period for a product that is defective because of the inclusion of a defective component he has bought out. If the defective component was produced over 10 years before the claim was initiated, its manufacturer would not be liable under the Act.

Exclusions of liability
Part 1 allows limited defence against claims:

- The product conforms to a legal requirement
- Defective stolen products
- Product supplied for a non-commercial purpose
- Defect resulted from misuse
- State of scientific and technical knowledge universally accept-able at the time (this is the particularly grey area, e.g. deaths from prescribed drugs which were not tested over a 'sufficiently' long period)
- By component manufacturers, only where they can show that the defect resulted by incorrect utilization of a component in the finished product or as a result of their compliance with instructions issued by the finished product manufacturer

Conclusions

The introduction of Part 1 of the Consumer Protection Act, 1987, means that manufacturers are required to direct much more thought and attention to the design, testing and extended trials of their products and to ensure that all related literature and packaging do not conflict with safe and proper use. The burden of proof has been lifted from consumers. However, manufacturers and suppliers do have limited defences against claims.

Appendix 3

Specimen general conditions of purchase — comments on particular clauses

Definition
'Buyer' means .... Limited. 'Supplier' means the person, firm or company to whom the Order is addressed. 'Goods' means the articles or services described in the Order. 'Specification' means the technical specification (if any) of the Goods referred to in the Order.

Quality and description
The Goods shall: (a) Conform as to quality, description and quantity with the particulars stated in the Order. (b) Be of sound materials and workmanship. (c) Be equal in all respects to samples, patterns or specifications provided or given by either party.

Variations
All variations to this Order must be agreed to by both Buyer and Supplier.

Identification
All Goods supplied against the Buyer's drawings must be marked with his drawing number except where such a number cannot be incorporated. Packages containing Goods supplied against the Buyer's drawings, part numbers or catalogues must be marked with the appropriate references.

Packing material
Packing cases, skips, drums and other packing material supplied against this Order are to be provided free of charge. Empties will be returned in 'as-received' condition at the Supplier's expense upon request, by the Buyer. Returnable

containers must be stencilled with the Supplier's name and address together with addressed reversible label.

Prices
Fixed prices agreed for this Order will remain firm for the whole of the contract period and not be subject to variation without the consent of the Buyer.

Goods receipt inspection
Goods may be subject to inspection on receipt. The Buyer shall notify the Supplier of any rejects. Rejected goods will be returned to the Supplier at his expense or be disposed of in some other way to be agreed with the Buyer.

Defects after delivery
The Supplier shall supply replacements, or make good by repair with the consent of the Buyer, goods which become defective within 12 months solely through inadequate design, faulty material or workmanship. Such remedial action taken will be provided free of charge including transport costs.

Patents
The Supplier shall indemnify the Buyer against any claims for infringement of letters patent, registered design, trademark or copyright (published at the date of the Buyer's Order) by the use or sale of any material provided by the Supplier to the Buyer against all costs and damages which the Buyer may incur in any action for such infringement for which the Buyer may become liable in any such action; provided always that this indemnity shall not apply to any infringement which is due to the Supplier having followed a design or instruction provided by the Buyer. The Buyer shall give the Supplier immediate notice of any such claim and permit the Supplier to defend the same and to conduct any litigation which may ensue.

Assignment
This Order, or any part of it, shall not be assigned or subcontracted to third parties without the Buyer's consent in writing. Any such consent shall not relieve the Supplier of any obligations to comply with the conditions of purchase.

Tools

Tools, gauges, dies, jigs, fixtures, patterns or drawings (hereinafter called 'Tools') specially made by the Supplier for the purpose of this Order and paid for by the Buyer, whether in whole or part, or supplied to the Supplier by the Buyer for the purpose of this Order shall be used for the manufacture of Goods exclusively to the Buyer's Order and not for any other purpose and not for any other customer.

Any such Tools shall be kept by the Supplier in good order and repair. The Buyer shall be granted right to acquire and use them elsewhere at his discretion where he has made full payment or where he has supplied the Tools. They are to be dispatched immediately to him on request.

'Free-issue' material

Material supplied by the Buyer 'free-issue' for the Order shall remain his property. The material shall not be used for the benefit of third parties or be transferred to any other premises. The Supplier shall fully indemnify the Buyer against any loss or damage resulting through spoilage or from any other cause.

Payment

Payment will be made on the 15th of the month following date of delivery except where special payments have been agreed for the Order. Invoices submitted must quote the relevant Advice/ Packing Note and Order numbers.

Suspension

If for any reason the Buyer is unable to take delivery of consignments to be made against the Order he reserves the right to instruct the Supplier to suspend the Order forthwith for a period to be stated, pending reassessment of the situation. The Buyer shall agree to consider all justified verified charges incurred by the Supplier up to the time of receipt of such notification.

Cancellation

Should circumstances arise where the Buyer has no recourse but to cancel the Order he shall give maximum notice of such intentions to the Supplier. The Buyer shall agree to pay justified cancellation charges incurred by the Supplier up to the time of receipt of such notification.

Arbitration

If at any time a dispute should arise between Buyer and Supplier in relation to the Order, one may give to the other notice of such dispute or difference and the same shall be referred to a single arbitrator in England to be mutually agreed upon, or failing agreement within 14 days of such notice, to a single arbitrator to be appointed by the President for the time being of the .... Institution/Association. The Arbitration Act or any statutory modification or re-enactment thereof for the time being in force shall apply.

Legal interpretation

This contract shall in all respects operate as an English Contract and be construed in conformity with English law.

Appendix 4

Specimen general conditions of disposal

Definition of terms

Four basic terms may need definition. These are:

- 'The Company', i.e. the selling organization
- 'The Merchant', i.e. the buying company
- 'Materials', i.e. the item(s) being offered for sale
- 'The Company's Premises', i.e. the site for collection

Subsequently, throughout the body of the conditions, the above terms would be used.

Inspection of Materials

These include:

- Merchants to satisfy themselves as to quality
- The Company does not hold itself responsible for inadequate description except in the case of hazardous Material, where it is a legal requirement to give full information
- Materials purchased without inspection is at the Merchant's risk
- Where samples are given, there is no guarantee on uniformity, except for hazardous Material where there is a legal requirement to do so

Removal of Material

Typical clauses related to theft or malpractice are:

- The Merchant's driver is to report to a stated point to collect the 'Disposal Authority' Note
- The driver shall be accompanied by the Company's representative while he is on the Company's premises
- The Merchant shall ensure that all Materials removed from

the Company's Premises are in accordance with the Disposal
Authority Note
- The Driver shall be required to sign for the Material and to
retain a copy to hand to the Merchant

Weighing of materials

Where weighing is appropriate, requirements include:

- The Merchant's representative can witness the weighing
- No claims for short weight can be considered later
- Where Material is sold by weight, which is beyond the
capacity of free-standing weighing equipment, the Merchant's
vehicle must be

  - weighed 'in' and 'out' on the weighbridge in the presence of
  the Company's representative or
  - weighed 'in' and 'out' at a local authorized public authority
  weighbridge in the presence of the Company's representative

Indemnities

This is of particular importance when the Company deals with
small Merchants who do not have the financial or legal sub-
stance enjoyed by larger companies. An accident might occur
while a Merchant's vehicle was on the Company's Premises.
There could be claims for heavy damages on behalf of the injured
parties. A small Merchant without adequate insurance cover
and with limited funds would be, to use a legal term, 'a man of
straw'. In such a situation the Courts would turn to the one only
alternative body who could make such payment, i.e. the
Company with its insurers. Comprehensive public liability and
third party insurance taken out by Merchants to meet
requirements of the Road Transport Act is only applicable to
accidents occurring on the Queen's Highway.

To avoid problems of this type arising in dealing with any
Merchant (or suppliers or contractors) bringing vehicles onto the
Company's Premises, suitable clauses of the following general
form are required.

- The Merchant shall indemnify the Company against all
claims resulting from accidents occurring during the period

his vehicle is on the Company's Premises and after the loaded vehicle has left the Company's Premises (both these requirements are subject to the satisfactory discharge of the Company's responsibilities under the Health and Safety at Work Act

- The Merchant shall produce documentary evidence of adequate and current insurance policies. These policies should be validated before allowing Merchant's vehicles and men to enter the Company's Premises

Workmanship

A Merchant's responsibilities can go beyond the mere collection of material. Dismantling work, loading of skips, cutting and bundling of materials may be involved and this would be catered for using a clause of the following form:

> Any work carried out by the Merchant or his employees is to be to the reasonable satisfaction of the Company.

Merchant's vehicle, plant, equipment and tackle

Accidents frequently occur resulting from misuse or by neglect of Merchant's plant, equipment and tackle. Hence there is a requirement to apply suitable clauses dealing with these aspects:

- The Merchant shall indemnify the Company against any loss or damage to the Merchant's plant, equipment and tackle while on the Company's Premises. This applies also to items hired by him
- The Merchant shall submit his lifting tackle for inspection on request by the Company's officials
- The Merchant shall offer for inspection on request by the Company's officials any of his plant, equipment or tackle requiring electrical mains supply
- In addition to accidents causing injuries or loss of life through electrocution, serious production stoppages can occur through cutting electric cables

Security and permits

Control must be exercised over people not employed by the Company while on the Company's Premises. This is of particular importance when the Company's operations are of a secret or highly confidential nature or where attractive or valuable material is stored or used on the site. Control may take the form of:

- Limiting the number of hours Merchant's employees are on the Company's Premises. A requirement could specify that permits are to be collected from the Works Police on arrival and handed in on departure
- Requiring Merchant's employees to keep to specified areas. This stipulation avoids interference with other work being carried on the Company's Premises

Payment

Methods of payment depend on the nature and value of the Material for disposal and a Merchant's status with the Company. Generally, arrangements made for payment are:

- Scrap material collected on a regular basis. The terms will be as per agreed procedures. Prices paid to be in accordance with schedules of rates currently in force which cater for market price fluctuations in special cases, e.g. steel scrap
- Non-standard parcels or lots. Prices to be negotiated following inspection of such material
- Plant and equipment. A price of several thousand pounds might be offered by a Merchant with whom the Company has not previously dealt. Such a Merchant could collect the plant and not make payment unless forced to do so through a Court action. Such action could be lengthy and unproductive, the Merchant being a 'man of straw' and unable to pay. To avoid such a situation arising, the cheque should be obtained and cleared with the bank before allowing the item to be removed from the Company's Premises

Recommended reading

Baily and Farmer, *Materials Management Handbook*, Gower
Baily and Farmer, *Purchasing Principles and Management*, Pitman
Burbridge, *The Principles of Production Control*, M & E
Compton, *Supplies and Materials Management*, M & E
Dobler, Lee and Burt, *Purchasing and Materials Management*, McGraw-Hill
Hill, *Production and Operations Management*, Prentice Hall
Jessop and Morrison, *Storage and Control of Stock*, Pitman
Leenders, Fearon and England, *Purchasing and Materials Management*, Irwin
Lockyer, *Factory and Production Management*, Pitman
Thomas, *Stock Control in Manufacturing Industries*, Gower
Wild, *Production and Operations Management*, Holt Rinehart Winston

Index